FACING
DEATH
and
FINDING
HOPE

CHRISTINE
LONGAKER

DOUBLEDAY

New York   London   Toronto

Sydney   Auckland

FACING
DEATH
and
FINDING
HOPE

A Guide to the
Emotional and Spiritual
Care of the Dying

PUBLISHED BY DOUBLEDAY
a division of Bantam Doubleday Dell Publishing Group, Inc.
1540 Broadway, New York, New York 10036

DOUBLEDAY and the portrayal of an anchor with a dolphin are trademarks of Doubleday,
a division of Bantam Doubleday Dell Publishing Group, Inc.

Library of Congress Cataloging-in-Publication Data
Longaker, Christine.
Facing death and finding hope: a guide to the emotional and spiritual care of the dying /
Christine Longaker. — 1st ed.
p.   cm.
Includes bibliographical references and index.
1. Death—Psychological aspects.   2. Death—Religious aspects—Buddhism.   3.
Terminally ill—Psychology.
4. Terminally ill—Family relationships.   5. Care of the sick.   6. Bereavement—
Psychological aspects.   7. Grief.   I. Title.
BF789.D4L664   1997   96-43278
155.9′37—dc20   CIP

ISBN 0-385-48331-7

This book is dedicated to my spiritual masters,
Sogyal Rinpoche and Nyoshul Khen Rinpoche,
in gratitude.
May Guru Rinpoche's blessing make their lives secure and firm,
and may their compassionate activity shine in splendor
in the ten directions.

This book is also dedicated to
Mother Teresa, Dame Cicely Saunders, Elisabeth Kübler-Ross,
and all those whose courageous work in the care of the dying
is an expression of reverence for life.

To you who read this book,
and all your relations,
may compassion and wisdom increase in your heart and mind
and so throughout the world.

CONTENTS

Contents

FOREWORD

BY

SOGYAL RINPOCHE

"LEARN TO DIE AND THOU SHALT LEARN HOW TO LIVE. There shall none learn how to live that hath not learned to die." These words, written hundreds of years ago in the medieval Book of the Craft of Dying, often come into my mind when I think about our understanding of death and its relationship to life. Because if we can only learn how to face death, then we'll have learned the most important lesson of life: how to face *ourselves* and so come to terms with ourselves, in the deepest possible sense, as human beings.

Yet all too often, it seems, we only start to think about death just before we die. Even those fortunate enough to receive hospice care only do so shortly before the end of their lives. Then again, the different religions, and near-death experiencers, speak of a life-review at the moment of death. But isn't that a bit too late? Shouldn't the knowledge and wisdom we need to negotiate death, and life, be available to us earlier on? Shouldn't our whole lives be devoted to such an education?

There can be few areas of life in which we need to make such a radical shift in our perspective as in our care for the dying. Amazing work has been done in the area of death and dying over the past few decades, and now more and more people appreciate that every attention must be given to the emotional and practical needs of the dying, so that they can die with dignity, without too much pain, and surrounded by love. Yet we are still lacking in our ability to offer spiritual help and care to the dying and to answer to their deeper needs. In a world like ours, fascinated by short-term goals and quick solutions, it's all too easy to assume that once someone has died, it's the end of the story. What characterizes spiritual care is its long-term vision, one which embraces the complete picture of the dying person and their future, and recognizes that we can help someone long before they die, at the moment of death, and even after they are dead.

What is the most important thing when we come to help a dying person, or a living one, for that matter? To give our love. With all our heart, without any conditions, and as free as possible from attachment. And yet our love can so often be entangled in all kinds of complicated stories, our history of suffering and pain, and what we take for love may in fact only be attachment.

Our task is to find that pure love, and curiously it is death, or rather impermanence, that can help us. The reason we become so fiercely attached to things—from our emotions, ideas, and opinions to our possessions and other people—is that we have not taken impermanence to heart. Once we can accept that impermanence is the very nature of life, and that everyone suffers, including ourselves, at the hands of changes and death, then letting go becomes quite natural.

With impermanence securely in our hearts, we'll see that if everyone were to realize its truth, then even in the thick of change and death and bereavement, we would not feel any great sense of loss. Our tears then would not be because death and impermanence are facts of life, but because of something much deeper: we would weep with compassion, because we'd know that all the pain and hurt and suffering we go through do not need to be there. They are only there in fact because we fail to understand that everything, absolutely everything, is transient.

What the teachings of all spiritual traditions offer us is the knowledge that even when the worst tragedy and suffering befalls us, there is still hope, there is something that nothing can destroy, or take away from us. There is a fundamental truth, a spiritual essence which lies within us all; and according to the teaching of the Buddha, the key to unlocking our limitless resources of wisdom and compassion is in understanding the innermost nature of our mind.

All of us need to give our love to a dying person, but if we have come in touch with the nature of our mind, stabilized it through our practice of meditation, and integrated it into our lives, then the love we have to give can only be deeper, because it comes from a different source: from our innermost being, the heart of our enlightened nature. It has a special quality of freedom. This kind of love, beyond all attachment, is like divine love. It is the love of all the buddhas, the love of Christ, of God. In that state, without contriving, and even without thinking, we can feel the presence of the Buddha or of Christ. It's as if we become their ambassador, their representative, our love backed by their love, and infused with their blessing. Love that springs truly from the nature of the mind is so blessed that it has the power to dispel the fear of the unknown, to give refuge from anxiety, to grant serenity and peace, and to bring inspiration in death and beyond.

As we will discover for ourselves, the more we can *embody* the spiritual teachings, the more natural and more effective we will be in giving spiritual care to a dying person. *How we are* is so much more important than what we say or do. Our presence, by itself, can reassure our dying friend, and evoke in him or her a fundamental confidence and trust, a sense of hope and meaning.

I believe that the ancient Buddhist teachings on death and dying have a tremendous gift to offer, to people of any faith or of none, one that is offered, in the spirit of Buddhism, quite freely and with no notion of conversion or exclusivity. Anyone should feel free to try them out. It is one of my deepest hopes that teachings such as these should be made available to people everywhere, and at all levels of education. To know that when we die we would be surrounded by the very best in spiritual care should be, I believe, one of our basic human rights. The kind of death we have is so important; death is the most vital moment of our lives, and all of us should be able to die in peace and fulfillment. I hope that in the years to come we can see a continuing revolution in our approach to caring for the dying, one which carries the deepest spiritual values at its heart, and which will give birth to different environments and places where people at all stages of living and dying can come to draw benefit.

Christine Longaker is one of my oldest students, who has devoted her life to helping the dying and their families, and to training others to do the same. I know there is much in this book which will inspire and strengthen you in finding the courage, compassion, and skill to help those who are very ill or dying, as much as in your own quest to come to terms with your own deepest self, your ultimate birthright as a human being.

Let me add my own prayers: For all who are engaged in the noble and often heartrending work of caring for the dying—may all their aspirations be fulfilled! May all those who are dying find a peaceful death, and may all who are struggling in life find happiness and a true spiritual path! May the blessings of the buddhas and all enlightened beings shine upon us, transforming our hearts and minds!

PROLOGUE

I EMBARKED ON A SPIRITUAL PATH OVER TWENTY YEARS ago, to free myself from the pain of my bereavement following the death of my husband and to begin preparing meaningfully for my own death. As my mourning gradually finished, I observed that many people were suffering unnecessarily while ill or dying, as had my husband. I also witnessed the profound challenges faced by medical caregivers, by relatives and friends of the dying, and by those journeying alone through the stark and unfamiliar territory of bereavement. Having completed a difficult yet ultimately healing journey through loss and grief on my own, I dedicated myself to helping others who were experiencing such crucial transitions.

During the year my husband was ill, I read an article about a new concept of care for the dying called "hospice." The principles of hospice care seemed to be exactly what our family needed: a humane and well-researched system for managing the discomforts and pain of terminal illness; support for families who bring a loved one home to die; care for the dying patient as a whole person (not just a disease) through the coordinated effort of an interdisciplinary team; and continued support for the family during the mourning process. However, in 1977 there were only four hospice programs in the United States, and none was available to us in Los Angeles.

After my husband's death, my four-year-old son and I moved to Northern California, and I was grateful to meet and begin working with a wonderful group of people who wanted to establish a hospice program. In another serendipitous development, my major in Community Studies at the University of California in Santa Cruz enabled me to combine my hospice work with my academic study.

At the same time, I began studying and practicing in the

Tibetan Buddhist tradition, which helped me to know that to truly serve others I needed to become more "free of myself" by working to attain enlightenment, complete liberation from suffering. Although attaining liberation is my commitment and highest intention, I am still working hard, and I know that I am far from free. Thus I write this book as a fellow traveler along the path of spiritual development.

My seven years of work with the hospice program in Santa Cruz concluded at the end of 1984, and since that time I have been able to share what I've learned through traveling and giving seminars for caregivers, the bereaved, and those facing chronic illness or death. Helping others learn a new and hopeful way to prepare for death—and witnessing their courage in applying what they have learned to their life—gives my husband's suffering, and mine, a greater meaning.

I have also spent many years working in a variety of capacities for Rigpa—a Tibetan Buddhist organization under the spiritual direction of Sogyal Rinpoche and Dzogchen Rinpoche—and have taken part in the initial development of a new program within Rigpa called Spiritual Care for Living and Dying. As I learned the teachings and practices for dying and death from the Tibetan Buddhist tradition, I felt moved to do whatever I could to bring the richness and wisdom of these teachings to a wider audience, especially caregivers and those presently facing death or bereavement. That is a principal aim of the Spiritual Care program, and also one of my aspirations for this book.

I have discovered, as have so many other professional and volunteer caregivers throughout the world, that some of the traditional Buddhist practices can be used readily by non-Buddhists as well, with remarkable results. I am presenting the practices in imaginative ways that I have found to be useful and valuable for caregivers and non-Buddhists who begin integrating them with their daily life and work. If the practices prove appealing and effective for you, you may wish to attend a course on Buddhism to learn more of the traditional teachings and meditations.

Please bear in mind that the teachings from the ancient wisdom tradition of Tibetan Buddhism on death, the after-death states, and the true nature of mind are extremely subtle and sophisticated, and thus difficult to convey in words. I will present here the teachings I have received from Sogyal Rinpoche to the best of my ability and within my present level of understanding. Yet, since I am still a student and have not fully actualized the truth of these teachings myself, I apologize to you, and my teachers, for any misunderstandings or errors in this presentation.

Whether we consider ourselves atheists, Jews, Christians, Muslims, Hindus, or Buddhists, whether we believe in rebirth or not, what is most important is that we develop a "good heart," by taming our selfish aspects and training ourselves constantly to express compassion, love, and forgiveness to others. Developing such a good heart throughout life enables us to heal our relationships with others, bring peace into this troubled world, and meet death without fear.

Of course, people can die well without Buddhist teachings and practices. Even though I find my own spiritual path very hopeful and inspiring, I am not interested in imposing these ideas on anyone. The spiritual views and practices presented here are offered for those who are interested in learning how they can prepare for their death in the best way possible, thereby developing the confidence and courage to be a genuine support for others. Please be sensitive when caring for those who come from cultures or belief systems that are different from yours, and support them in ways appropriate to their own understanding. Whether or not you can speak about spiritual matters with people who are suffering or dying, you can always quietly offer your prayers and meditations on their behalf.

The dying would like us to relate to them as people who are *living,* compassionately accepting their vulnerability and suffering while still seeing them as whole. We can do this most effectively by having thoroughly prepared for our own death, and by training in meditation which enables us to connect with the innermost essence of our being. Then, when we are by the side of the dying, we will have the assured knowledge that they are more than their suffering, more than whatever is temporarily manifesting on the surface—confusion, anger, denial, dementia, and so on. We can recognize and honor the inherent goodness within each person, no matter how clouded over it might seem at the moment.

When this understanding becomes our authentic way of being, then we won't feel driven to give someone who is afraid and confused little snippets of philosophy or platitudes. We can give instead from the fullness of our heart. *Spiritual care is an expression of our inherent compassion and wisdom; thus it is our entire way of being.*

Prologue

. . .

What I have learned from professionals and volunteers who lend vital support and care for those living with HIV—and from people with AIDS themselves—is woven throughout this book, yet here I would like to express one more message connected with the AIDS epidemic.

I have heard tragic stories of gay men who found themselves judged and rejected by their own families after revealing their diagnosis. I can also appreciate the extreme difficulty some parents face when going through bereavement after their son has died, particularly in communities where they are afraid to mention the death or show their grief for fear of ostracism. My plea is that we acknowledge any fear we may have of those who choose a lifestyle different from our own, and then take courageous steps to overcome our fear. Our task in life is to learn to love. Love is built on a foundation of understanding and acceptance; understanding comes by initiating a dialogue of open and honest communication. Every single person is worthy of our utmost respect, as each of us is a "child of God," with the potential to become a buddha, or enlightened being.

The person living with life-threatening or chronic illness, the bereaved parent, the person paralyzed by a stroke and living in a convalescent hospital—all those who need our support also have a gift for us. When we truly connect with others, lending them our understanding and friendship, we receive from them much more than we give. What we receive is more satisfying to the spirit than any amount of money, prestige, or power.

By volunteering to work with those who are ill, suffering, or dying—as either professional or lay caregivers—we can come to know ourselves better, learn to speak the truth with kindness, and uncover our own wholeness, or "holiness." Most important, we must be willing to be open, realizing that the more we learn, the more there is yet to learn. Whenever we enter the world of the suffering, we thus have a unique opportunity to discover the "unfinished" aspects of ourselves and, by so doing, begin to heal our lives and grow.

Lest you assume that the "facing death" of this book's title refers to those already diagnosed with a life-threatening illness, you will be reminded as the book unfolds that we are all facing death in this very moment. This is a book for and about the living, too. "Living" concludes soon after we breathe out our last breath. Since we don't know when that last breath will come, preparing for our death begins right now.

Although this book includes stories of people within traditional family structures, please consider that the message within each example applies equally to those in other forms of relationship as well.

The names and locations connected with the stories described in this book have been altered. I am extremely grateful to all those who, through sharing their lives, their most difficult struggles, and their insights and remarkable courage, have not only enriched my life but continue to relieve unnecessary suffering for so many others who have begun a similar journey through suffering, bereavement, or death.

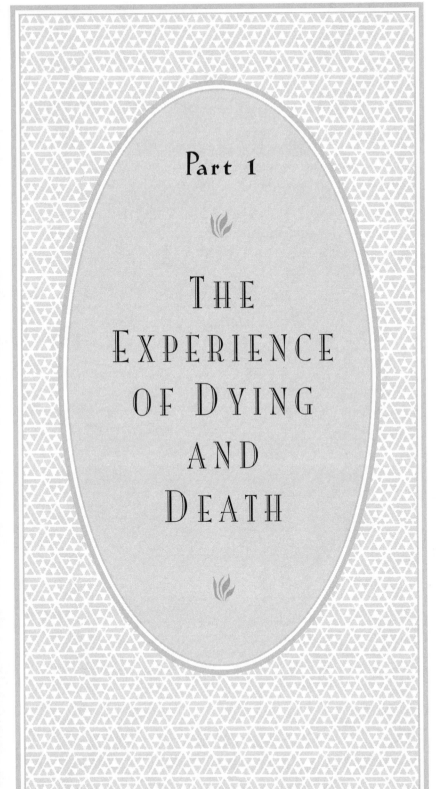

Part 1

THE EXPERIENCE OF DYING AND DEATH

Chapter 1

FACING DEATH

"WHY IS THE SHIP ROCKING SO MUCH!?" MY HUSBAND cried out, sitting bolt upright in bed, his body bathed in sweat. "How did my back get broken?"

"It's all right, Lyttle," I said as calmly as I could. "You're all right. It was just a bad dream." I tried to sound soothing, but in fact I was terribly afraid. Lyttle was obviously racked with pain, and this delirium was yet another sign that something was seriously wrong with his health.

Lyttle was twenty-five years old and had not been feeling well most of the summer. Lately there were disturbing new symptoms: his calf had grown so swollen and painful that he could no longer walk without support. One testicle had also enlarged. Two previous visits to emergency rooms had brought us only superficial reassurance and medicine which didn't seem to have any effect. I had been taking care of Lyttle and our three-year-old son, Donovan, after strenuous days at work. His unexpected illness and these new symptoms had been deeply unsettling these last weeks, but now I was truly afraid.

Lyttle was clearly getting worse. After he woke, his pain and confusion intensified. Fortunately, a friend of his, Cecil, was staying overnight with us, and Cecil and I quickly drove Lyttle to yet another emergency room. They drew blood from him almost immediately, but told us that until the tests were completed, the doctors could not prescribe anything for Lyttle's pain. We sat together for over three hours under the bright lights of an unheated examining room while Lyttle moaned with agony.

Finally, around 6 A.M., a doctor burst through the door with the blood test results, took one look at Lyttle, and said, "No, this can't be right, it must be a mix-up," and promptly disappeared. Soon a nurse came to draw more blood, yet after repeated painful attempts

1

she couldn't get the needle into a vein, since Lyttle's arm was almost blue from lying still for hours in the cold room.

At 7 A.M., a doctor announced that Lyttle was going to be admitted to the hospital. A cheerful young nurse brought us to a warm and sunny room—seemingly a world away from the harsh emergency area—and piled heated blankets onto Lyttle to help him get warm again. The first blood tests indicated Lyttle might have something serious, but we were told not to worry about it until they had the results from more exhaustive tests in a few hours. Lyttle was finally given something for his pain, but with little effect. His dosage had to be significantly increased two more times within the first hour. Only as he became groggy from a strong dose of narcotic did his suffering and tension seem to ease a bit.

I don't know which is harder: experiencing unbearable pain or helplessly witnessing such pain in someone you love. After all that had and had not happened during our long wait for care, I felt angry and increasingly anxious.

At 9 A.M., a female intern hastened into Lyttle's room and gave us the news: "The tests have been completed and they confirm that you have acute leukemia. We don't know how extensive it is yet, but . . ."

At that moment the door banged open and a young man pushing a gurney tried to enter, but the intern waved him back into the hall. Her grim bulletin continued:

"We have a group of specialists discussing your case at this moment. Because of your symptoms, particularly the delirium you experienced last night, we are concerned that the leukemia has infiltrated both your brain and sexual organs, two places where chemotherapy will have no effect. The entire course of your treatment has not yet been decided, but right now a radiologist is waiting to give you your first treatment. We'll provide you with more details after you come back to your room."

We were in shock, but there was no time to absorb this news. Lyttle was hastily transferred to the gurney and wheeled down the hall and the three of us were on our way to the radiology department. Standing transfixed and trapped in an elevator full of strangers, I watched the heavy steel doors close in front of us. Nothing seemed real anymore; the past had suddenly and irretrievably closed and an unwelcome future seemed to be rushing forward beyond control.

This feeling of unreality was reinforced when we met with the radiologist inside a tiny cubicle. The doctor wanted our consent to dose Lyttle with 300 rads, to destroy the leukemia cells that he believed had infiltrated the testicles. This treatment would foreclose any opportunity to have another child. In the specialist's opinion, the treatment was necessary and urgent, a matter of life and death. He left us alone for a few minutes to make our decision.

Ironically, Lyttle had just finished four years of training as a radiology technician before becoming ill that summer.

"Is three hundred rads a lot?" I asked him quietly.

"Yes, it's a lot," Lyttle replied. "In our job it's considered unsafe for us to receive over five rads a year." Then he fell silent, and I saw tears in his eyes.

"You've been wanting to have another child," he said, "and I was putting it off. Now I'm glad that we had Donovan when we did."

The doctor reappeared to take Lyttle to the treatment room, and I had no place to go but the busy hallway, where I found Cecil waiting. My legs suddenly buckled underneath me as I leaned against him, feeling as though the world were collapsing around me. Even as I sobbed in panic and grief, I was aware of people talking around us, going about their business. I was shocked and angered at the insensitivity of the medical staff and the uncaring environment. There was no place to go, no privacy or shelter for my grief, and Lyttle and I had been abruptly separated soon after hearing the most devastating news of our lives.

The Mirror of Death

After Lyttle's radiation treatment we were finally able to speak privately together, at the end of that long and hellish day in which we learned his diagnosis. We didn't know exactly what lay ahead, but we both knew that we were facing the very real possibility of his death. I realized then that all I had learned about death up to that point in my life was that dying was something very tragic, hopeless, and sad.

"If that's all that death is," I said to Lyttle, "then the remainder of your life will just be our tragic story playing itself out. We'll only see ourselves as victims of this terrible illness. I don't want to think of us that way. I don't really know what death is, and I'm not sure if anything continues after death. But I'd like to find a more positive way to view what's happening to us. Maybe we can consider the fact that you might be facing death as a gift in our lives, instead of a tragedy. This experience could help us to really appreciate our life, and use the time we have together well."

We committed ourselves that day to use whatever experiences we would have in the best possible way, as a catalyst for our own growth. And this more positive and empowering view of death helped bring a richness and courage to the ensuing months that wouldn't have been possible otherwise.

Of course, the process we went through that year was quite difficult. We had no guide or models to show us how to prepare for a "good death," nor many clues on how to live while facing the mirror of death. We did not understand the process which was unfolding, we did not have much support beyond our nuclear family, and we made many mistakes—sometimes hurting each other and often missing opportunities to connect more genuinely.

Still, the commitment we had made imbued our good days, bad days, and worst nightmares with meaning. We were determined to keep living until Lyttle's death. Small acts of kindness, generosity, or sacrifice took on a greater significance. Through such acts we appreciated our connectedness with others, tested our understanding of life's unfolding, and deepened our trust in the fundamental goodness of human nature. Some of the most important learning I did was to surrender my attempts to be consistently "independent," swallowing my pride to ask for what I needed. Those who offered support gave me much more than they knew.

A Glimpse of the Future

A few weeks after his diagnosis, Lyttle and I still had reasons to be hopeful. He had acute lymphocytic leukemia, a form of leukemia which usually occurs in children. In 1976, the treatments given to children had a good success rate. And we were encouraged about Lyttle's being treated at the UCLA Medical Center, a major leukemia research center. Specialists there had access to the latest findings and treatment protocols.

Lyttle's first round of chemotherapy for his leukemia proved rather innocuous. The drugs he received would normally have induced remission in a child patient, but this didn't happen for Lyttle. Now Lyttle had to be admitted to the hospital to receive a stronger regimen of chemotherapy. On a late September afternoon, we sat in a cool, semi-dark hospital room, telling stories and joking with my sister and a friend.

Something caught my eye and I glanced through the door and into the room across the hallway. That room had a western exposure and was flooded with sunlight. On the bed I saw the profile of an old man, frail and thin, moving ever so slowly. He had no hair and wore wire-rim glasses. He sat upright in bed, facing away from the open door, and removed his pajama top, and I could see that his back was fragile, the skin stretched over protruding bones. Since the old man was beginning to change his clothes, I looked away and returned my attention to our own room.

In marked contrast with the man across the hall, Lyttle looked youthful, with high cheekbones, clear green eyes, and light brown hair falling to his shoulders. His body was still strong and tanned. He was enjoying the attentions of the two young women, and they all laughed easily together. Even though Lyttle had been admitted to the medical center to receive a new and more potent course of chemotherapy, he and I were confident that we would overcome all adversity. Watching him in the warm afternoon light reaffirmed my confidence.

After five minutes or so, my curiosity got the better of me and I stole another glance across the hall. The old man was almost fully dressed, and I felt happy for him, thinking that today he was probably going home. Tentatively he began to walk across his room toward the window, his back to me. He turned around, and I was stunned to see that he had the face of a young man—he couldn't be older than thirty-five! He was entirely bald, extremely frail, and devoid of energy, and appeared to be close to total collapse.

Suddenly he rushed toward his bed, grabbed a metal basin, and began vomiting violently. Horrified, I looked away, toward my husband, and our eyes met. Lyttle had witnessed the same scene. In that moment of shock, we must both have been thinking: That won't happen to Lyttle. *That couldn't happen to Lyttle.* He was too young and strong, he had too much of his life ahead of him to end up like that. The nurses had already warned us that the new chemo was very different from those which Lyttle had received before. For one thing, these drugs would make his hair fall out. But at this moment we understood that the loss of his hair was only a small part of a grim picture.

By evening Lyttle's visitors had gone and the hospital was quieter. An intravenous line had been inserted in his arm and a nurse sat by his side to monitor any allergic reaction to the new drugs. Seeing his long and healthy brown hair, she gently reminded him, "Don't be alarmed if some of your hair starts coming out after this."

Although she said no more, the nurse certainly knew the severity of the transition we had entered. Working in the leukemia ward, she had repeatedly seen the indescribable suffering that results from this illness and its aggressive treatments. What hung in the ensuing silence was our new unspoken knowledge. We had glimpsed the future and we were deeply shaken.

Encountering the Moment of Death

I had never seen anyone die before, so I didn't know what to expect. During the year of his illness, with repeated health crises, setbacks, and missed opportunities, Lyttle and I had learned that it was always best to seize the moment, to acknowledge with honesty what was happening, no matter how difficult, and to speak clearly from our hearts.

The day before his death, a year after he was first diagnosed, Lyttle had been transferred to Intensive Care because blood clots had damaged a lung and he was having difficulty breathing. When the doctor met with us, he admitted that every aspect of Lyttle's condition was serious. A normal white blood cell count is between 5,000 and 10,000; over the previous year, Lyttle had been given chemo whenever his count neared the 100,000 mark. Now Lyttle's white blood cell count was up to 685,000. Hearing that figure, I felt my knees go weak. We all understood it was the beginning of the end for Lyttle.

I pulled the flimsy yellow curtain around his bed to shelter the two of us from the view of the other Intensive Care patients and staff. He was hooked up to all sorts of monitors and IV lines, and it was impossible to get close physically. Aware that he was going to die soon, we took this moment to speak openly with each other, knowing we might not have another chance.

"Lyttle, I'm sorry to be losing you. I love you so much. Even though this was a difficult year, I am so glad we had this time to be together. I feel our love has really deepened. I still don't know what death is, or if any aspect of your being will continue. Yet when I look at all we have learned about being more honest, about forgiving and accepting each other, I can't believe that this will be wasted. In one way or another, I know that our love will continue after you die. Even so, I'm going to miss you very much."

Lyttle replied haltingly. "I don't know how I could have made it through this illness without you, Christy. At the start I was so afraid you would leave me. Instead, you stayed by my side through everything, and you've done so much to help me. Thank you for all you've done; I know it wasn't always easy. I'm also really grateful that we had this year together. I love you."

Twenty-four hours after our talk, Lyttle's urine was increasingly darkened with blood. In the morning, an intern flashed a light into Lyttle's eyes and turned away with a grim look. By looking at the blood vessels at the back of Lyttle's eyes, the doctor could see that the veins in his brain were hemorrhaging. Later Lyttle's clinic doctor, to whom we'd grown very close during the year, admitted that this hemorrhage would be difficult to stop.

"But it might stop spontaneously," he said optimistically.

Lyttle had survived many crises in the last year, in which medical intervention had brought him back from the threshold of death. It wasn't clear to me if this was the end, or if there was hope. I needed to know if Lyttle had entered the final stage of dying, but I didn't have the courage to ask directly. Instead I said, "What about the high white blood cell count? Can you do something for that?"

The doctor mentioned several alternatives, making it sound as if there might be effective solutions to Lyttle's grievous and accelerating problems. I continued to grope for a way to learn the truth, finally asking, "Should I call his brothers and sisters and tell them to come?"

"Yes," he replied gently, "tell them to come."

Even though it was hard to hear, I needed to have the truth confirmed. I told the doctor I wanted Lyttle to die naturally, without heroic resuscitation attempts. The doctor agreed that this was appropriate. Since Lyttle's doctor was not likely to be present at the time of death, I asked him to inform the Intensive Care staff of our wishes.

A nurse from the leukemia ward had grown close to us over the year of Lyttle's frequent hospital admissions. She came that afternoon to say good-bye to Lyttle, and left with tears in her eyes. I was very touched and grateful for her courage, for showing her love openly this way. By evening, Lyttle was drifting in and out of consciousness, giving his final messages to family members who had gathered around.

The physical changes that are part of the dying process were startling. At one moment Lyttle was burning up with heat, and then he would suddenly be shaking with unremitting chills. His bed became soaked with sweat. As he came back into consciousness at times, Lyttle's face would once again register his pain, and then he would drift away. Hours later, we heard a terrible gurgling with each labored breath and I pleaded with the nurses to do something. I was sorry in the next moment when I saw what happened. After they put tubes down his throat to suction out the fluid filling his lungs, I could see that Lyttle was more pained from the procedure than from the shallow breathing, and I asked them to stop.

Shortly after midnight, the heart monitor began flashing a warning and the staff rushed all of us out of the room, away from Lyttle's side and into the hallway. I was sad and frightened and frustrated: contrary to my wishes, they were attempting to resuscitate him!

After a few minutes, a doctor came into the hall. "Mr. Longaker's heartbeat was restored for a few minutes and now it has stopped again. We're not going to be able to revive him."

Lyttle's mother and I requested to go to his side first. Lyttle lay on the bed, eyes closed and body still, his breathing stopped. Was he dead? The heart monitor still showed an erratic heartbeat, in jagged peaks and valleys. Lyttle appeared to be alive and only resting; I understood then that there is no single, clear moment when death happens.

All through the past year I had helped take care of Lyttle. Now I felt utterly helpless and wondered: *What can I possibly do for him now?*

A story I had read in a magazine article a few months earlier came back to me, about a Tibetan lama's advice on helping a loved one at the time of death: "There are two vital things you can do for someone at the time of death," he said. "Giving your dying relative all your love, let him or her go. Let him die in peace, feeling loved. And whatever spiritual practice the dying person has faith in, encourage him to do this practice meaningfully and regularly, in preparation for the extraordinary spiritual opportunity dawning at the moment of death."

Then the Tibetan lama told the story of an elderly nun who was very close to death; she was conscious yet unable to speak. An old man who had been her spiritual brother and friend came to her room early in the morning to give her his loving encouragement and say good-bye. Her friend reminded her to rely completely on the spiritual teachings and practices she had received for the time of death, for in fact this was the moment for which she had prepared her whole life. He encouraged the old nun to not worry about anyone else, but to concentrate on her spiritual practice until her last breath, and then, he reassured her, she would be fine. Finally, he said, "I am going shopping now, and perhaps when I come back, I won't see you. So, *good-bye.*" Understanding the heart of his message, the old nun nodded and smiled a good-bye to her friend.[1]

Lyttle and I had no spiritual practice to rely on at that point in our lives, but remembering this story as I stood by his side at the time of his death, I encouraged him to let go, expressed my love, and said good-bye, silently wishing him well on his journey. In my heart, I felt peaceful and loving in letting him go.

As I observed Lyttle's body lying still on the Intensive Care bed, I had a clear realization that one day I, too, would be on my deathbed. Facing that truth, I found I could accept it, but with one condition: When it is my time to die, I want to have a clear understanding about what death is, and I want to be fully prepared for that moment.

Lyttle's death was the beginning of my very personal research into the subject of dying and death, research that profoundly altered the direction of my life.

Chapter 2

FALLING INTO GRACE

"YOU YOUNG PEOPLE, YOU DON'T REALIZE HOW LUCKY you are." Science-fiction writer Ray Bradbury was speaking to a youthful audience at UCLA in 1977 about how to develop the breadth of perception necessary to become successful writers. "You must pay attention and notice what is happening on a larger scale than your everyday lives; otherwise, you won't know how fortunate you are.

"For example, it's only been a few decades since modern medicine has enabled the prevention of many deadly childhood diseases. If I had given this talk fifty years ago, more than half of you wouldn't have survived childhood to be here today. . . .

"When I was a child, families experienced death all the time. A woman might have eight babies, but half of them wouldn't live past the age of five. People were dying all the time. We took care of them at home, watched them die, and then washed their bodies and carried them in coffins to the graveyard. We had to have a belief in God, because we had to have a way to make sense of all that dying."

It's true that we don't know how lucky we are. We also do not realize what we've lost. While I stood listening to Ray Bradbury, I was aware that my husband was hospitalized only a few hundred yards away at the UCLA Medical Center. Before his diagnosis of leukemia, Lyttle and I had rarely thought about death, suffering, or momentous change. Having a husband and child was the center of my life, but like most people, I took my situation for granted. When you imagine that people are going to be around forever, you rarely cherish them or give your full attention. It's easy to hold on to grudges, and deal with those closest to you in unconscious, conditioned ways.

Lyttle and I felt we had everything we wanted, and that life was simply there for enjoyment. Although we were both raised in a Christian tradition, as adults we weren't affiliated with any religious tradition. In spite of this, we shared an appreciation that there is some kind of spiritual reality beyond the material dimension of life.

When my husband suddenly fell seriously ill, "cut down" in the middle of his happy but spiritually neutral life, some might have called it a fall from grace. But I know now that living in blissful ignorance is not grace, or even a desirable way of existence. For one thing, it can't last. The vicissitudes and suffering of life are inevitable, and they can easily catch us unprepared to weather their storms. Without a sense of the "bigger picture," it is unlikely we will appreciate the preciousness of life and of our loved ones.

In truth, facing illness, suffering, or death is a *fall into grace*. When Lyttle and I were forced to acknowledge his eventual death, we finally understood the truth that *everything is impermanent*. Gazing continually into the mirror of death during the year of his illness encouraged us to find and commit to a meaningful direction in our lives. Rather than feeling we were helpless victims, we committed to creating the kind of life we truly wanted in our final year together. This change came about in the way we decided to view death on that very first day in the hospital.

During my year of caring for Lyttle with his illness and many health crises, I anticipated that this would be the most painful and difficult time of my life. For a while, this seemed to be true.

For four months after Lyttle's death I was relatively numb, existing in a prolonged state of shock. Once in a while I was sad, but the full awareness and finality of the loss I had suffered had not yet hit me. When it did, the sensations of excruciating emotional pain and personal disintegration were so powerful that I felt sometimes that now I was dying. At other times, I feared that I was simply losing control of my life, going crazy with grief and disorientation. This painful process of mourning, and the fear that I might not be able to keep body and soul together, continued for many months.

Even more than Lyttle's illness and death, the experience of bereavement effected a profound change in my life. In despair, I began to pray, even though I didn't believe in anyone or anything at the time. I was the proverbial "atheist in the foxhole." I prayed for help, I prayed to find something reliable which could help me get through my suffering. At times I was in such deep loneliness and despair, I imagined that only my own death would bring any respite from my pain.

The two years following Lyttle's death were the hardest period of my life, as the experience of grieving and letting go led to the experience of my own "inner death," in which it was necessary to release all the references from my former way of life. I became much more attuned to the fragility of life, with an acute awareness that I would suffer even more losses in the future, particularly the loss of my son, whether by his death or mine. So I prayed because I felt lost, alone, and desperate, and I knew that I did not want to ever experience such deep despair and helplessness again. I knew that I needed a spiritual path to help me find the way out of my suffering.

A Deeper Understanding of Death

From out of my husband's suffering and death, I gained two exceptional life experiences which dynamically shaped my perspective on life and its meaning: working in a hospice program and learning the Tibetan Buddhist teachings and practices for death and life from Sogyal Rinpoche.

One year after Lyttle's death I moved from Los Angeles to Santa Cruz and helped to develop a hospice program there. I spent seven years working with the hospice, serving on the board, training the volunteers and staff, and visiting the dying, their families, and the bereaved. One invaluable gift which came from Lyttle's suffering and death was that I could now help families understand how they could use the time of dying well, and thereby alleviate much of the unnecessary suffering of dying and death.

Working for seven years in the hospice program, helping others face death and find hope, was a tremendous gift for me as well. This work allowed me to continue viewing life in the mirror of death and to clarify my priorities and choices. Every experience was more vibrant than it would otherwise have been, and I felt a daily gratitude for my work and my life.

A few years into my hospice work, a volunteer in the program suggested I come to a talk being given by Sogyal Rinpoche, a Tibetan Buddhist master, on the subject of death. I agreed, although I had my doubts. I had looked into *The Tibetan Book of the Dead,* and felt the teachings it contained wouldn't be relevant to my work supporting the dying and their families in modern America.

Thus, what happened came as a pleasant surprise. Rinpoche didn't describe elaborate visions we might have after death, but instead he talked about the very real process of dying—the dissolution of the physical elements, senses, and physical powers which I had repeatedly witnessed in dying patients. Everything Rinpoche taught was practical, and his manner revealed qualities of deep understanding, compassion, and openness. He described, from the Tibetan Buddhist perspective, the supreme way to prepare for death, and then proceeded to show a variety of methods for offering those who are not Buddhist appropriate spiritual support.

Sogyal Rinpoche emphasized the importance of speaking honestly with the dying, of giving our love fully, and especially of making the dying person's last months or weeks sacred, by creating an environment imbued with spiritual practice.

Then he began to tell the story of his great-aunt, Ani Rilu, an elderly Tibetan nun who was very near to death in Sikkim. An old man who had been part of the family for many years and whose job it was to cook for the household heard that Ani Rilu was close to death, and so early in the morning, before going shopping, he came to her room. He reminded the dying nun to practice continuously and intensively in preparation for her death, and to not worry about those she was leaving behind. And then, with great love, he said his final good-bye to her.

Listening, I was riveted in my seat, tears of gratitude in my eyes. This was the same story that I had remembered at the moment of my husband's death! If what Rinpoche taught had already helped me once, and enabled me to give my husband the gift of a peaceful death, then I was certain he had much more wisdom that could benefit my life and work. I felt especially blessed when Sogyal Rinpoche agreed to return and continue teaching and giving retreats in the United States. Thus I took my first steps toward an authentic path and a spiritual master who has a very important message of hope for the modern world.

The Tibetan Buddhist teachings have expanded my understanding of life's potential. I have learned that it is possible to work with and transform suffering and that I can use my life to prepare spiritually for death. I have come to clearly appreciate—through the presence and blessings of many great spiritual masters I have met as well as through their teachings—that each of us has an inherent innermost essence which is our original and true nature, an unchanging pure awareness which underlies the whole of life and death. And, although I may have confusion and suffering at times, I know now that I am *not* my emotions, my confusion or negativity or fear. The spiritual path offers me many tools to understand and transform these painful emotional habits so that I can slowly become free.

Facing death and bereavement so early in my adulthood brought me this precious gift of a spiritual path. Awaiting everyone who is facing the struggles of dying, death, or bereavement is the same secret gift. A gaze into the mirror of death each day reveals to us how to live more meaningfully, and provides the impetus for changing ourselves and transforming our suffering. Our deepest experiences of suffering and loss can inspire us to take the first step upon the path toward spiritual liberation.

The Four Tasks of Living and Dying

Drawing upon my personal experience, from years of hospice visiting and providing education and training to professional caregivers, I have formulated "The Four Tasks of Living and Dying" which are vital to our process of living and dying well. These four tasks, described in detail in Part 2, are:

- Understanding and transforming suffering
- Making a connection, healing relationships, and letting go
- Preparing spiritually for death
- Finding meaning in life

Since death could come at any time, working with these tasks now not only enables us to prepare for our death but provides us with the keys to living fully and finding meaning throughout all of the unwanted changes, losses, and painful circumstances of our lives.

How much we suffer as life unfolds depends on whether we can use these experiences of impermanence and change as opportunities to "practice dying" and learn to release our strong grasping toward whatever we are losing. Familiarizing ourselves with this nongrasping attitude, when we "let go" with each change we can begin to uncover something even greater: the openness and freedom of our skylike nature—the deathless, unchanging innermost essence of our being.

Thus all the things that happen—especially the "deaths within life" that we necessarily experience—are markers along our path, pointing the way toward learning how to live, and in so doing, how to die.

Chapter 3

THE NEEDS OF THE DYING

Afᴛᴇʀ ʏᴇᴀʀs ᴏꜰ ʟɪsᴛᴇɴɪɴɢ ᴛᴏ ᴍᴀɴʏ ᴘᴇᴏᴘʟᴇ ᴡʜᴏ are dying, hearing them try to articulate what they need during this most difficult passage of their lives, I will try to speak for them to you, their loved ones and caregivers. I will speak with one voice representing all their many voices, communicating the emotional, practical, and spiritual needs of a human being facing imminent death.

I need to talk about my thoughts and fears. I am going through so many changes; I feel so uncertain about my future. Sometimes all I can see in front of me are those future things I am afraid of. And each day, my fear ignites a different emotion. Some days I can't take it in and I need to believe it isn't happening. So there might be days or even weeks that I will feel sad, or act irritated. If you can listen and accept me, without trying to change or fix my mood, I will eventually get over it and be able to relax, and perhaps even laugh with you again.

Until now, you may have always expected me to be emotionally strong and in control. Now I'm afraid that if I honestly reveal myself, you will think less of me. Because of the extreme stresses I am going through, it might happen that the very worst sides of my personality, the real dregs, will get stirred up. If that happens I need permission to be "lost in the woods" for a while. Don't worry, I will come back.

Do you know that I'm afraid to express my true thoughts and feelings? What if everyone I care about runs away and leaves me all alone? After all, you might not believe how hard this really is. That's why I need you to reassure me that you understand my suffering, and that you are willing to stay with me through the process of my dying. I need to know that you will listen to me, respect me, and accept me, no matter what sort of mood I am in on any particular day.

The Needs of the Dying

Here's the most important thing: I want you to see me as a whole person, *not as a disease, or a tragedy, or a fragile piece of glass. Do not look at me with pity but rather with all of your love and compassion. Even though I am facing death, I am still living. I want people to treat me normally and to include me in their lives. Don't think that you cannot be completely open with me. It is okay to tell me if I am making your life harder, or that you are feeling afraid or sad.*

More than anything, I need you to be honest now. There is no more time for us to play games, or to hide from each other. I would love to know I am not the only one feeling vulnerable and afraid. When you come in acting cheerful and strong, I sometimes feel I must hide my real self from you. When we only talk of superficial things, I feel even lonelier. Please, come in and allow me to be myself, and try to tune in to what is going on with me that day. How healing it would be for me to have someone to share my tears with! Don't forget: we're going to have to say good-bye to each other one day soon.

And if we have a rocky history between us, don't you think it would be easier if we could start by acknowledging it? This doesn't mean I want you to rekindle the same old disagreements. I would like it if we could simply acknowledge our past difficulties, forgive each other, and let go. If we don't communicate like this, and instead stay in hiding from each other, then whenever you visit we will feel the strain of that which remains unspoken. Believe me, I already feel much more aware of my past mistakes, and I feel bad about the ways I might have hurt you. Please allow me to acknowledge them and say I am sorry. Then we can see each other afresh, and enjoy the time we have left together.

Now more than ever I need you to be reliable. When we make plans and you are late, or do not come at all, you don't realize how much you've really let me down. Thinking that I will have one visitor on a given day can make all the difference in how much I am able to bear my pain or emotional distress. Each moment spent with a friend who really loves and accepts me is like a warm light shining in a very difficult, lonely, and frightening existence.

When you come into the room, can you meet my gaze? I wish you would take the time to really look into my eyes and see what I am truly feeling. I long for friends to embrace me, or at least touch my shoulder, hold my hand, or gently stroke my face. Please don't hold back your affection and your love. In the hospital, I sometimes feel more like an object or a disease rather than a human being. Please, bring in your humanity and kindness to ease my suffering. Because no matter how I might seem on the outside—gruff, withdrawn, cheerful, bitter, or mentally impaired—inside, I am suffering and I am very lonely and afraid.

Even though this is a difficult time in my own life, often my main worry is about how my condition is affecting my loved ones. They seem so lost, so burdened, so alone with all of the changes they are experiencing, and all the responsibilities they shoulder. And what about their future? How are they going to cope after I am gone? I'm afraid I am leaving them stranded and alone. Some days, when everyone comes in with different emotions and needs, I am too weak to handle it all. I can't possibly listen to everyone and all of their burdens. I would be so relieved if someone could help my closest family members contact a counselor, or an organization like a hospice, who could support them, listen to their needs and their sadness, and maybe even help out in practical ways.

Saying good-bye is so very hard for both of us. But if we don't, and if you are resisting my death when I have begun the process of dying, it will be even harder for me to let go. I would like to live longer, yet I cannot struggle anymore. Please do not hold this against me, or urge me to fight when all my strength is gone. I need your blessing now, your acceptance of me and of what is happening to me. Tell me it is all right for me to die, even if I appear unconscious or in great pain, and tell me you are letting me go, with your warmest wishes and all the courage you can muster in this moment.

One of my deepest, most powerful fears is that I will be reduced to the situation of an infant, helpless and incoherent. I fear that you will forget who I am and treat me with disrespect. Even thinking about others taking care of my most intimate needs makes me feel ashamed. And every step closer to death makes me realize I will soon be totally dependent on others. Please try to understand when I resist giving in to one more change, one more loss. Help me to take care of myself, even in little ways, so that it will be easier to tolerate the bigger changes which are coming. Speak directly to me, rather than over my head, or as though I were not in the room. Find out what my wishes are for my medical care during the time of dying while I can still articulate them. And please honor and respect my wishes, ensuring they get written down and communicated.

When everyone treats me as though they know what is best for me,

The Needs of the Dying

I get so angry. Aren't I the person who is ill? *Isn't this my life, and my body? Don't I have a right to know what is going on, to know if I am living or dying? I need to know what my condition is. I need to know, in the doctor's best estimate, how much time I have left. If you find the courage to tell me what is going on, then I can decide which type of care is right for me; then I can make decisions about my life. If we stop hiding the truth about my imminent death, I will be able to wrap up the details of my life, and prepare my family to survive after I'm gone.*

You know, the pain can be unbearable sometimes. On other days, the pain is just there, *like a bad toothache, and I get tense and irritable. Please forgive me when I am in a bad mood; you may not know what it is like to live with constant pain and discomfort. What is hardest is when no one believes the amount of pain I am having; that makes me feel crazy. I need to be believed and I need to have my pain relieved. But please don't knock me unconscious to do it. I would rather experience a little pain, and still be conscious—to enjoy my life and my family, and to do my spiritual practice—while I am in the last few weeks of life.*

One of the most important ways you could offer practical help would be to act as an advocate for my needs. When I am ill and weak, I may lose my ability to communicate what I want and need. Perhaps some hospital rules can be relaxed to accommodate my lifestyle, my family, and my personal needs. My loved ones might need reassurance, or encouragement to take a break from caregiving duties when they become too emotional or stressed. And legally, help me to plan ahead of time whatever practical arrangements are necessary so that I can prepare for a peaceful atmosphere at the time of my death.

And what happens if my mind starts to disintegrate? How long will you visit me then? I hope you will not give up communicating with me when my words come out garbled, or when I can't speak at all. Do not forget that underneath the seeming confusion—or unconsciousness—I am still there, I can still hear you, I can even feel the quality of our relationship. I might be feeling lonely and afraid, though. I always need your love and your reassurance. In order to help me, I hope you can learn to be deeply peaceful inside and receptive, so that you can sense what I am feeling and needing and know how to respond appropriately.

As my body and mind disintegrate, remember that inside I am still the person I was when my life was at its peak—and thus I am always worthy of kindness and respect. No matter how far gone I appear to be, trust that your love and your heartfelt prayers really do get through and deeply reassure my entire being. Please don't give up on me when the going gets rough. This is our last chance to heal our relationship, and to give to each other our last gifts of love, forgiveness, and wisdom.

Being in the hospital makes me feel so restricted. It's hard to give up the patterns of my normal lifestyle: my ability to enjoy the company of my friends, my favorite activities, and even my usual waking and sleeping patterns. It's hard to lose my privacy; in the hospital I feel so exposed and vulnerable. I miss the home-cooked meals, the family celebrations, and my favorite music. It's hard, in this controlled and public environment, to find a space to share our intimacy and our grief without fear of being interrupted. When I'm hospitalized, I yearn to have a connection to the outside world, to nature, to the beautiful changes of weather and seasons and wind. Do I have to be cut off from all that I love and cherish even while I am living?

I might prefer to die at home. If you called a hospice program, they could show you how to arrange for me to be cared for at home as long as you can manage it. Being at home would make the process of dying more bearable. I understand that if you have the responsibilities of work and raising your family, you might have to put me in a hospital. But please, do not abandon me there! Help make the hospital environment more like home; try and spend the night when you can. And, even if I have to be hospitalized for most of the period of my dying, I would be grateful if you could arrange with the hospice nurses to bring me home for at least the last few days of my life. What a relief that would be, to be cared for in my familiar surroundings, with family and friends keeping vigil—meditating, praying, or simply talking with me, to help relieve my fears and my loneliness.

I need help reflecting on my life, so I can make sense of it. What meaning did my life have? What have I accomplished? How have I changed and grown? I need to know you will not judge me, so that I can honestly face and reveal my life to you. Encourage me to acknowledge my regrets, so that I can make up with anyone I've neglected or harmed and ask for their forgiveness. Sometimes when I look back on it, my life seems to be one continuous string of mistakes, or a legacy of selfishness and disregard for others. Remind me of what I have accomplished, of any good I have done, so I can know that in some way I have contributed to your life.

The Needs of the Dying

Please don't feel you must have all the answers or wise words to assuage my fears. You might come to my side feeling anxious, not knowing what to say. You don't have to pretend or keep up a strong façade. To really offer me spiritual support, I need you to be a human being first. Have the courage to share with me your uncertainty, your fear, your genuine sadness for the immense loss we are facing. Going through these difficult feelings together, establishing a deep bond and trust, I will feel safe enough to begin letting go, and I'll be able to face my death with more equanimity and an open heart.

After you have listened to my painful stories or complaints, remind me that I am more than my fear or my sadness, my pain or my anger. Help me understand that whatever suffering I am going through is natural; it's part of the human condition. Remind me that my painful emotional or physical condition, no matter how seemingly solid and real, will pass.

If I seem to be lost in my own suffering, help me to remember that there is still one positive thing I can do: extend my love and compassion toward others. Tell me the ways my life has touched yours. In whatever way you can reach me, help me connect to the inner goodness which is the most essential part of my being.

How can my process of dying have meaning? When I am lying here, weak and helpless, I am tempted to feel that the remainder of my life is useless. Everyone has to do everything for me, and it's so hard to feel that I have nothing left to contribute. If you ask, you might find there is something I do have to offer you: the insights about life and about death that I've recently gained. Would you allow me to give you whatever final gifts I have?

Sometimes the thought of death terrifies me. At the same time, I also feel strangely peaceful and even curious about the adventure that is ahead. Yet it is a journey for which I may not have prepared. It won't help if you try to give me your own beliefs and answers about death; I need you to help me discover my own philosophy, my own inner resources and confidence. But if you are grounded in a spiritual tradition which gives you strength, which helps you work through your own suffering, perhaps you can find ways to open windows and doors of hope for me. Perhaps all you need to do is tell me your own story, without any expectations attached. With time, if you give me your love and your trust, I will work something out deep inside me.

The Experience of Dying and Death

What will happen to me after I've died? What will count then? Help me find images of death which inspire rather than frighten me, so I can trust that what I am going toward is good. What I don't like is to feel I must simply "give up" and die. Perhaps you can help me find a way to meet death in a more positive way, calling on the best qualities of wisdom and authentic compassion within me. Maybe, like the prodigal son, I have been wandering far away from my home and my truth. Dying might be the process to help me find my own way home, so I can make my peace with God or my inner truth.

Perhaps you could learn which spiritual practices—prayers or meditations, sacred readings or music—are inspiring for me, and sit by my side and practice with me, whenever you visit. Finding a spiritual practice that fills my heart with confidence, devotion, and compassion will help me to feel more prepared for death. I would be grateful if you could arrange whatever is necessary with the hospital staff and my family, so that the atmosphere when I am dying is loving and peaceful, and will be conducive to spiritual practice.

And please do not worry or feel bad if I die when you are not by my side. Sometimes your presence is soothing, but sometimes your being there makes it harder for me to leave. Please say and do whatever you need to early on, and then you won't have regrets if I should die unexpectedly soon. And when you learn I have died, please let go of any guilt! Remember that I am grateful for all you have done—and what I need most is your kindness, your sincere and heartfelt prayers, wishing me well and letting me go.

Chapter 4

DISCOVERING HOPE IN DEATH

As a young child I enjoyed a warm and close relationship with my grandmother. She was a devout Catholic and often expressed her personal devotion to the Virgin Mary. Each day she would recite the rosary in front of a small shrine in her room, and whenever I visited her, I came along and watched. As Grandmother did her spiritual practice, the atmosphere in her room always felt peaceful, full of love and trust.

Years later, when she was near death, she lay unconscious in a convalescent hospital. My mother told me that just before Grandmother died, a priest whom she didn't know came to her room to give her the Sacraments of the Sick, a series of prayers and rituals to prepare a seriously ill or dying Catholic for the moment of death. When the priest had concluded all that was required of him, he opened the door to leave, but then had a strong intuition that his work remained unfinished. He turned and came back to recite the rosary by Grandmother's side. This was the last imprint on her mind and heart before she died.

After learning of her death, I expected to feel sad and a little guilty, for I had not visited her much toward the end of her life. Yet in the ensuing days, every time I thought of her, I saw her surrounded by light, radiating happiness and joy. And I myself felt an inexplicable joy and all-embracing love.

Only when I heard Sogyal Rinpoche teach many years later on the spiritual dimension of the dying process did I begin to understand the experience I had after my grandmother's death. The Tibetan Buddhist teachings say that whatever happens at the moment of death has a very strong impact on the dying person's mind and heart. The last thought or emotion we have in this life is what we will wake up to in the after-death state. Reminding a dying person of her strongest refuge, the deep wellspring of her devotion and trust—as the young priest did by saying the rosary for my grandmother—can help the dying person transcend the suffering of death and set her on the path toward liberation.

Perhaps more than any religion in the world, the ancient wisdom tradition of Tibetan Buddhism has thoroughly charted death's territory, revealing what we will experience during the time of our dying and death and after our death. Whether or not you embrace the rest of Tibetan Buddhist philosophy, gaining an understanding of what survives after death—as well as how to take advantage of death's unique "window of opportunity"—may help deepen your appreciation of the teachings and practices for death within your own spiritual tradition. All the world's major religious traditions are valid and valuable spiritual paths, showing us how to live well and meet our death with hope, by connecting us to our inherent compassion, devotion, and wisdom.

Images of Death

Death is not our enemy. In woodblock prints from the Middle Ages, death was depicted as a skeleton dancing with a living human. Death is a part of the reality of life, our constant companion; whether we are aware of it or not, we dance through life in the embrace of death. The real "enemy" is our deliberate ignorance, because the more we avoid thinking about or preparing for death, the more we are bound to suffer when we ourselves—or a loved one—are faced with it.

We can, however, *imagine* death to be our enemy. In woodblock prints from the nineteenth century, death is depicted as a skeleton carrying a scythe ready to cut down a living person in one stroke. In the early part of the twentieth century, prints depict a courageous physician in a heroic stance, protecting the person lying on her sickbed from this ever-threatening figure of death.

For many people, facing death is just such a battle with a merciless force that wants to rob them of their life and everything they cherish. Healing and continued life are seen as victory in battle; accepting one's death as akin to "giving up," admitting defeat and giving in to hopelessness. While it is sensible to do whatever we can to heal, if we continually avoid death or view it as our "enemy," we will arrive on death's threshold feeling heightened tension and fear, because we have failed to prepare for the inevitable.

People who have left the religious tradition of their upbringing might claim they do not believe in anything spiritual—no God, no soul, no form of existence after death. Yet standing on death's threshold, they may begin to wonder, and worry: *"What if there is a heaven and hell? And if so, what are my chances of going to heaven?"* If they surmise that they are not worthy to go to heaven, the other alternative, hell—an existence of eternal suffering with no reprieve—becomes a frightening prospect. Some people who believe that their existence ends at death may or may not be especially afraid of death. They may feel fear or hopelessness in facing death if they go through the process of dying without proper care—devoid of dignity or the love of others.

As a result of the pioneering work of Dame Cicely Saunders (founder of St. Christopher's Hospice in London), Elisabeth Kübler-Ross, and other leaders in the modern hospice movement, an old image of death is being reintroduced to our culture: death as something natural—a part of the *whole* of life. Death is neither evidence of personal failure nor a problem due to an unhealthy psyche. Death is universal: it will come to everyone. And it can come at any time, not just to the elderly or those diagnosed with a life-threatening illness.

Popular stories about near-death experiences have caused many people to view death as a simple process of "going toward the light." Many have been lulled into complacency, assuming that they will easily achieve happiness at death. But not all near-death experiences are positive ones; people do experience suffering even after death. And unfortunately, the entire experience of death takes much longer than a few moments. The quality of our existence after death depends on how we have lived, and more importantly, on how we have prepared spiritually for our death.

Hope in Death

Most of us feel that living is hopeful and that death represents the loss of hope. Yet hope can be experienced on many levels, and what is hopeful while we are living is in fact the same hope we can cultivate when we are dying. To feel that we can face our death with hope, then, we must be willing to take our life seriously now, and use its rich potential for our own change and growth.

Whether we're living or dying, we can hope to heal our lives and purify and atone for our past actions. Even if we realize we have lived in unconscious or selfish ways, we can always change and begin to extend our compassion, appreciation, and love to others. We can seek forgiveness and heal our hearts by extending forgiveness to others.

We all hope to be loved, to be accepted; and we desire to express the love in our heart to others. We hope to *mean something* to someone else. We hope that we have contributed to others in our life, and that our life has meaning. We hope that even our suffering can ennoble us as we draw on our resources of grace and courage to help us go through the process of dying with dignity.

We hope to be respected, regardless of the deterioration of our body or cognitive functions. We might hope that there is a hospice program of care in our community available to support our loved ones, and to relieve, skillfully and humanely, the physical, emotional, and social pain we may experience while dying.

We hope to grow personally and spiritually, so that when we come to die, we are confident that we will experience happiness in our future state of existence, and have the opportunity to continue our spiritual evolution.

Those who are not religious can look with hope toward what they accomplished in life, in their capacity to give and receive love, and the extent to which they have cultivated peace of mind.

These are all different levels of hope we can find in dying. We can exchange our hope to live longer with a hope to live in a meaningful way, finding a purpose in our suffering and peace of mind as we are dying. We all have the potential to die a good death. With the love and encouragement of others, and with the support of hospice programs, it is possible to experience the end of our life with dignity and peace.

The Tibetan Buddhist teachings—which I received from Sogyal Rinpoche and present here to the best of my ability—are based on a centuries-old wisdom tradition that reveals the deeper, spiritual dimension of life and death, and describes a very special hope we can find in death. For an individual who takes the teachings to heart and cultivates a deep experience in her meditation practice, applying herself with sustained commitment to realize her highest spiritual potential, death can be an extraordinary opportunity to reach enlightenment—complete liberation—a state that is totally free of all suffering, fear, and delusion.

The Opportunity of Death

In the Buddhist view, life and death are not seen as two separate things, but as different aspects of one whole. As an end to this life, death is very real. Yet death is also the doorway into another type of existence, where our evolution continues.

Our present life, dying, and even our states of existence after death are presented in the teachings as *bardos,* periods of transition in which we are suspended between two states of existence, our past and future reality. There are six principal bardos: life, sleep and dream, meditation, dying, and the two after-death bardos—*dharmata* (intrinsic radiance), and becoming, or rebirth. The term *bardo* is most commonly used in reference to the bardo of becoming— a transitional existence we enter into after our death and before taking our next rebirth.

A bardo is an experience of profound change and uncertainty, since the past—our known world—is dissolving, and the future— our next existence—has not yet manifested. Nowhere is this more evident than when we are dying, as we anticipate the loss of all our life's references and security, while our future remains shrouded in uncertainty.

Yet, since life is a continual movement through change and uncertainty, we experience bardos—deaths and rebirths—all the time: when we first leave our family to live on our own; when we bring home our first newborn; when we lose a job in the middle of life; when we must reenter the workforce after the dissolution of a marriage; when we are wheeled into surgery for diagnosis of an unidentified illness. Even on subtle levels, we are constantly experiencing transitions, because everything is changing from moment to moment. Perceptions, thoughts, and emotions come into being, and then dissolve again.

Bardos are also opportunities. Because they are periods of transition, each bardo is an opening or gap in our seemingly "solid" reality, presenting us with the potential to change: to transform our attitude, choose a fresh direction, or, through meditation, to release our grasp on the material world and discover, when we turn inward, the innermost essence of our being, which is unchanging and deathless, our true nature of mind.

Some bardos are more charged than others, and whatever we do while going through those transitions has a very potent and far-reaching effect. One of the most powerful bardos is the moment of death.

Although our body and our ordinary mind both die, another aspect of our being—our skylike innermost essence—continues after death. Like heavy, dark storm clouds blown apart at the end of the night by a strong wind, just at the moment of death our emotions, our suffering, and our "self-grasping" are swept away, and a radiant pure awareness dawns like a vast, clear, and powerfully brilliant sky. This is a glimpse of our enlightened essence, and this is the profound opportunity that is revealed at the moment of death. Yet whether this enlightenment endures depends entirely on whether we are able to let go of our confused and conditioned identity and *recognize* and unite with our true nature when it dawns. As Sogyal Rinpoche writes:

> Realization of the nature of mind, which you could call our innermost essence, that truth which we all search for, is the key to understanding life and death. For what happens at the moment of death is that the ordinary mind and its delusions die, and in that gap the boundless sky-like nature of our mind is uncovered. This essential nature of mind is the background to the whole of life and death, like the sky, which folds the whole universe in its embrace. . . .
>
> If all we know of mind is the aspect of mind that dissolves when we die, we will be left with no idea of what continues, no knowledge of the new dimension of the deeper reality of the nature of mind. So it is vital for us all to familiarize ourselves with the nature of mind while we are still alive. Only then will we be prepared when it reveals itself spontaneously and powerfully at the moment of death; be able to recognize it "as naturally," the teachings say, "as a child running into its mother's lap"; and by remaining in that state, finally be liberated.[1]

Although liberation is possible at death, it is far from easy. Since it is our inherent nature that is being freed, all of us will have a glimpse of this clear luminosity as it dawns; yet our ability to recognize and *remain* in that state depends on how thoroughly we have prepared, on the state of our mind and heart at the moment of death, and on how we have lived.

The Tibetan Buddhist teachings encourage us to apply ourselves assiduously to the practice of meditation and learn to stabilize the flow of our true nature *before* we come to die, so that we will have gained the familiarity and confidence that can enable us to unite with our nature at the moment of death.

THE "ORDINARY MIND" THAT DIES

Imagine responding to the question: Who are you? Most of us would describe the trappings of our present "identity": our sex, occupation, marital status, the family, ethnic group, or culture to which we belong, our economic status, our religion and nationality. Now, if we lost all those external references, would we still exist? We might then identify the internal references that appear to define our existence as a separate and unique individual: our history, thoughts, and memories, our hopes for the future, our feelings and emotions, our desires, our values and judgments, perhaps even a particular "personality type."

Most of us believe that an independent "I" exists, and this "I"— associated with our thoughts, feelings, beliefs, history, personality, and even our body—is our real identity. However, this identity or ego is not our true nature, but only the self-grasping aspect of our mind.

Sogyal Rinpoche suggests that we imagine ourselves in the circumstances of someone who, after having an accident, now has total amnesia. Since we have forgotten our original identity, people begin to tell us our name, our history, and our cultural beliefs, which, over time, we accept as who we really are. Our original identity, our true nature, is still there, yet our amnesia prevents our awareness of it.

Our ordinary, discursive mind, which sustains this illusory identity, is the aspect of our being that feels separate from everything, relating in a dualistic way to external references. Our self-grasping ego feels always insecure and incomplete, and is never content. Our minds are forever moving—running toward whatever we believe will make us happy or fulfilled, or running away from whatever we imagine brings us pain or disappointment. This subtle resonance of hope and fear lies beneath all our thoughts and conflicting emotions.

Like a versatile con artist, our scheming mind convinces us that if we can *only* acquire the next wonderful thing (maybe a racy red sports car, or an exciting new relationship), we will finally be satisfied and happy. So we invest a lot of hope and energy in acquiring whatever we want, only to find ourselves still feeling empty and dissatisfied. The car develops mechanical problems; the person we desire turns out to be yearning for someone else.

Our troublesome ego is a false identity, a temporary personality we have developed and strengthened throughout life. Our personality did not exist before we were born, and it will cease to exist once we have died. Like a flash of lightning, our present identity *appears* to exist because of certain causes and conditions that have come together. Yet when these causes and conditions begin to disintegrate—as they will in the process of dying—then our seemingly real and permanent identity begins to disappear as well. If we think of this self-clinging ego as our true identity, then no wonder the thought of death is terrifying!

Yet behind the clouds of our ordinary mind's projections and emotions lies a deeper aspect of our being—our deathless, unchanging, innermost essence.

OUR DEATHLESS ESSENCE

Our innermost essence—our original, deathless nature—is sky-like: open, free, boundless, and all-embracing. Like the sky, our true nature is unchanging and indestructible, unborn and undying. Like the sun in the sky, our nature is clear, luminous awareness; awake, rich, self-sufficient, and whole. Like the sun's brilliant clarity, our nature is wisdom; and like the sun's warmth, our nature is the radiance of limitless, unconditional compassion and love for all beings.

Our innermost essence is not a "thing," like a personal soul which survives death. Even though we use words to give an example of our nature, our nature is utterly free of all concepts and words, an uncompounded, naked simplicity. Our true nature is the presence of awareness existing in every moment, before the ego's machinery begins to react to pure experience with commentaries, judgments, thoughts, and emotions.

Our true nature is no different than the true nature of all existence. It is like the space inside a vase: There is no difference between the space inside and the space outside—they are the same. The vase, like our ordinary mind, limits and contains the space inside it. Yet when the vase shatters—when the ordinary mind dies—our true nature is released and freed, becoming indistinguishable from the space outside.

This essence is the inherent source or seed of enlightenment within our being, which can only blossom fully when we have relinquished our attachment to our false identity and learned, through meditation, to recognize and sustain the luminosity and all-pervading space of our true nature.

The Tibetan Buddhist teachings say that because this innermost essence is inherent within all life, each of us will have a glimpse of our true nature, our essence, at the time of death. And the accounts of those who have survived a near-death experience seem to bear this out. After the moment of clinical death, many survivors describe a sensation of utter darkness, a state of absolute peace, free of any physical pain or suffering. Yet the total darkness is not a void, for there is still an awareness experiencing this state. This awareness is often experienced as being near, or directly above, the person's body.

A man who suffered a heart attack said, "It seemed like I was up there in space and just my mind was active. No body feeling, just like my brain was up in space. I had nothing but my mind."[2]

When the experience of "clinical death" occurs for more than a few moments, the dead person's consciousness moves through what feels like a dark tunnel, toward a brilliant light that gets closer and brighter. Finally, there is a sensation of merging with this radiant light. One person said, "As you gradually draw nearer to this extremely brilliant light there is no sensation of an abrupt end of the tunnel, but rather more of a merging into . . . this magnificent beautiful blue-white light."[3]

Another person described the light differently: "It was not a light, but the absence of darkness, total and complete . . . you didn't look at the light, *you were in the light.*"[4]

People who entered this brilliant light describe an overwhelming sense of joy and happiness beyond anything they'd previously experienced. They say that if we combined all the happiest and most loving experiences of our life and multiplied them a thousand times, it would not come close to this state of bliss and infinite peace. As one man said, "I went forward towards the light and as I did so I had such a feeling of freedom and joy, it's beyond words to explain. I had a boundless sense of expansion."[5] Another man recounted, "This was the most beautiful feeling I have ever known, it's absolute pure love. Every feeling, every emotion is just perfect. . . . Everything there is absolutely vivid and clear."[6]

This glimpse of our true nature reveals the hope there is in death. But *a glimpse is not enlightenment,* and those who experienced the radiant light when they were "near death" agree. Many of them describe painful aspects of their experience as well—feelings of profound remorse about the selfish or negative way they had lived, or anguish over their separation from loved ones. Coming back into life, many of those who have had a near-death experience realize that their role in life now has a greater meaning and purpose, and they are confident that death is not a final end.

If our innermost essence is our inherent, true nature, why then don't we experience it in everyday life?

Our skylike, true nature is utterly open and free, indestructible and unchanging. It's always there. Yet we fail to recognize it because our dualistic mind is continually generating clouds of emotions, thoughts, concepts, fantasies, and memories which obscure the pure presence and clarity of our nature.

Sometimes, when the sky is obscured for many weeks with deep layers of clouds, we might come to believe that only the clouds exist. Yet if we could find a way to fly above the clouds, we would experience the vastness of the sky and the sun's brilliant radiance. In the same way, no matter how dense the clouds of our emotional confusion, the all-embracing radiant expanse of our true nature is always there, forming the backdrop of our existence.

WHAT COUNTS AT
THE MOMENT OF DEATH

Given the extraordinary opportunity for gaining liberation which is presented at death, we need to understand how to prepare meaningfully for death while we are alive. The teachings emphasize that *two things count at the moment of death: how we have lived our life and the state of our mind in that moment.*

"How we have lived our life" has two implications. The results of our wholesome and negative actions—and our habits—will follow us when we die. Buddhist teachings describe the principle of karma: our every action has a consequence, or reaction, on our self. Even though we don't immediately witness the effects of our actions, nonetheless they are there. All of the actions of our life—including our words and thoughts—are like seeds that we are sowing, and later in life or after we die, those seeds will mature and bear fruit. The effects of our actions will be our harvest at death, for better or worse, and they will have an impact on our experiences in the after-death states, determining the quality of our next existence.

Those who survived clinical death and had a prolonged near-death experience have described witnessing a complete review of everything they had done in life, even scenes they didn't consciously remember. However, they don't just passively watch what they've done; those who entered death's threshold describe experiencing the effect of their actions on others, *as though they were now receiving it.*

"Everything in my life went by for review—I was ashamed of a lot of the things I experienced because it seemed I had a different knowledge. . . . Not only what I had done, but how I had affected other people. . . . I found out that not even your thoughts are lost."[7]

"It was a total reliving of every thought I had thought, every word I had ever spoken, and every deed I had ever done; plus the effect of each thought, word, and deed on everyone and anyone who had ever come within my environment or sphere of influence whether I knew them or not."[8]

One woman who had two near-death experiences in her life told me, "After death, when you see the effects of your actions and even your thoughts on everything and everyone, *that is hell.* In all of the seemingly insignificant encounters of your life—perhaps your reaction to a stranger who walks into a shop—you see how you are constantly projecting your judgments, your selfish or negative motivations, and you yourself now feel the effects of them."

It is clear that people who have survived near-death experiences are lucky, for now they have another chance to live, to atone for what they had done, to use their minds and hearts in a positive way, bringing kindness and good circumstances to others. Yet we who hear their message are no different. We can honestly assess our lives, heal our past actions, forgive others and ask forgiveness, and resolve to live in a different way, beginning now.

Another type of seed we are sowing is our habits. Our mindstream is a continuous flow of untamed and negative emotional habits that are the source of much of our suffering in life and untold suffering after we die.

Many years ago I brought a young Tibetan master, Dzongsar

The Experience of Dying and Death

Khyentse Rinpoche, to meet a woman who was dying. When he came into her room he introduced himself, and she expressed gratitude that he had come to see her. She said, "In the last few weeks, I was resisting my death, but now I think I have accepted it."

He looked at her with a twinkle in his eye and said, "I don't think so!"

She laughed and then admitted, "Yes, you're right."

After pulling up a chair to sit beside her, he turned and asked me in a stage whisper, *"What should I tell her?"* I suggested he tell her about the bardos, those periods of transition where we are suspended for a time between two seemingly real states of existence. I expected he would speak about the first bardo of death, when the nature of mind is fully revealed. But what he talked about was the third bardo of death: the bardo of becoming, the period between lives, from the moment when the person's consciousness leaves the body and begins to roam, until it takes rebirth.

Rinpoche proceeded to tell her: "After you die, everything will go on the same as it does now. You will have the same awareness as you have now; you will experience everything just as you do now." As he spoke these words, I reflected on how the dying woman might feel reassured to view death not as an end but simply as a continuation of awareness, independent of the body. But what he said next came as a complete surprise:

"Not only does your awareness continue, but after death your *habits* continue." As I watched her face registering this message, I imagined we shared the same response: *"Oh, no, not my habits!"*

Death is truly the fruition of all the seeds we have sown in this life, and a continuation of whatever is in our mind and heart from moment to moment. *Death is a continuation of how we are right now, in life.*

THE WINDOW OF OPPORTUNITY

The second thing that counts at the moment of death, "the state of our mind," reveals that how we are when we die is of crucial importance. At death we don't meet anything new. Instead, we experience ourselves nakedly—both our absolute nature and our ordinary, relative condition. Yet how well do we really know our *true self*? How much have we worked with our conditioned habits, or learned to cultivate compassion and wisdom in our mind and heart? Here, what I mean by "mind" embraces our whole attitude, and the spirit in our heart. Our true mind is not restricted to our intellectual or cognitive power, but is a fundamental goodness or "good heart" which is at the core of every being.

Dying is a process of gradual dissolution—of our physical powers, our senses, the gross and subtle elements of which our body is composed, and our cognitive abilities. The external aspect of this dissolution concludes when we exhale our last breath. Yet after this point, an internal process of dissolution still continues, during which our internal energies collapse along with the thought-states of anger, desire, and ignorance which had supported our ego. The conclusion of this inner dissolution is the final moment of death, which most of us will experience as "fainting" into a dark void— a space which is peaceful and free of pain.

As explained earlier, when our consciousness awakens from the utter darkness of death, the Ground Luminosity—our true nature of mind—dawns like an immaculate, clear, and radiant sky. The key to this moment is *recognition*: if we recognize the Ground Luminosity as our true nature when it dawns, we can unite with it and attain liberation. Therefore, "how our mind is" at the moment of death means, for those who gained stability in resting in the nature of mind during life, simply remaining in that pure awareness while dying, and uniting naturally with the Ground Luminosity.

However, since most of us meet death unprepared for this moment, lacking familiarity with resting in our true nature, or in an emotionally confused state, we will fail to recognize the Ground Luminosity. By sheer force of habit, we will begin to react emotionally and separate ourselves from the pure experience, thus regenerating our ego's self-grasping, fear and negativity, and all our patterns of suffering. Even though we have a momentary experience of complete freedom, we will resume the mind's habitual grasping and aversion, which propel us helplessly into the confusion and suffering of the after-death bardos and our next existence.

Since the attitude in our mind and heart—our very last thought or emotion—is what we wake up to just after the moment of death, then even when we are dying we have the potential to change our habitual grasping attitude, release our attachments, give up our judgments and aversions, and develop a kind heart. In fact, all of the suffering, changes, and losses we experience in our life offer us countless opportunities to "practice dying," training ourselves to let go of our grasping habit and to release and relax into our true nature. And we have many opportunities to heal our relationships, purify our wounded heart, and transform our response to suffering. Thus there is no moment in life when we are not preparing for death.

Through spiritual training, we can learn meditative practices that enable us to connect with our inherent wisdom and compassion. When our mind settles deeply in meditation, the conceptual mind and ordinary sense of self may temporarily dissolve. Then we experience a gap or space between our thoughts: a wakeful, clear, radiant awareness unstained by hopes, fears, or habitual projections. Pursued deeply and sincerely, spiritual practice enables us to purify and release the emotional conditioning and self-grasping ego that separate us from reality. Meditation connects us ever more reliably and profoundly to a natural, effortless awareness, in which there is a deep relaxation and spaciousness, an unbounded gratitude, and an all-embracing, joyful compassion. As Sogyal Rinpoche writes:

> The fundamental message of the Buddhist teachings is that if we are prepared, there is tremendous hope, both in life and in death. The teachings reveal to us the possibility of an astounding and finally boundless freedom, which is ours to work for now, in life—the freedom that will also enable us to choose our death and so to choose our birth. For someone who has prepared and practiced, death comes not as a defeat but as a triumph, the crowning and most glorious moment of life.[9]

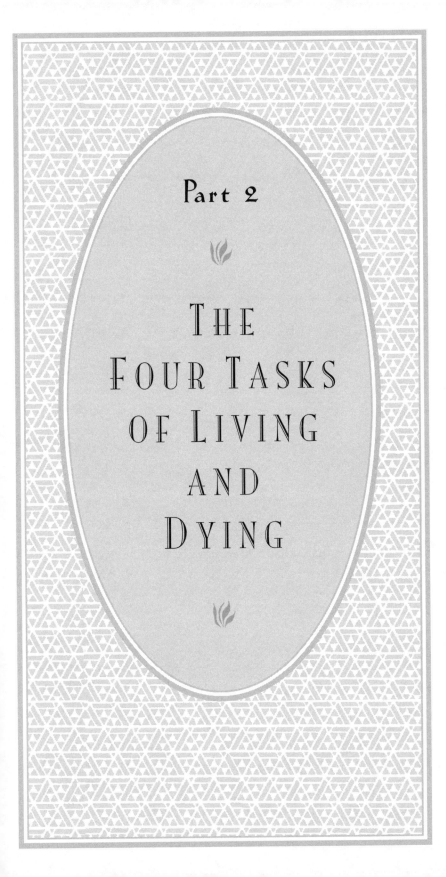

Part 2

THE FOUR TASKS OF LIVING AND DYING

Introduction

WHAT CAN I DO IF MY DYING FRIEND KEEPS DENYING his death and won't allow me to talk about it? How can I help a patient who is comatose, or extremely confused with dementia? What can I offer someone who feels completely depressed and hopeless, and refuses to talk about the spiritual dimension of death? How can I respond to the heartbreaking situation of a young mother who has to leave behind small children? What do I say to someone who is so afraid of the deterioration and pain of dying that he is planning to take his own life?

When we have a friend, family member, or patient whose suffering is immense, who is struggling against some inevitable aspect of dying—physical or emotional pain, or an inability to communicate—what can we do to help? First we need to understand that dying is not a passive activity. Accepting our death does not mean giving up, feeling as though we are helpless victims of our circumstances. Actually, dying is the last stage of living—an opportunity for growth if we see clearly the tasks we are facing. In this stage of growth we are challenged to complete our life well, and to prepare to meet death with true peace of mind.

The Four Tasks of Living and Dying described in this part of the book are specific to dying only if we've never addressed them while living. They represent the principal challenges we face in negotiating any of the unavoidable changes and sufferings of our lives, such as illness, loss, or bereavement. Understanding and fully undertaking the Four Tasks of Living and Dying enables us to face ourselves and to understand how and why we are choosing to live, even in the midst of our deepest pain. The Four Tasks offer us the opportunity to let go of past habits and commit to a positive direction for our lives, enabling us to evolve into more genuine and compassionate human beings.

Life is already a path, a journey toward the ultimate destination of death. We can commit to making that journey a spiritual one, whether we call it developing a good heart, becoming a genuine human being, or realizing our wisdom nature and attaining liberation. We have the potential to discover a playful spaciousness, generosity, and humor to touch others' hearts with kindness and thereby bring more goodness into this world. And when we finally experience our own death, we will know, without a doubt, that we have done something useful with our lives.

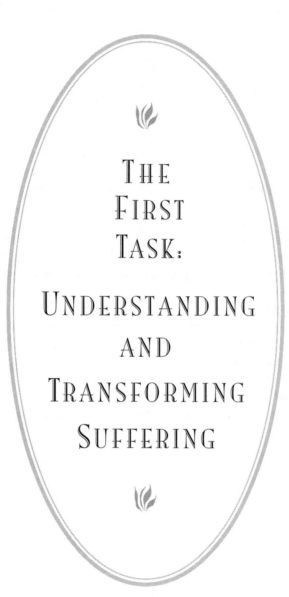

The
First
Task:

Understanding
and
Transforming
Suffering

Chapter 5

UNDERSTANDING AND RESPONDING TO SUFFERING

IT IS DUSK, THE END OF AN AUTUMN AFTERNOON. FOR you, it is the end of a long series of tests. The waiting room of the doctor's office is empty now, and you sit down for a few moments to collect your thoughts before heading home. You need time to absorb the impact of the news your doctor has just given you: your condition is not curable, and you have approximately six months to live. Take a moment to consider: How do I feel now? What are my principal concerns? What do I need?

Reflect on how you normally live day to day, and on what you expected to be doing with your time and energy during the next six months. Is there anything you would do differently? Are there any activities you would stop, any things you need to finish?

Now consider the impact of this news on your friends and family. With whom would you first share the news? Imagine telling him or her. Who else would you tell at some later time over the months to come? Imagine what it will be like to share the news of your impending death with each of your loved ones.

The months are going by. See yourself receiving different treatments for your illness, and experiencing their side effects; new and changing symptoms; physical discomfort and pain. You spend part of each month in the hospital. As your strength deteriorates, you lose the ability to do the many things you're used to doing, and you spend more and more time in a wheelchair. Strangers, professional people, are taking care of the practical details of your daily life, and eventually, even the most intimate aspects of your physical care. Your body, skin, and hair are aging quickly and you begin to look frail. As you imagine this process of illness and deterioration, take a moment to consider: What do I most need? What would help me? What do I fear the most, in this process of illness and facing death?

The Four Tasks of Living and Dying

What you fear most deeply—the worst situation or suffering you can imagine—may actually happen. If it did, ask yourself: What would help me? What external or internal resources could I call on that would help me get through the hardest part of dying? Imagine that you are calling on those invaluable resources to support you during this process.

Many months have passed, and you are in the hospital now, aware that you have only a week or so to live. You begin giving away your possessions, deciding and writing down who will receive each thing. You also write out the final directives for your medical care and the disposition of your body, and conclude all the practical details of your life. Imagine saying a final good-bye to each close friend and family member. Is there a last message you would want to leave for anyone?

Next, as though you're viewing the scene from above, consider it is the actual time of your death. You see your body below, on the hospital bed, and your last few breaths are very faint and shallow. Whom do you want to be in the room with you? What would you like them to be doing at the time of your death? As you see yourself breathing out your final breath, consider: What would be in my mind and heart in the final moments of my life?

This exercise of the imagination may give you deeper insights into the experience and needs of someone who is facing death, and help you understand what life is like from their perspective. I hope it also enabled you to see what dying might be like from your own perspective—if you were to die as you are now, somewhat unaware and probably unprepared.

To offer the most effective and compassionate care for the dying, to truly understand their experiences, difficulties, and needs and help them begin preparing meaningfully for death, we need to overcome our own hesitation and do the same. So now it is time to do exactly that. The most valuable asset we can offer to others facing death, loss, or bereavement is the confidence we will embody once we have found meaning in our life, healed our relationships with others and with ourselves, learned how to understand and transform our suffering, and prepared spiritually for our own death.

The Necessary Suffering of Dying

Dying, for most of us, will mean experiencing a certain amount of unavoidable suffering. Yet too often the dying experience *unnecessary* suffering, magnifying their feelings of helplessness and isolation and even exacerbating their physical pain.

What is the necessary suffering of dying? In the process of illness or aging, we experience physical discomfort and pain as the functions of our body slowly diminish and break down. Not all illnesses bring increasing and unbearable pain in the last months or weeks of life. Yet since pain is frequently an element of illness, the dying often unnecessarily fear that pain will only increase as death approaches.

As our body deteriorates, we lose our strength and ability to care for ourselves, and we become increasingly dependent on others to manage the details of our life and even to perform the most intimate aspects of physical existence. This dependence, and the loss of control it implies, is often what people dread most about dying.

When we're faced with the reality of dying we may also be facing, for the first time, the emotional process of letting go of our attachment to life. Understanding and working through this emotional pain, like every other task of dying, becomes a huge problem for us if we have never learned how to let go gracefully throughout the many losses in our lives.

To understand the immensity of emotional pain experienced by a dying person, reflect on a period in your life when you lost something that you greatly cherished: perhaps a beloved home, the possibility of a future career, or your partner or spouse. Remember how you reacted when you first experienced this change or loss: "I can't believe this is happening to me." You were in shock; you hoped it was a bad dream that would soon go away.

When the shock wore off, and the "bad dream" didn't go away, you probably began resisting the change. Perhaps your resistance was expressed as anger, resentment, or frustration, while you lashed out at anyone who tried to come near; as deep-seated fear of vulnerability and grief, causing you to close your heart and withdraw from loved ones; as strong judgment, where you blamed others for your suffering or criticized yourself for losing control; as resignation or hopelessness; or as denial, where you suppressed or attempted to hide from your pain.

Eventually, though, when your resistance wore down, you were able to fully acknowledge the change, and begin mourning and letting go. Depending on your level of attachment, this process of grieving and letting go, of prolonged sadness and pain, may have taken a year or more to finish. Or, as you reflect on it now, you may be aware that you have never fully let go and accepted this significant loss.

Seeing how painful and difficult it is to come to terms with just one loss in our life, we may understand more clearly the extreme circumstances of those facing death. They're not just losing one thing or one relationship they cherish—they're losing everything and everyone, all at the same time!

Thus the dying are often feeling a depth of grief, fear, and resistance that we can barely imagine. People facing death may also sense that they carry a reservoir of unfinished grief accumulated throughout their life. Allowing themselves to open to the profound losses of dying may bring them face to face with a deep pool of pain that they have never felt safe to heal.

Although modern writers decry our fear of death, I find we have an even deeper fear of grief. We equate grieving with dying, hopelessness, and helplessness. We don't have cultural models of people going through bereavement, loss, and grief, and coming out the other side. We don't trust that we *can* come out the other side, so we resist grieving as though it were the worst thing that could happen. Yet we don't just grieve once, at the very end of our illness, and then come to accept our death peacefully. *We die a thousand times before we die,* and each new change requires a new level of grieving and letting go.

Once we develop a chronic or life-threatening condition, we have the sensation we've "fallen out of the healthy world." Later, when we learn our illness cannot be cured, we will have entered the bardo of dying, which concludes at the moment of death. These transitions can evoke extreme anxiety and fear, as we sense that our known world is dissolving and the future—the form our existence will take after death—is uncertain. When we're dying, there is nothing from our former life we can grasp on to for security. When our mind and body gradually begin to disintegrate in the process of dying, we are faced with the ultimate experience of "losing control." Experiencing the bardo of dying—with its accompanying uncertainty, disintegration, and fear—can reveal our deepest vulnerability. Thus any reaction or emotion a dying person expresses is perfectly understandable, given the emotional pain, resistance, fear, and extreme vulnerability which usually accompany the dying process.

The Unnecessary Suffering of Dying

A middle-aged woman was dying in a major city hospital. Rose was receiving palliative treatment for her cancer and she spent most of her days alone. In the last few weeks of her life, as her condition slowly deteriorated, she kept ringing the nurses' bell, complaining of pain. Although her doctor adjusted the medication dosage a number of times to ensure that her pain was well managed while keeping her alert, Rose continued to ring the nurses' bell, over and over, complaining of pain. A psychiatrist was called in, yet before going to the patient's room he learned from one of the nurses that Rose had never been informed of her diagnosis or prognosis.

After greeting the dying woman, the doctor was honest about the reason for his visit. "I've been asked to see you because you keep calling the nurses and complaining of pain, but the nurses and your doctor have done all they can. So I'm here to spend time with you, to see how I can be of help. Tell me, what is it you need?"

"All I need is a cup of tea, but they keep bringing me these little pills."

"A cup of tea, is that all you want?"

"No, I am frightened, and I really need to talk, but no one has any time."

"What do you want to talk about?"

"Well, I've got cancer, haven't I?" Rose asked.

The doctor asked the dying woman to tell him how she felt about cancer. She had heard of another patient with cancer who had terrible pain, and was worried that this would happen to her. The doctor did his best to reassure her that her pain could be managed quite well until she died.

"Are you in pain now?" the doctor asked her.

"No," came her surprising reply.

"Are you afraid of death, Rose?" he asked.

Rose wasn't afraid of death, as she had a confident faith in God and in the hereafter; principally, she was anxious about the process of dying. After this long and reassuring talk, Rose was much more relaxed and no longer complained of pain. The nurses continued to connect with her and reassure her. And, once her family realized she did not have long to live, they were frequently by her side, until Rose died peacefully a few weeks later.

As this woman's experience reveals, a large part of the unnecessary suffering of dying comes from not feeling safe to acknowledge or express our natural fears and sadness, and no one taking the time to communicate honestly or appreciate us as a "living person."

Usually, neither the dying nor their families fully understand the physical and emotional process they are going through in facing death. In experiencing the dying process of a loved one, family members may feel as though they themselves are dying. They do not realize that their conflicting emotions, anticipatory grief, feelings of helplessness, anxiety, frustration, and guilt are perfectly normal. They lack the validation and support that they desperately need during this extremely difficult time. "Dying" is sometimes a harder process for the loved ones than it is for the person facing death.

One of the greatest sufferings a dying person experiences is his family's attachment and grasping, their suppressed emotions, or their inability to accept the death and let go. Lacking the personal support they need, family members often lean heavily on the dying person for support that he or she can no longer give. And, fearing to speak honestly and share their feelings and natural grief, the family members' communication becomes increasingly strained as death nears, and everyone suffers more as a result.

Another source of unnecessary suffering is when the dying person and his family do not know the resources in the community that might be available to them; sometimes they are not even sure what they need, let alone how to ask for it. Thus they are often forced to "go it alone," and endure more misunderstandings and suffering as a result.

If his doctor lacks training in effective pain management for the end stages of illness, the dying person may not be believed when he describes his pain, with the result that he is undermedicated; he may suffer unnecessary cycles of heightened pain and anxiety every few hours whenever his previous dosage begins wearing off. Alternatively, when the medical staff respond to the dying person's pain with their own fear, they may overmedicate him, rendering him confused or unconscious in the last weeks of life. Caregivers are often unaware that the physical component of pain is only one part of the distress experienced by a dying person; he may also suffer from emotional pain, social pain, financial pain, or spiritual pain that could be the largest factors in his experience of "pain."

Finally, another unnecessary suffering is the lack of control over our physical environment; having our preferences for medical care and life-sustaining measures disregarded; and being unable to complete the practical arrangements necessary for a peaceful and dignified death. Spending his last weeks in a hospital or Intensive Care setting can effectively prevent the dying person from having his most important needs during this time fulfilled: regular contact with a select few loved ones in an atmosphere where they can openly share their affection; the private time and space to share their grief and say their final good-byes; the clarity and support to finish with the practical details of his life; the freedom to sleep, eat, and wake in his own rhythm; the ability to enjoy some views of nature, or to die at home in his familiar surroundings; and the possibility to create with friends and loved ones an environment of meditation, prayer, and spiritual practice as the time of death draws near.

With better understanding, education, and support, and resources such as those offered through hospice programs, a lot of the unnecessary suffering of dying can be entirely relieved. Yet a certain amount of suffering in the process of dying is unavoidable, and will come to each of us. Thus to really prepare for death, each of us must develop the understanding and courage that can help us accept and go through—or even transform—the inevitable losses and suffering of our life.

Suffering in Life

At the core of any suffering is a glimpse of death. We all have had experiences of profound suffering and loss—shocking changes such as being robbed, losing our home, betrayal by a co-worker, experiencing a prolonged illness, or the grief of losing an intimate partner. Life is a continual dance with change, impermanence, and loss. When we really look into our most painful life experiences, then, we realize that death is no stranger to us. Even though death may seem like a remote event that will be unlike anything we've experienced, we actually suffer many losses in the midst of life that feel as uncompromising as death itself.

Suffering profound losses, prolonged emotional or physical pain, serious illness, or bereavement are the "big deaths" we repeatedly face in life. Some people call them "little deaths," but those who are seriously ill or bereaved attest that their experience parallels the emotional pain and disruption felt by those who are facing death. To prepare for the profound "letting go" of death itself, we can use these adversities as opportunities to "practice dying," so that we begin accepting our losses with courage and dignity and learn how to let go gracefully.

Yet how do we usually respond to the painful circumstances of life? We hide, resorting to a wide array of diversions: turning on the TV, working long hours, making phone calls, going shopping, having another beer or pill or fix, generating a personal crusade, or crawling into a shell of isolation and silent despair.

Pain is inevitable, suffering is optional. Suffering comes from our aversion and resistance to our painful circumstances, not from the pain itself. Suffering is our agony at losing our hopes and expectations, being forced to relinquish control, and feeling vulnerable and powerless against the undesired change or loss. Until now, we've trained ourselves to resist, deny, or hide from our pain. But how long will these hiding places help us when we're finally faced with death?

Whether we are dying or experiencing one of the "big deaths" within life, we suffer more when:

- No one believes our pain, and it is denied, diminished, or shamed.
- We are not given permission, by ourselves or others, to grieve.
- We, or those we love, judge our responses and expect us to always stay in control.
- We withdraw into a shell of isolation, not letting anyone in.
- We identify with our suffering, perceiving ourselves as helpless victims.
- We continually deny or repress our pain and give up our power to find a way through it.

Reacting to unwanted suffering with aversion, indulgence, blame, or hopelessness only compounds and prolongs our pain. Not only do these reactions make many difficulties for us now, at the end of life we will be left without any resources to help us face and go through the extraordinary multilayered sufferings of dying.

Negative Interpretations of Suffering

While visiting countless dying people and their families, I've seen how their painful circumstances can be magnified by the way they interpret the meaning of their suffering. The dying, or their loved ones, may respond to the question *Why do you think this is happening to you?* with one of the following negative interpretations:

"All day, I lie here and wonder: Why me? Why is this happening to me? All I can think is that God is somehow punishing me for something bad I have done in my life." The result of this interpretation is that during this critical time in a person's life—when he most needs to turn toward his ultimate refuge—he may conclude instead that God has judged and abandoned him, and he will feel even greater despair.

When we lack an understanding of the spiritual dimension of our being, then it is easy to conclude that a human is merely a machine that should be turned off when it's beyond fixing: "There is no purpose at all to this suffering. I know my pain will only increase as I get closer to death, and it will be impossible for me to cope with it then. My life is meaningless now that I am weak and unable to care for myself; I am only a burden to those who love me. Please put me out of my misery now." This interpretation makes the dying person feel powerless to enjoy the opportunities in his life even while dying, or to view his suffering as ennobling rather than degrading.

Alternatively, an ill person who learns he is now dying may feel he is a failure, or be tormented with guilt: "I must have a lot of emotional blockages, or the wrong kind of personality to have gotten this illness. And since I failed to heal myself, I haven't learned the 'lesson' this disease was bringing me. It's my fault I'm dying; perhaps I have a death wish." If the dying person's family also holds this belief, they may feel that he is "choosing" to die and therefore abandoning them, or they may pressure him to "not give up the fight" even during the marked deterioration of the dying process.

· · ·

Each of these interpretations is based on the premise that something is wrong with suffering, that dying is unnatural, degrading, or the result of a personal or moral failure. And these negative interpretations exacerbate our suffering by piling on feelings of hopelessness and despair. Interpreting suffering more positively will not make our painful circumstances disappear, but it will change how we feel about ourselves and offer us the potential to grow, or change, as we experience our pain.

Rabbi Pesach Krauss works as a chaplain in a large cancer hospital in New York, where he meets hundreds of people at major turning points in their lives. He writes:

> Every human being has certain aspects of his life that touch other human beings. We want to feel that we are worthwhile, that we do count, that we have dignity and a sense of responsibility. We are all subject to events and environments that we didn't create. And everything depends on how we respond to them, how we interpret them, and whether we are submerged by them or surmount them. If we can go beyond them, we can use the most difficult circumstances as rungs on a ladder, in a sense, heavenward.[1]

We can see how important it is that we develop a framework of understanding that enables us to accept the *whole* of life, with all of its joys and sorrows, accomplishments and disappointments. The Buddhist teachings reveal that suffering is universal, an inevitable and natural part of being alive; and show how—if we use them wisely—our deepest experiences of pain or loss can reveal an essential "next step" along our spiritual path.

The Buddhist Understanding of Suffering

After the Buddha fully realized his true nature and attained enlightenment—the state of complete freedom from suffering—he began teaching in order to reveal a path, a way for all beings to realize the same freedom he had found. The first message the Buddha communicated was intended to wake us up to reality, so that we might discover for ourselves the source of wisdom and compassion within. This teaching is known as the Four Noble Truths:

- Knowing that suffering pervades our existence
- Discovering the cause of our suffering

- Understanding that we can bring an end to suffering
- Entering the path which enables us to become free of suffering [2]

SUFFERING PERVADES OUR EXISTENCE

We won't even be interested in becoming free if we do not first realize that we are trapped, imprisoned by the unfolding harsh realities of life, over which we have little control. Instead of hoping our suffering will disappear, running from it, or trying to anesthetize ourselves from it, we need to understand the universality of suffering. That's our first step toward real freedom.

Our present existence is one of continuous suffering, from the gross to the most subtle levels. Although we yearn for a lasting happiness and peace, it seems to elude us, and we are never satisfied. We might work very hard to attain good situations that we imagine will bring us pleasure or comfort, but the nature of everything in this world—circumstances or people or even our present comfort—is imperfect, unreliable, unsatisfactory, and impermanent. Since nothing is perfectly satisfying or unchanging, we feel constantly let down, frustrated, and disappointed. Even our ordinary mind is insecure and untrustworthy, its cravings and delusions ushering us into difficulties and heartbreak over and over again. Thus mental suffering and dissatisfaction pervade our experience of life.

This could be depressing news if you want to hang on to your belief that "other people" are happy, and that you could eventually attain the satisfaction you imagine they feel. But even the *appearance* of happiness in the material world is an empty facade. People enjoying good circumstances are still frustrated with constant craving and insecurity, expectations and disappointments, just like you. *Suffering pervades our entire existence.* Therefore, if you are suffering, there's nothing especially wrong with you—in fact, you're on the right planet! And you have a lot of company.

Another fundamental characteristic of life on earth is that everything and everyone we grasp on to is subject to impermanence, disintegration, or death. When we do attain some pleasurable or comfortable situation—a wonderful job, building our dream home, finding the perfect partner—we will eventually experience the suffering of change. Even though we already have experienced such changes, each time we attain something that makes us happy, we fall into the same trap: believing that *this time* our situation is permanent and reliable and that we won't be disappointed. And then our situation changes or dissolves, and we end up hurt, bitter, or angry; but who is really to blame? Our expectation is a premeditated disappointment.

If this weren't enough, finally there's the suffering of suffering itself. In the course of our life we inevitably experience physical pain, illness, old age, and death. We are often thrust into unwanted or fearful experiences, and rarely attain what we most desire.

Contemplating the truth that suffering is universal—and unavoidable—is meant to wake us up, and motivate us to change our approach to life. A traditional metaphor for our dangerous ignorance of *samsara*—these endless cycles of suffering—is that of children playing games inside a burning house. Not only will all our time- and energy-consuming games to attain happiness consistently frustrate us, but eventually the house—our human body—is going to collapse. And what can we take with us when we die?

DISCOVERING THE CAUSE
OF OUR SUFFERING

If we want to become free, the next step is to ascertain the true cause of our suffering. We might be tempted to point to external circumstances or people as the source of our frustration or pain. But if they were the cause, then each of us would suffer to the same extent when we found ourselves in the same distressing situation. Those who care for the ill and dying report otherwise: two people on the same hospital ward may have the same illness, with similar complications, yet the extent to which each of them suffers varies greatly. All of us experience painful circumstances, but whether or not we suffer because of them is due to our reaction.

The next time you experience emotional or physical distress, try looking inward, at your state of mind. If you are generating strong thoughts of fear or aversion, of grasping, jealousy, pride, or blame, doesn't your experience of pain intensify? If you honestly examine your condition, you'll find that it's your own mental states of craving, grasping, or aversion which are the cause of your suffering. And ignorance, or unawareness, is the source of all these negative and troubling emotions. We are ignorant that our own grasping and selfish habits are the cause of our suffering; and we are unaware of our true nature—thus we keep identifying with our self-grasping ego and getting hurt. We don't engage in the positive actions and compassionate attitudes which could bring us happiness; and we continually indulge in the selfish and negative attitudes and actions which result in more unhappiness. Thus we remain trapped in endless, vicious cycles of expectation, fear, grasping, disappointment, and pain, repeating moment to moment, year to year, lifetime to lifetime.

Like an impoverished man who bears great hardships in search of fortune while unaware of the treasure hidden in his own home, we are unaware of who we really are, and keep looking in the wrong direction for the source of true happiness. *Ignorance is the jailer who keeps us imprisoned in suffering.*

BRINGING AN END TO SUFFERING

When we finally come to accept that suffering, impermanence, and death are facts of life, we are freed from our unrealistic expectations, our grasping, and our subsequent disappointments and grief. It may not seem logical at first glance, but contemplating impermanence and death is thereby life-affirming.

When we truly know that things won't last, we find we are more aware and appreciative of what we already have in our life. We slow down and begin enjoying life, with its precious experiences of beauty, friendship, and love. When we realize that we don't know when we will die, we see the wisdom of making choices that express our true values and priorities. And we will then be motivated to find a way out of our endless cycles of suffering.

It is possible to end this cycle and bring an end to suffering by removing its cause—our identification with this self-grasping ego—and by realizing our true nature of mind. Stabilizing the realization of our true nature until it becomes our unbroken experience is the means by which we are liberated—freed, once and for all, from suffering.

ENTERING THE PATH TO BECOME FREE OF SUFFERING

We can free ourselves from the prison of suffering by entering a spiritual path, where we contemplate daily the truth of impermanence and death, accumulate positive actions, purify and tame our negative propensities, and gradually, through the practice of meditation, come to realize our wisdom nature.

Instead of looking outward toward the world, in meditation we shift our attention inward, to help us connect with our innermost essence—a pure, boundless awareness and natural simplicity. Training in meditation, we can experience breaks in our endless mental suffering—moments of freedom, spaciousness, and deep peace. By committing ourselves to study, contemplation, and meditation, we can learn to sustain and integrate into our entire way of being the openness, clarity, and boundless compassion of our true nature, until we transcend suffering entirely.

What if we haven't gained this confidence of our wisdom nature and we are presently in a state of extreme suffering? The next chapter describes how, through spiritual practice, we can learn to accept and transform our experiences of emotional or physical distress.

Responding to the Suffering of Others

One of the hardest parts of caregiving work—or life, for that matter—is being asked to help someone whose particular form of suffering we have not experienced ourselves, perhaps one that triggers our deepest fears—for example, the sudden death of a child. How can we respond to a young father's pain when we don't even want to imagine what he is going through? What can we possibly offer him?

Over years of traveling and teaching, I've heard many stories of unimaginable suffering, and have gleaned one truth from them all: irrespective of our particular circumstances, each of us has the same needs when we are suffering.

We all need to have our suffering and emotional pain validated. We need to feel safe speaking about and expressing our pain, and to trust that others will understand our feelings. *We need to feel that no matter what our experience or circumstances, we are respected and unconditionally accepted.*

We all need basic human kindness—the reliable presence and love of another person, someone willing to be in regular contact with us for the duration of our journey through suffering. We need others to simply listen and bear witness to our pain, offering support, encouragement, and honesty tempered with compassion.

What helps us endure suffering are frequent expressions of affection, love, and hugs; sometimes we need laughter to lighten our pain. We need time to withdraw and heal our wounds, balanced with encouragement to take steps back into life's enjoyable activities. We need friends who can sometimes offer new ideas or perspectives, without any expectations attached.

And we all need to be reminded that our suffering and painful circumstances do not constitute a new "tragic" identity. We need others to view us always as a whole person, facing yet another of life's transitions. If others can respond to our needs with courage and love, this gives us hope that we can bear our suffering with dignity.

When a friend is in tremendous emotional or physical pain, sometimes we're afraid to go and be with him or her, or afraid to communicate honestly when we visit. We think we should know how to relieve his pain, or have just the right things to say. Yet what a person suffering needs most is our presence. The Greek word for comforter is *paraclete,* meaning "one who comes to walk alongside." What we bring to support a friend is our loving presence, with perspective.

More than anything we do or say, what helps a person who is suffering is how we are. "How we are" is a reflection of the unified perspective we have on the whole of life, which includes experiences of joy and adversity. Our presence is also an expression of our confidence, the profound love and unqualified respect for others we have come to embody through our spiritual practice. "How we are" is connected to our awareness of our own suffering and the extent to which we have worked through our grief. And finally, our loving presence depends upon our ability to acknowledge and then release our fears and expectations, remaining compassionate and receptive toward the other person.

You can obtain valuable insights for responding to another person's suffering from your own experience. Take some time to reflect on a period in your life when you went through a deep experience of suffering, loss, or grief. Remember what it was you really needed during that time. Recall what helped you to face and heal your pain, and what resources—either internal or external—you called on for help. Or if you never received what you most needed, reflect on what you *wished for* to help you get through your painful distress.

Finally, you might ask yourself: What benefit did this suffering bring to my life? Can I appreciate now that my suffering played a purposeful role in my development? Was I able to give a meaning to my difficulty by the way I chose to respond?

Reflecting on your own experiences of deep suffering will enable you to realize that you have the necessary skills for supporting others, the confidence that suffering is not hopeless, and an appreciation that suffering presents us with an opportunity to change or find meaning in the midst of our adversity.

Before meeting a friend who is experiencing physical or emotional pain, sit quietly for a few minutes. Become aware of any thoughts or fears that might impede your receptivity, and connect again with your inherent openness and love by reflecting on your friend's suffering.

As you settle quietly in meditation and watch your thoughts, you might find that you have fear about the other person's anguish, or concern about your ability to make him feel better. Perhaps you're already trying to plan what you will say, to feel some control in the uncertain situation ahead. Acknowledge these thoughts and fears, and then allow them to dissolve. You might imagine setting your fears, plans, and thoughts in a box next to you and leaving them behind, before going into your friend's room.

Reflect on your friend's situation, and let his suffering touch your heart, awakening your compassion and love. No matter how painful the circumstances or how disturbing the physical appearance you will encounter, remember that your friend has, at the core of his being, an innermost essence of wisdom and compassion. *Your role, then, is not to rescue him or give him your solutions, but to help him recall and turn toward his own inner resources.*

After becoming aware of yourself and compassionately opening your heart to your friend, you'll feel more ease in communicating authentically with him or her. You don't have to have all the answers or be perfect; *you can simply be yourself.*

You might begin: "I'm at a loss here because I don't know what to do. And I can't even imagine how difficult this is for you. Still, I've come because I want you to know that I care about you, and that you are not alone. No matter what happens, or what you're feeling, I love you. Please tell me what is happening for you now."

Then *listen* as your friend expresses who he is and how he is feeling. And you must listen with your whole being, not just your ears. Listen with your body, your heart, your eyes, your energy, your total presence. Listen in silence, without interrupting. Fill any spaces of silence between you with love, with silent permission for the other person to go on and to go deeper. Once in a while, perhaps, ask a question to draw your friend out even further:

"What else are you going through; what else is happening in your life right now? What are you thinking about as you go through this difficulty? What's the hardest part of this for you? What is your biggest fear?"

If he can't talk directly about the immediate suffering he is going through (for example, if he is dying and doesn't want to speak about it yet), then you might say: "Tell me about your life. What has happened to you? What did you do that you feel good about? What was the happiest part of your life? What have you accomplished? What challenges or difficulties have you had to face?" Or: "How have you coped with your illness up until now? Has being ill brought you any new insights about life?"

Give space for his answers and acknowledge his pain. Don't immediately jump in with your stories or brilliant ideas. Silently acknowledge your rising thoughts and feelings, and *continue to be there for him.* Focus on what he is communicating on every level— through his body, his expression, the tone of his voice, his energy, and his words. Listen to what is said and also to what is not said, yet implied. Validate the feelings he has expressed, and through your intuition and questions, slowly draw out even more of his thoughts or needs.

You might reflect back to your friend: "This must be very hard. You are going through a great difficulty right now, do you realize that? As I listen to you, I feel your distress, your sorrow, your frustration or fear. This must be really, really hard. Whatever you are feeling is perfectly understandable, given the circumstances you are facing."

After encouraging your friend to describe his deepest fears, angers, regrets, or sadness, you can acknowledge his pain and let him know that it may take a while for it to diminish. By fully listening to and accepting your friend's pain, you help him accept himself and his present condition, thus alleviating a great deal of the emotional suffering that can result from guilt or harsh self-judgment.

While it's good to reveal yourself at times, be aware of how much you reveal, and when, and, most important, why. When you do speak, communicate clearly, with honesty and kindness.

At a later time, when the person's emotional suffering has somewhat lessened, you may see an appropriate opportunity to expand your friend's awareness beyond his immediate situation. You could choose words and images of hope which come from phrases your friend has already used; or you might express something like the following:

"I hear your pain and confusion, and I understand how very bad things are for you right now. I know you may feel lost in the dark sometimes, or fear this suffering will never end. But even though it won't go away quickly, your pain won't last forever.

"Your suffering might seem like a heavy cloud covering up every trace of hope at the moment, yet remember that there is another aspect of your being that is always whole, peaceful, and loving. This aspect of you has known joy and happiness, and can experience happiness again. Remember this and please do not judge or abandon yourself as hopeless. No matter what happens, I am going to stay in contact with you, and keep visiting. I love you."

Finding a Direction in Our Suffering

We cannot control the hand that life deals us; all we can do is decide how we will play the hand we've got. Thus we can use experiences of suffering as opportunities for focusing the energies of our heart and mind in new ways: by strengthening our positive qualities, changing a destructive habit, healing our unfinished business, or deepening our trust in our spiritual path. The challenge is to find a way to grow, or give ourselves a positive direction in the midst of our suffering, rather than agonizing about what we are losing.

One friend described his own appreciation of this process to me: "It deepens my soul to suffer, forcing me to go down and under, to find the gem in all that darkness. I go through a time of darkness, and when it lifts, a whole new level of integration happens. Although it seems hopeless, if you go through it you find something necessary and precious for you. There are things you need to learn, and you can only learn them through suffering."

Since it is impossible to know all of the causes for whatever difficulties we experience, it is certainly not helpful to imagine that suffering is our punishment for having been bad, or to rail against our fate. I find the following perspective from Buddhism very helpful: In any situation, no matter how difficult, we have the power to affect our future by bringing our suffering onto our spiritual path, and expanding our awareness of and compassion for the immense suffering that all beings experience.

Choosing a positive response to our suffering may not immediately dispel our pain, but over time such a response generates the causes and conditions for our future happiness. Intense experiences of adversity often become strong incentives for entering a spiritual path. Since we have finally awakened to the universality of suffering and impermanence, and realized that there is no hiding place, we make a decision to become free. As Elisabeth Kübler-Ross said:

All the hardships that you face in life, all the tests and tribulations, all the nightmares, and all the losses, most people still view as curses, as punishments by God, as something negative. If you would only know that nothing that comes to you is negative. I mean *nothing*. All the trials and tribulations, and the biggest losses that you ever experience, things that make you say, "If I had known about this, I would never have been able to make it through," are gifts to you, opportunities that you are given to grow. That is the sole purpose of existence on this planet Earth. You will not grow if you sit in a beautiful flower garden and somebody brings you gorgeous food on a silver platter. But you will grow if you are sick, if you are in pain, if you experience losses, and if you do not put your head in the sand, but take the pain and learn to accept it, not as a curse or punishment, but as a gift to you with a very, very specific purpose.[3]

Chapter 6

SPIRITUAL PRACTICES FOR TRANSFORMING SUFFERING

In the journal she kept during her illness, Treya Wilber wrote:

> Learning to make friends with cancer, learning to make friends with the possibility of an early and perhaps painful death, has taught me a great deal about making friends with myself, as I am, and a great deal about making friends with life, as it is. I know that there are a lot of things I can't change. I can't force life to make sense, or to be fair. This growing acceptance of life as it is, with all the sorrow, the pain, the suffering and the tragedy, has brought me a kind of peace. I find that I feel ever more connected with all beings who suffer, in a really genuine way. I find a more open sense of compassion. And I find an ever steadier desire to help, in whatever way I can.[1]

After searching unsuccessfully for some sort of "lesson" or assigned meaning in her illness, Treya decided instead to invest meaning in her situation by choosing a positive response. As she was able to embrace and accept her own suffering, she opened to the immense suffering in the world around her, and deepened her love and compassion for all other beings.

Most of us want to feel that our lives and our daily activities have meaning. Caregivers going to work in a busy hospital, those who cannot work due to chronic illness or debilitation, people who work each week in a mundane office or factory job, or a parent who stays home to raise small children—all may wonder how their daily life and work can have any meaning.

If we start each day and every positive activity or spiritual practice by reflecting on the Three Noble Principles, we can imbue all our actions with a sacred meaning. The Three Noble Principles are known as "good in the beginning, good in the middle, and good in the end." They help us connect to the positive, compassionate aspect of our own nature and deepen our experience of wisdom.

"GOOD IN THE BEGINNING"

At the start of our day or meditation practice, we can arouse a motivation of "profound compassion." Ordinary compassion is limited and conditional, and it comes from a dualistic perspective: there is "me" feeling compassion for "you" (as long as you appear miserable and do not do anything to make me unhappy). Profound, transcendent compassion is limitless, unchanging, and free of any bias. It is a pure, unconditional love and compassion for all beings which radiates from our wisdom essence and is often referred to in Buddhism as *bodhicitta*—"the heart of our enlightened mind."[2] Profound compassion is based on the recognition that from the viewpoint of our true nature, all other beings are, in their essence, the same. And since we are all connected, all beings are worthy of respect and love, like our own family or dearest friends.

Begin by reflecting quietly for a few moments on the many direct and subtle ways that you experience suffering, and recognize how much you yearn to be free of suffering. Acknowledge as well that at the very core of your being is your *innermost essence*—an openness, radiant clarity, and boundless compassion that is entirely free of suffering.

Reflect next on how many others are suffering at this very moment: thousands with the same problems you have, and many in circumstances far more painful or desperate than your own. Reflect on those who have been in a recent disaster, or who live in a country where there is war or famine; remember a person you saw while walking down the street, or a co-worker or family member who has tremendous physical or emotional suffering. As you think of those who are in great distress, allow their suffering to touch your heart, so that you generate a deep desire to truly help them.

Reflect as well that even though so many people appear to be strangers, you are actually related to them as members of the human family. In different circumstances, any stranger could become your most cherished friend, or could save someone you love from a fatal accident. You might consider the possibility that you are connected from having gone through countless lifetimes with all these so-called strangers; everyone having been your partner, child, parent, or dearest friend in former lives. In the same way you would want to help your closest friends when they're in distress, allow your compassion to become limitless and unbiased, so that you embrace everyone with the same profound compassion and love.

These reflections may awaken in you the noble aspiration to do everything possible to benefit others: sharing all the positive power and merit of your spiritual practice with them, and committing to relieve their suffering and bring them happiness in whatever ways you can, through your actions, words, prayers, or thoughts. Then conclude with a heartfelt prayer. Here's a very beautiful one composed by the great Tibetan saint Jigmé Lingpa:

> Mesmerized by the sheer variety of perceptions, which are
>   like the illusory reflections of the moon in water,
> Beings wander endlessly astray in samsara's vicious cycle.
> In order that they may find comfort and ease in the
>   Luminosity and All-Pervading Space of the true nature of
>   their minds,
> I generate the limitless Love,
>   limitless Compassion,
>   limitless Joy, and
>   limitless Equanimity of the Awakened Mind,
>   the heart of Bodhicitta.

"GOOD IN THE MIDDLE"

The second of the Three Noble Principles refers to the fact that during our daily life or our spiritual practice, we commit to sustaining the presence of awareness of our true nature. This view helps us approach every situation with more generosity, kindness, ease, and humor. If we cannot remain in our true nature of mind throughout the day, we resolve to prolong the inspiration of our practice, maintaining an open, peaceful, lighthearted, and nongrasping attitude toward everything we encounter, remembering all the while our sacred and compassionate motivation in life and toward all beings.

"GOOD IN THE END"

At the conclusion of our meditation and at the end of each day we dedicate the merit—the spiritual benefit and power our positive actions generate—to the immediate and ultimate happiness of all beings. We pray deeply that any merit our virtuous actions have generated might help to relieve the suffering of others, bring them happiness and peace, and contribute to their ultimate enlightenment. Dedicating our merit reaffirms our compassionate motivation and seals our practice, so that the benefit of it is never lost. Dedicating our merit to others unites our activity with the enlightened activity of all saints and enlightened beings, making our merit more vast and inexhaustible. As the Buddha said:

> A drop of water
> Falling into the vast ocean
> Will never evaporate
> Until the ocean does.
>
> Just so, merit
> Fully dedicated toward enlightenment
> Will never vanish
> Before enlightenment is reached.

When our positive actions are motivated by compassion, when we keep our heart and mind pure in the midst of our work or spiritual practice, and when we dedicate the merit to others at the end, then whatever we have done becomes a meaningful part of our spiritual path, our evolution toward our highest potential. Through employing these Three Noble Principles every day, and keeping them in mind during our every action, we will gradually begin to see the sacred in everything we do and in everyone we meet.

We can pray and dedicate with words like these:

> *By the power and the truth of this practice,*
> *May all sentient beings enjoy happiness, and the causes of*
> *   happiness,*
> *Be free from suffering, and the causes of suffering.*
> *May they never be separated from the sacred happiness which is*
> *   free of suffering.*

And may they dwell in the great equanimity that is free from pas-
sion, aggression, and prejudice.

Meditation: Inspired Openness and Pure Presence

Sogyal Rinpoche wrote a beautiful description of meditation:

The Buddha sat in serene and humble dignity on the ground, with the sky above him and around him, as if to show us that in meditation you sit with an open, sky-like attitude of mind, yet remain present, earthed, and grounded. The sky is our absolute nature, which has no barriers and is boundless, and the ground is our reality, our relative, ordinary condition. The posture we take when we meditate signifies that we are linking absolute and relative, sky and ground, heaven and earth, like two wings of a bird, integrating the sky-like deathless nature of mind and the ground of our transient, mortal nature.[3]

The real meaning of "meditation" is to sustain the flow of pure awareness, free of duality—pure, simple, naked presence—an awareness without commentary or reactions, a pure presence of profound peace and unbiased love, free of grasping after external things and free of our sense of self, the "grasper." And this is the ultimate relief from suffering—dissolving our habitual identification with the selfish ego and arriving at the profound peace and bliss of our true nature.

Meditation is more than a relaxation exercise; it is a practice designed to connect us to our innermost essence of wisdom. Still, we must be relaxed in order to meditate. The following instructions on how to meditate include techniques for settling and relaxing your body and mind, details of the methods and the spirit of meditation, and insights that may help you understand and accept your present circumstances or even transform your experience of suffering.

Meditation practice helps us become more accepting of ourselves, especially when we are suffering. When we're in physical or emotional distress, meditation helps us disengage from our reactions such as aversion, depression, or fear, and from the self-clinging which tends to grow stronger when we have pain. Fighting suffering is like riding a bicycle uphill against the wind. Meditation practice is akin to turning your bicycle around and flowing smoothly with the wind, as you learn to accept your suffering and find that every situation in life is workable.

Meditation isn't something we can *do* so much as a state we naturally arrive at through training and practice. The methods of meditation create the positive conditions—a spacious and open-hearted attitude, along with the grace and wakeful dignity of the physical posture—which are most conducive toward arriving at the state of carefree ease and clear awareness of our true nature.

AN ALERT AND GRACEFUL POSTURE

Sit quietly and settle down, breathing normally through both your mouth and nose, leaving your eyes open and gazing gently downward. Check that your torso is neither collapsed forward nor unnaturally rigid. Sit with a strength and dignity in your shoulders and upper body, with alert wakeful presence. One image from the Zen tradition suggests your posture should be "like a tiger about to pounce."

If you're sitting in a chair, choose one with a straight back, or use a cushion to support your lower back so you can sit upright with your feet touching the ground. If you are on a cushion on the floor, sit with your legs lightly crossed. Ensure that your cushion is high enough so that your bent knees can touch the ground and your pelvis and hips are stable and grounded. This will also enable you to keep your torso upright with a minimal effort of your back muscles.

Rest your hands lightly on your knees. This is called "the mind in comfort and ease posture." Remember, as you assume the posture, that meditation is nothing extraordinary; you are simply assuming your original nature.

Keeping your eyes open makes it easier to sustain a mindful, alert awareness because your senses are open to your present experience. And, it's easier to stay awake! When you begin to sit, if your mind and senses are overexcited, you can spend the first few minutes of meditation calming yourself with your eyes closed, but then gradually open them and direct your gaze downward at a 45-degree angle.

Allow your abdomen, legs, and arms, your face muscles, and even your jaw to relax and soften, as though you are having a day off from your troubles and relaxing in the warm sunlight of a spring afternoon. Leave your mouth slightly open, as if you are about to say "Ahhh." Extending compassion toward yourself, simply ease yourself and rest naturally, dropping any traces of struggle or self-concern.

THE METHODS AND SPIRIT OF MEDITATION

Since the purpose of meditation practice is to arrive at a state of clear awareness, openheartedness, and carefree ease, approach the practice in the same spirit. When you first begin to sit and settle down, you may find that your mind is agitated and scattered everywhere. There is nothing wrong with your meditation; you are finally noticing the chaotic stream of thoughts which has been untamed until now. Meditation is not meant to be a new struggle or inner battle. Instead of trying to accomplish a "good" meditation or banish your "bad" thoughts or feelings, let go of any judgments, expectations, or concerns about what rises in your practice.

As Sogyal Rinpoche describes: *Meditation is bringing the mind home, releasing any tension or struggle, and relaxing into the clarity and peace of your true nature.*

Allow all the scattered energies of your mind to settle like sediment in a glass of turbulent muddy water. What happens when you set the glass down on a table? The mud swirls for a while, but eventually it settles to the bottom. The clarity of the water, which was always there—only temporarily obscured—naturally begins to manifest.

To enable you to eventually arrive at the state of pure presence in your practice, there are many methods of meditation which can slowly tame and settle your agitated mind, disarm your negativity and fear, and help you make friends with yourself, and thereby the world around you. The practice of Shamatha or "Peacefully Remaining" is a method in which you lightly focus your awareness on one object or activity, thus giving your mind one very simple thing to do. One focus of Shamatha meditation is the breath itself.

When you meditate, breathe naturally, and bring your awareness to the physical sensation you feel each time you breathe out. Feel the air moving out of your lungs, passing through your throat, and leaving your body from your nose and mouth. Simply focus your attention lightly on each out-breath. When your exhalation is complete, as the air from inside mixes with and dissolves into the space in front of you, consider that your ordinary mind, with all its grasping, dissolves into the space as well.

You don't need to especially focus on the sensation of breathing in. Simply take a break on the in-breath, and then once again focus your attention on the sensation of breathing out.

This method—focusing your awareness on the sensation of breathing—is meant to deliver you to the state of natural and care-free ease, free of thought and emotion. If you find you are already in that state of pure presence and inspired openness, you can drop the method and simply remain. Once thoughts and emotions come back, as they will, then return to the method.

When you are first learning to meditate, it's important to take frequent short breaks of a minute or two while still sitting, although you may want to stretch every so often. Drop the method during the break, along with all your distractions, while remaining present and clear. Then, resuming the posture and the method, alert yourself and begin once again.

Rather than focus on the sensation of breathing, you can focus your attention on an object—a sacred image or photograph, a flower, even an ordinary rock or a pen. You don't need to gaze intensely, simply practice "being with" whatever you are looking at, training yourself to stay concentrated on the object of your meditation. When your mind wanders, so does your gaze, so it is easy to catch yourself when you are distracted.

Keep bringing your awareness gently back when it wanders, and focus again on whatever you have chosen as the object of your meditation; doing this is like setting the turbulent glass of muddy water down. And keep breathing.

Focusing your awareness in this way will allow the mud of your "ordinary mind"—the turbulence of your energy and thoughts—to settle down. As you become more still and peaceful, aware and present, you may also become aware of all that is going on in your life right now, the many gross and subtle layers of your suffering. You may be tempted to judge your present condition harshly or reject it, but doing this will only close your heart and bring further harm. Instead, extend an openness and ease toward any experiences of suffering or pain or grief that you may be freshly aware of. Be compassionate with yourself, as though you were watching your dearest friend suffer with the exact same problem. *Be kind to yourself; be spacious.* And continue breathing naturally.

While you are practicing meditation, thoughts and emotions will continue to capture your attention. By themselves, your thoughts and emotions are not a problem; they become so when you believe they are real and take them seriously, either by chasing after them or by trying to suppress them, which only gives them more power to create agitation or suffering in your mind. Simply acknowledge your emotions, even the difficult ones, accepting them as if they were slightly eccentric members of your own family. Instead of struggling with or reacting to your rising thoughts and emotions, view them with detachment, "like a wise old man watching children play." Your thoughts and emotions are just the mud settling, they are not *you.*

Don't take refuge in emotions; don't even indulge in the thought "I am suffering." Simply allow yourself to become aware of your suffering, and with kindness accept yourself exactly as you are. Take refuge instead in the luminosity and all-pervading space of your true nature.

When you are suffering, then, shift your perspective. Instead of identifying with your difficulty, sit in meditation as though you are the sky, watching the clouds of suffering float by. The more you train yourself to connect with this skylike aspect of your being, the more you will be able to embrace experiences of suffering or happiness with the same peaceful, nongrasping equanimity. This takes training and consistent commitment, yet eventually you will find this shift comes more easily. Remembering and assuming your true nature again and again through the practice of meditation, you can finally become free.

INSPIRING YOURSELF

Often meditation can devolve into watching memories or fantasies, making lists of errands, or getting sleepy. Thus it's important to recognize when you are distracted and be creative in finding ways to bring your mind home each time you practice. Choosing a vivid image with which to inspire yourself before you begin meditating, such as the ones that follow, will enable you to keep your mind and heart open, clear, awake, and connected.

If you are feeling sleepy or caved in, straighten your body and imagine you are a rocket rising. You can adjust your gaze slightly upward into the sky to help wake up your body and mind. If you are very tense, imagine you are a piece of butter or a block of ice melting in the sun. If you are feeling agitated or lacking in confidence, sit like a mountain: solid, stable, and majestic. A mountain is not moved, harmed, or excited if there are clouds, storms, or brilliant rainbows overhead. A mountain doesn't get emotional or take things personally; it just *is*.

If you feel a bit self-absorbed or close-hearted, invoke again the compassionate motivation of your practice: the wish to come closer to realizing your wisdom nature so that you may be of greater benefit to all beings. Imagine that in your daily meditation you are surrounded by others who are suffering, and share your practice with them—perhaps your friends or family members, or someone you have just heard about in the news.

Each time you meditate, find ways to adjust yourself so that both your physical posture and your inner attitude are attuned to support your practice. Before meditating, you might listen to music that inspires you, or read a passage from a book that reawakens a recognition of your wisdom nature. Whenever possible, meditate in beautiful natural settings, where you can listen to a flowing river or gaze into the sky, to help open your heart and expand your awareness.

On a deeper level, "inspiring yourself" means that you are able to connect with your true nature in your meditation. Two very skillful approaches to help you make that connection are the meditation practices that arouse your deepest devotion or awaken your boundless, unconditional compassion and love.

The Loving Kindness Meditation

One of the hardest things about suffering is the feeling that we are trapped in our painful circumstances—lost, hopeless, and alone. We fear our suffering will go on forever, and that there is no way out of it. And when we don't know how to transform or heal our own suffering, we may find it difficult to be with and support others in distress. Before we can extend compassion toward others, we must first feel love. If we find our own heart is wounded or walled up, the Loving Kindness Meditation can help reconnect us to the source of love within. Once this love opens our heart and heals our pain, then we will be able to offer our genuine love and fearless compassion to others.

Sit quietly, and allow all the scattered aspects of your mind and energies to settle down. Acknowledge and embrace gently any suffering or struggle you become aware of.

Now, remember a person from your life who once loved you very much. Imagine this person sitting in front of you at this very moment, extending his or her love to you once again. It's all right if you can recall only one happy memory with the person—make that memory of love your entire experience, and bathe in its healing warmth.

Feel the other person's love coming toward you like warm rays of sunlight, permeating your entire being, and especially filling and warming your heart. If there is an old barrier around your heart, see it not as a massive or impenetrable wall, but as fragile as a thin layer of ice. Let the love flowing toward you melt the ice of your old hurt or fear, warming and nourishing your heart.

As this healing love comes into you, you feel your heart overflowing with love and gratitude. You feel peaceful, whole, and replenished with love. Naturally, your love and gratitude goes out now to the person who evoked it, wholly and unconditionally.

Once this giving and receiving of love is flowing strongly, expand the direction of your love another degree. Imagine that on either side of this person in front of you are other people in your life whom you love and cherish, and extend the same love to them, fully and joyfully. Then consider that on either side of this central person are also people you don't know very well: co-workers, shopkeepers, neighbors, even strangers you pass on the street. Extend the same love to them, fully and wholeheartedly. Expanding your love further, visualize that on either side of the central person loving you are those who irritate you, those you've been angry with, or who seem to be your enemies. Extend the same love to them, fully and unconditionally, loving and accepting them exactly as they are.

Finally, expand your love to embrace all beings. Consider now that the whole space in front of you is filled with beings throughout the universe, all forms of conscious life, including the tiniest insects, and even those who have died. Now your love is boundless and unbiased, and it shines powerfully onto each and every one, extending happiness to all existence.

As you conclude the practice, don't shake off the inspiration, awareness, or limitless love it has aroused. Instead, as much as you can, continue practicing the essence of this meditation throughout your day, extending unconditional love toward yourself and everyone you meet.

Training in the Compassion Practices of Tonglen

The Loving Kindness Meditation helps to reawaken our inherent capacity to give and receive love, and the compassion practices take us one step further. They are designed to completely eliminate the source of suffering: our belief in and identification with our selfish ego.

By reflecting on the immense suffering that all beings, everywhere, experience, our compassion becomes deeper and more limitless. We wish to free all beings from their suffering and even its causes; we desire, more than anything, to bring them happiness and peace. The more we meditate on suffering, the deeper our compassion becomes, until one day we finally realize that to be of the greatest help to beings, we ourselves must attain enlightenment for the benefit of all others. As Sogyal Rinpoche writes:

> This compassionate wish is called Bodhicitta in Sanskrit; *bodhi* means our enlightened essence, and *citta* means heart. So we could translate it as "the heart of our enlightened mind." To awaken and develop the heart of the enlightened mind is to ripen steadily the seed of our buddha nature, that seed that in the end, when our practice of compassion has become perfect and all-embracing, will flower majestically into buddhahood. Bodhicitta, then, is the spring and source and root of the entire spiritual path.[4]

The compassion practices described in this section—Tonglen for an Uncomfortable Atmosphere, Self-Tonglen, and Tonglen for Others—are intended to uncover and awaken our bodhicitta, our enlightened courage, and thus bring us close to realizing our wisdom nature.

Tonglen means "giving and receiving." In the Tonglen visualization, we receive, with a strong compassionate motivation, the suffering and pain of others; and we give them, with a tender and confident heart, all of our love, joy, well-being, and peace. Normally, we don't want to give away our happiness, nor do we want to take on another person's suffering, but this not-wanting is the voice of our selfish ego. We cherish "I" more than we do "others" and thus everything we think or do has a self-centered motivation. Following our ego's commands all the time keeps us trapped in cycles of hope and frustration, fear and disappointment.

The voice of your ego may warn you that Tonglen could "harm" you, but this is not true. The compassion practices are designed to unravel the selfish patterning of the ego and gradually reinforce your confidence in the radiant wisdom and compassion of your true nature, which is indestructible. Tonglen is a skillful training in a completely new way of being, in which you begin to develop a limitless, fearless, and unbiased compassion toward all creation. One key to attaining enlightenment is to develop your compassion so profoundly that you come to love and cherish all other beings more than yourself.

Thus although at first the Tonglen practice appears to be a courageous response to the suffering of others, you will find that training in compassion is actually benefiting you and bringing you further along the path to liberation.

The Tonglen practices may also enable you to:

- Bring difficulties and illness onto your spiritual path
- Heal your past and present suffering
- Prevent or relieve burnout
- Transform your relationship with others

The Tonglen Practices

Before beginning any of the following Tonglen practices, spend some time in meditation, settling your mind and energies, and arousing your compassionate motivation for doing the practice. To nurture the confidence and fearless love that will enable you to take on others' suffering, it is important, before you begin practicing, to shift your perspective and connect with your true nature. In practicing Tonglen, then, "ordinary you" should never be doing it! The preliminary meditation practice is intended to help you release your identification with your limited and fearful "self-grasping" with all its conditionings and barriers, and shift your perception 180 degrees.

As you sit in meditation, then, playfully "pretend to be a buddha," an enlightened being. Imagine now that you are viewing things from the perspective of your true nature—the aspect of your mind and heart that is clear, infinitely spacious, and naturally radiant with unbiased compassion and love. And from this perspective, begin the Tonglen practice.

TONGLEN FOR
AN UNCOMFORTABLE ATMOSPHERE

If either your physical environment or the atmosphere inside your mind is uncomfortable or tense, transform it with a simple form of Tonglen. Begin by centering yourself, meditating quietly and invoking your compassionate motivation. Now, shift your perspective and consider that radiating from your innermost wisdom essence is a clear, unbiased compassion and love.

With each in-breath, take in the negativity from your external or internal atmosphere, in the form of a dark cloud, and consider that this dark cloud of negativity is transformed at your heart center, the way hot air is cooled by an air conditioner. With every exhalation, send out and fill the atmosphere with calm, clarity, and joy in the form of light.

SELF-TONGLEN

Sit in meditation and consider that the pure aspect of your being—yourself as the embodiment of enlightened compassion—is the aspect of you sitting on your meditation cushion or chair. Directly in front of you is the "ordinary" aspect of you that is suffering; perhaps feeling lonely, fearful, misunderstood, angry, or troubled by physical illness or grief.

As you gaze toward your ordinary self and become aware of the suffering you've been carrying, you feel a deep warmth and tenderness, a sense of friendship and unconditional love. You accept the suffering of this other part of yourself, you understand it. Your awareness of this pain or difficulty opens your heart and generates a fearless wish to release and transform the suffering of the "ordinary" you.

Consider that the suffering of the "ordinary" you takes the form of a dark cloud, and with each in-breath, visualize that you breathe it in. As the dark cloud of suffering enters your being, it disintegrates any final traces of egoistic clinging or fear in your heart, and reveals your bodhicitta—the radiant source of wisdom and compassion at the core of your being—which shines out even more powerfully, like a brilliantly shining sun.

As you exhale, freely give out understanding, joy, unconditional love, and peace, in the form of light, to the suffering aspect of you. Continue this giving and receiving with each breath for as long as you like.

As you continue the practice, visualize that the "ordinary" aspect of you is gradually becoming relieved of suffering and filled with well-being and joy. Each time you conclude, consider that the practice has been completely effective: the "ordinary" aspect of you is released of all pain and distress and is now radiantly happy and at peace. And since there is no difference now between these two aspects, dissolve the visualization and remain in meditation.

TONGLEN FOR OTHERS

Begin the Tonglen by sitting quietly and bringing your mind home through the practice of meditation. To inspire your practice, meditate deeply on the suffering that all beings experience, and allow their suffering to open your heart and awaken your compassion.

To help you develop confidence, you can do the following meditation as a preliminary to your practice of Tonglen. In the sky in front of you, invoke the presence of a Divine Being for whom you feel devotion, or the presence of many saints or enlightened beings. Pray that through their inspiration and blessings the seed of your compassionate essence, your bodhicitta, may be awakened in your heart. Visualize that these enlightened beings respond to your prayer, sending tremendous rays of compassion and wisdom into you, dissolving the ego's clouds of selfishness and fear, and revealing your bodhicitta. At the end, visualize that all of these enlightened beings dissolve into you, becoming one with your wisdom mind—which shines out even more brilliantly with compassion. From this perspective, begin the Tonglen.

Visualize that sitting in front of you is someone in your life whom you know to be suffering. Open yourself to this person's suffering, allowing yourself to feel connected with her and aware of all of her difficulties. Feel rising in you a strong compassionate intention to release the person from her suffering and even its causes.

Breathe in the other person's suffering, in the form of a dark cloud, and visualize it coming into your heart center, where it dissolves any final traces of self-grasping, thus fully revealing the heart of your enlightened mind, your bodhicitta. As you breathe out, consider that you are sending to the other person, in the form of brilliant light, all your healing love, warmth, energy, confidence, and joy.

Continue this "giving and receiving" with each breath for as long as you wish. If you like, you can even imagine your bodhicitta has transformed your heart or your whole body into a brilliant wish-fulfilling jewel that is able to fulfill any special needs or desires of the person for whom you are practicing. At the end of the practice, consider that your compassion has completely dissolved all the person's suffering and even its causes, filling him or her with well-being, peace, happiness, and love.

As your Tonglen practice becomes stronger and more confident, you can gradually imagine others who are suffering in front of you—co-workers, patients, relatives, or even strangers—and practice taking in and transforming their suffering, extending to them all of your happiness, clarity, understanding, forgiveness, and love. While doing the Tonglen, as the light of your bodhicitta touches and fills those for whom you are practicing, feel a firm conviction that all of their suffering and traces of negativity have been purified. Knowing this practice can bring such benefit, you feel a sense of joy that it has enabled you to successfully free others from their suffering or pain.

As you conclude each session of Tonglen, dedicate its positive and healing power to those you had visualized and pray that the merit of your practice of compassion may benefit all other beings, who are as limitless as space.

ADAPTING THE TONGLEN FOR DAILY LIFE

Sometimes when you bring the Tonglen practice to your daily encounters with suffering, you may find you still have a subtle hope or fear: a hope that the person will be grateful, or change, as a result of the practice, or a fear that you will experience his or her suffering. If this happens, then use one of the following methods to adjust yourself or adapt your practice:

- Do the Tonglen mentally, as an aspiration: "May I be able to relieve the suffering of all beings; may I give my happiness to all beings."
- Do the Tonglen for your own aversion to the other person's suffering.
- Focus on the Loving Kindness or the Self-Tonglen meditation.

The Tonglen practices should be approached as a training, so that as you gain familiarity with each part of the practice, you are able to engage in the next stage with greater ease and confidence. I have found that before applying Tonglen in everyday situations it is important to first spend some time doing the preliminary Tonglen practices in your daily meditation—Tonglen for an Uncomfortable Atmosphere and Self-Tonglen—so that you learn to extend a genuine acceptance and compassion toward your own suffering and even your fears. Then train in doing Tonglen for Others as a meditation. With the increased confidence and familiarity this brings, you'll find that when you encounter suffering in your daily life, you are able to naturally do the "giving and receiving" practice of Tonglen with genuine love and fearlessness.

If you find you have difficulty extending compassion toward yourself, you can consider that, with each in-breath, you are taking in and transforming the suffering of all others who presently experience the same kind of illness, loss, pain, or emotional distress as you. This may help you begin to accept your own painful circumstances with more awareness and compassion.

It was this tonglen practice, more than any other, that so deepened Treya's compassion for all those suffering. She talked of the deep connection she felt with all beings, simply because all beings suffer. And doing tonglen allowed her, in a special sense, to redeem her own suffering, her own ordeal with cancer. Once you are proficient in tonglen, you find that every time you have pain or anxiety or depression, on the inbreath you almost spontaneously think, "May I take all such suffering into me," and on the outbreath you release it. The effect of this is that you befriend your own suffering, you step into it. You don't recoil in the face of suffering, but rather use it as a way to connect with all beings who are suffering. You embrace it and then transform it by giving it a universal context. It's no longer just you and your isolated pain, but rather a chance to realize that "inasmuch as you do this to the least of my brethren, you do this to me." In the simple practice of tonglen, of compassionate exchange, Treya found much of her own suffering redeemed, given meaning, given context, given connection; it took her out of her "own" isolated woes and into the texture of humanity on the whole, where she was not alone.[5]

Finally, doing the Tonglen practice while we are ill or disabled is an extraordinary way of bringing meaning to our suffering, and it enables us to begin using each life experience as a preparation for our death. The Tonglen practice enables us to transcend our suffering by dedicating it to others, thus literally "forgetting ourselves" in the process.

Dedication

We are not helpless as we experience painful or distressing situations if we can creatively respond to those circumstances with dignity and courage. Dedicating our suffering to the benefit of others is a way of imbuing our experience with a sacred meaning. The practice of dedication is taught in many religious traditions, and I have found that even those who are not familiar with traditional spiritual concepts resonate very strongly to the principle of dedication. We can dedicate our suffering, our grief, our illness, or even our death with words like these:

Through the suffering I am enduring now, may I be able to benefit and help all other beings, who are like my own cherished friends. May I take upon myself the suffering of all others who are ill or in pain, grieving or dying, and may they all enjoy happiness and good circumstances. May they have peace of mind and freedom from fear; may they have everything they need: love, shelter, food, and medical care. May whatever suffering I am enduring now or will endure help all others experience happiness in this and future lives, and ultimately attain liberation.

. . .

The Four Tasks of Living and Dying

The practice of dedication enables us to expand our perspective beyond our ordinary self-centered concerns and learn to cherish others more than ourselves. Thus dedicating our suffering to benefit others can transform our present experience of suffering and even remove the cause of suffering: our self-grasping ego.

Father David, a retired priest and hospice volunteer, was conducting his weekly visit with an elderly, wealthy widow who was very bitter and suffering greatly. All Norma talked about were her troubles and her blame of others—the caregivers who neglected her, the doctor who didn't listen, the pain which was not relieved, her loneliness and abandonment by her children, whom she resolved to disown. Week after week, Father David listened patiently and wondered if his presence made any difference at all.

Then Father David was called in on an emergency to see a young woman whose husband had died suddenly at work. Laura had four small children at home, all of them under the age of six. She was in great distress and emotional pain, confused, in shock, weeping profusely, and unable to cope with her children's incessant demands. Laura wondered out loud about how she was going to support her children emotionally and financially. In witnessing her distress, Father David's heart went out to Laura, and he promised to continue giving her his presence and support.

When Father David next visited Norma, the elderly widow, and heard her continuous stream of blame and self-pity again, he lost his patience and said, "I know this is very hard for you; I see that you are suffering and feel all alone. I wish I could make things better for you, but I can't. If you continue thinking only of yourself, you will only feel trapped in your suffering. A few days ago I met a young mother whose husband died suddenly, and she doesn't know how she is going to survive. Why don't you dedicate your suffering and pain to Laura, so that she might find a way through her troubles and heartbreaking loss?"

After speaking so strongly to Norma, Father David wondered if he would be welcomed back, but when he next entered Norma's room, he saw a complete transformation. "I don't use this word lightly—in fact, I have never used it to describe a living person. But when I came to see Norma, she had completely changed; she was a saint. Her whole being, and even the room, was infused with radiant love. Her first words to me were: 'How is that young woman doing? I have been thinking about her and praying for her all week, and dedicating my dying to her. Is there anything she needs? How else can I help?' "

Since the practice of dedication is one of the Three Noble Principles, we should train in this practice throughout our life, whether we are in happy or difficult situations, sharing the merit and positive spiritual power we generate each day with all other beings, and praying that everything we do may only benefit and help them.

When concluding any of the meditation practices described here, always remember the two essential points that will make the meditation effective in your life. First, if during the practice you experience more clarity, awareness, peace, or compassion, recognize this inspiration and keep it with you. Resolve to sustain the flow of this clear and compassionate awareness throughout your next activities, in your perceptions, and in your way of relating to others and to yourself. It is only through integrating the inspiration of your meditation practice with your daily experiences that you will feel a beneficial change in the quality of your life.

And finally, remember to seal each practice, and the end of each day, with a dedication. To paraphrase Sogyal Rinpoche:

> May whatever merit and benefit that comes from these practices be shared with all beings, who are like my own dearest friends; may this merit become a drop in the ocean of the activity of all the enlightened ones in their tireless compassionate work for the liberation of all beings. May there be peace between individuals, in every home, and in all the nations of the world. May all beings have everything they need, may they be entirely free of all kinds of suffering, and may they experience total well-being and lasting happiness. And ultimately, may the positive and sacred power of these practices bring all beings to enlightenment, the peace which is beyond all suffering.[6]

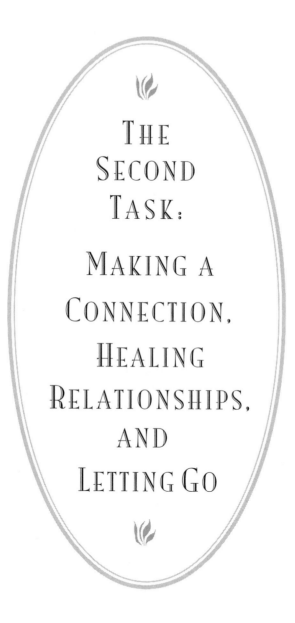

THE
SECOND
TASK:

MAKING A
CONNECTION,
HEALING
RELATIONSHIPS,
AND
LETTING GO

Chapter 7

CREATING A GENUINE CONNECTION

A young man told me of his father's last days:

"My mother didn't want my father to be told he was dying. She was afraid he couldn't handle it. She had committed herself to caring for him at home as long as she could manage his physical needs. When the family came to visit—my sister, myself, and my brother and his wife—we felt extremely awkward, looking at his emaciated body and talking normally about the sports and weather as though nothing had changed.

"We could see his symptoms were getting worse, and each day he was having more difficulty getting up and walking. There was a lot of tension and fear in the house. Then one morning, my dad's breathing began to worsen, and we rushed him to the hospital, where he was admitted to the Intensive Care Unit. He looked very far away, lying on the hospital bed with its bars on the sides and with all the tubes going into his arms and the machinery surrounding him. I didn't know how to get close.

"We were warned that he might not get better, but when we insisted, the doctor admitted that it was possible that Dad might pull out of this crisis. So we pushed away our sadness, hoping and praying for the best. Each of us hoped to have a chance to speak with him if the time came that he was actually dying. We began a vigil by his side, and day and night there was always someone with him.

"After five days, we were all pretty tired. The nurse persuaded Mom to go home for the afternoon, have a bath and a good sleep. The rest of us went together to the coffee shop down the block from the hospital, and we sat and talked about the whole problem. My older brother was really agitated, so he went for some cigarettes, and must have smoked a few before he rejoined us. Finally we started back for the ICU. My feet felt like lead, I was so tired.

"We were stopped at the door. The nurse called for the doctor, and he said that Dad suddenly stopped breathing a short while before. They had tried everything they could to bring him back—but he was gone. Gone!

"My older brother immediately went into a rage, attacking the doctor and the staff for letting him die, while his wife stood there frozen in fear. My sister began sobbing hysterically, and though I wanted to stay by Dad's side for a while, I realized I had to keep it together and be strong for everybody else, so I took her into the hallway to calm her down. Later, they all told me that it looked like I didn't care that he died.

"My brother insisted on calling Mom, and he gave her the news in a pretty stark way. She knew he was going to die, but still the news was like a lightning strike. She was really overwhelmed. She kept saying it was her fault, that she'd abandoned him in his hour of need. I never saw my mother like that, she was so out of control.

"The funeral was a travesty—everyone was blaming everyone else. Nobody wanted to see my sister's and mother's tears, and we were judging each other's reactions as a measure of how much we loved Dad. We all thought we had abandoned him, though, and nobody but my mom would say it. Pretty soon, we stopped talking about his death, because we just wanted to forget it."

One of the most poignant and unnecessary sufferings experienced by the dying or their loved ones is the failure to connect with each other before the moment of death. And yet many people—facing death unprepared—don't communicate all they would have liked before a loved one dies. This is even more likely to be the case when our loved one dies unexpectedly. If reading the preceding story evoked painful memories of your own, be kind to yourself. It's important to accept that you did the best you could with what you knew at the time.

Acknowledging your regrets can inspire the courageous resolve to live and communicate in a different way now. It's even possible to conclude your relationship with a loved one who has already died. The purpose of this task—making a connection, healing relationships, and letting go—is to chart the journey of death, and offer tools for communicating and healing relationships, tools that will enable you to navigate your present or future life situations with greater awareness, compassion, and skill.

At the time in their lives when they are the most vulnerable and distressed, those facing death need comfort, reassurance, affection, and love. Tragically, they often get just the opposite.

There are many reasons for this situation. One arises from the family patterns we were raised with, where communication may have been primarily superficial or polite. In some families, emotions such as anger, grief, or fear may be judged, shamed, or entirely suppressed. Yet during the process of aging or illness, both the dying person and her closest loved ones are at times experiencing the deepest emotional pain of their lives. It takes a lot of energy to hide this from each other.

Another typical communication problem arises from a relationship—perhaps between siblings, or between the dying person and a parent—where both have taken well-entrenched "positions" against each other. Having related with each other in a judgmental or defensive way for years, it's extremely difficult to change this habit, even when death is approaching. Regardless of how much they may both desire more authentic communication, they find their conversation remains distant and polite, or devolves each time into a familiar argument.

Finally, many of us carry a load of heavy baggage—the emotional unfinished business of our entire life—and we haven't a clue about how to resolve and release it. When we carry these unacknowledged burdens with us into the room of a dying family member, it is impossible to communicate authentically and openly.

Even in a family that usually gets along well, the potential for unsatisfactory or blocked communication is intensified by the fact that one family member faces illness or death. Family members— or the intimate partner of the dying person—usually don't understand their own emotional process and their own needs. They are often confused about whether, and *when,* they should begin letting go of this person they dearly love.

The family also may not be aware of resources in the community or wider circles of support, including extended family or friends, whom they could call on. Thus, most of the stress and responsibility usually falls on one or two people during a prolonged illness. And when they lack other sources of support, family members may unwittingly burden the dying person with their troubles.

It is common that the intimate partner is informed first that his or her loved one is facing imminent death, and that partner sometimes colludes with the doctor in keeping this vital information from the dying person. As a result, the partner, other friends and family members, and even the medical staff must hide their natural feelings, communicate superficially, lie about the person's condition, and generally walk on thin ice to avoid revealing the truth.

Even when the individual has been told she is dying, the family may be in denial or have a general aversion to acknowledging the coming death. They may fear that speaking about death will either hasten it or plunge the dying person into a state of hopelessness or depression. Yet when we fear sharing our natural grief, we are forced to hide from each other. The resulting inability to make a genuine connection—and all the superficiality and pretense that goes along with it—will intensify the dying person's sense of isolation and despair.

Finding the Courage to Communicate

It was late afternoon on Christmas Eve, and my husband, Lyttle, and I were at the leukemia clinic for his checkup. The doctor examined the recent swelling in Lyttle's leg and frowned. "It looks like a new blood clot is forming in your left leg," he said. "This is very dangerous. If you are walking around, part of it could break away, like the last one, and destroy your lung or heart. I want to have you admitted to the hospital today."

This was a devastating blow. Lyttle hated being in the hospital. Since his diagnosis in late August, he had been hospitalized for three weeks out of every four, dealing with one life-threatening crisis after another.

We looked at each other, already aware that this would be our last Christmas together with our family and our young son. Lyttle told the doctor, "No, I want to be home for Christmas. It's very important to me, and I'll take my chances. I will come back to the hospital the day after Christmas."

We returned home and celebrated Christmas with our family, without mentioning the new danger to his life. Neither of us spoke about it or revealed our disappointment and fear. We wanted this last Christmas to be a happy one, so we carried our sadness in silence. As promised, the next day Lyttle came back to the hospital for treatment of his blood clot.

A week later, he was still in the hospital, impatient and unhappy. Now it was New Year's Eve, and once again we did not want to show each other the sadness we felt. At midnight most people celebrate the new year, but Lyttle and I knew that in the coming year he would die. Unable to face my pain, I made an excuse to leave his hospital room before midnight.

One week later, our wedding anniversary approached. Lyttle's doctors said going home was too dangerous, but it was a risk we were willing to take. We tugged on the heartstrings of one recently married physician, explaining how important this anniversary was to us. He said Lyttle could go home on one condition—that he take his next dose of chemo before leaving. What we didn't know was that the drugs he would receive were new and even more toxic in their effects.

Arriving home, Lyttle felt extremely weak, confused, and nauseated, and he immediately went to bed. His condition persisted for two weeks; he could barely stand up and walk through the house without collapsing. It wasn't possible to celebrate our anniversary; Lyttle couldn't even leave the house. Our grief, fear, and frustration were mounting, but we held it all inside.

Finally Lyttle confessed his pent-up despair: "I don't want to go on like this. You had better hide my pain pills, or else I will probably take them all and get it over with. I just can't keep going like this."

I looked inside the medicine cabinet, filled with a variety of very strong narcotics, and wondered where I could hide them in our small house. With plenty of time alone each day while I was at work, Lyttle would be able to find them. So I decided I would have to carry the bottles with me. I looked again at the rows of bottles and the size of my purse, and realized they wouldn't fit. It was then I realized that I had to speak openly about my feelings.

I went back to Lyttle and said, "Your being sick is not easy for me. I'm either taking care of you at home or visiting you every night in the hospital. I look after our son, go to work each day, and manage the house without you. And I know that one day I will be all alone after you're gone. None of this is easy, but I'm willing to go through it all, because I love you. But if you were to take your own life, I couldn't handle that. That would be too much."

All the sadness, tears, and disappointments we had held inside over the last month spilled out in the ensuing conversation. Finally we connected. Finally we were being honest with each other. And rather than feeling a heavy cloud of gloom descend on us, it felt like a cloud had lifted! After sharing our tears and grief, we were then able to share and express our love, and even our laughter and joy. It was like coming alive again, for both of us.

Coincidentally, Lyttle's condition stabilized. Although he still received chemotherapy regularly, over the next nine months he was briefly hospitalized only one time before his final process of dying began.

A person who is suffering or dying needs to feel a deep and meaningful connection with her closest loved ones. To engage in genuine communication, no matter how painful the subject matter, is to tap into the healing power of love.

When family members are not communicating openly, we might ask them, "If you cannot take away the reality that your loved one will one day die, what do you most yearn for in the time you have left?" Their answer will likely be: "To enjoy our relationship and share our love in the time we have left together." The problem is that they may not know how to begin.

Sometimes what stops us from connecting is simple fear: How can we break through a habitually superficial pattern of communication? First we need to acknowledge our fear, and then we can stop taking it so seriously. Fear is a signal that *I am worrying too much about "me," and my heart is closed.* It's vital to shift this orientation to our concern and love for *the other person.*

We've all experienced genuine connection with others in the past. I always encourage family members to remember a satisfying communication they have had, and to reflect on the qualities which made it go well, which they can draw on once again. These qualities probably include:

- Openness without expectations
- Really listening to and getting to know the other person
- A sense of play, an easy humor
- A sincere willingness to reveal oneself

The key is to be natural and to speak from our heart. When we first go to communicate with a dying friend, perhaps we'll feel afraid, upset, or sad. Our friend might be relieved to hear us admit this right at the start. Finally someone is being honest! When we take the risk to reveal our vulnerability, the dying person may then feel safe to reveal her own difficulties or pain.

Perhaps our difficulty in making a connection stems from an older and deeper problem: the old unresolved hurts or grudges in our relationship. This imminent death challenges us to find a way to heal our relationship while we still have time.

When there has been a long history between family members, not every communication attempt will bear immediate and positive fruit, yet still we must begin to release our old positions and fears, so that we can spark a change in the relationship. It's vital to remember that the source of any change is in ourselves; we must become more free, more loving, more willing to take a risk and speak with honesty and kindness. Whether or not the other person is able to change, we'll be able to understand and connect with him or her more easily.

Healing Relationships: Dissolving Your Position

When your motivation in communicating with others is to "win" the discussion or change the other person, you are doomed to fail. If you truly want to heal the conflicts in a relationship, first you need to sit quietly and become aware of your own thoughts and feelings, the hopes and fears that are operating behind your perceptions and communications. In your previous communication, what were your expectations of this person? That she would admit she was wrong, or promise to change? That she would never make another mistake, or would promise never to hurt you again? That she would extend her love to you in the exact way you think it should be shown?

Similarly, you must become aware of your fears about communicating with the other person. Are you afraid of being rejected or misunderstood, of feeling ashamed or foolish? Afraid of having your feelings hurt once again? The hope that another person will never hurt you, or will always love you perfectly, is unrealistic, as is the expectation that the other person must change in order for you to be happy. The only freedom you have is to change yourself.

Thus, you need to become aware of your habitual identification with the "selfish ego" and realize you can identify instead with your true nature: a clear and fundamental goodness, or "good heart." Meditating and connecting with this highest aspect of your being will help you tap into your own wellspring of love and meet the other person without fear.

The next step, before actually communicating face to face, is to establish your motivation. In meeting someone with whom you normally have a problem, imagine that your intention now is simply to listen to the other person's feelings and experience, and to express your natural self. That's all. See if you can be willing to "meet" the other person as she is. If you've been holding on to old judgments that would make this difficult, then first do the following reflection, which may help you understand the other person's experience in a new way, and thus have more compassion for her. There are two steps to this reflection: Seeing the Other as Another You and Exchanging Places.

COMPASSION REFLECTION:
SEEING THE OTHER AS ANOTHER YOU
AND EXCHANGING PLACES

Instead of seeing this person in their usual role—parent, sibling, or boss—see him or her in your mind's eye as just "another you." Consider that this person is just like you, with the same desires for happiness and with the same fears of suffering.

Once you have established this feeling, then imagine changing places with the person. Now you are in her life, standing in her shoes. Imagine you have this person's history—with her possible past experiences of rejection, grief, trauma, or fear. Consider that you have whatever constitutes her present suffering as well: feelings of being misunderstood and unfairly judged, deep experiences of pain or fear, or hidden insecurities and frustrated cravings which give rise to constant states of unhappiness. Imagine and consider the suffering this person may yet face—the physical deterioration and pain of aging or illness, the grief of future losses, the loneliness of dying or feeling abandoned.

From this perspective of seeing the world through the other person's eyes, now imagine seeing "you" enter the room to have a talk. Ask yourself: What would I most want from this person coming to see me? What would I most need from him or her?

. . .

Once you have completed this meditation for awakening compassion, if you find that your heart is more open and understanding of the other person's suffering, you may want to include him or her in your daily practice of Tonglen.

If the person with whom you have a communication problem is not facing imminent death, you may feel more willing to let go of your old hurt or anger by *imagining the person is dying*. By summoning the courage to heal your relationship now (since the time of death is uncertain), you will have fewer regrets if either you or the other person should die suddenly. You may harbor a hope that if you do not heal your bad feelings, they will simply dissolve once the other person dies. Yet death does not release your old wounds and the wall of fear you've erected around your heart. What releases you is your willingness to communicate and let go of the past. Healing the relationship is healing your own heart, thus it is your task—whether the person is living or has already died.

Joe's children and grandchildren were so warm and loving and their communication was so open that Mark, the hospice volunteer, wondered if he should have himself assigned to another family. Before asking for a transfer, Mark privately approached the dying man and asked, "Is there anything you can think of, anything at all, that I can help you with before you die?"

"I'm so glad you asked," Joe said. "I've been troubled by one thing that I really want to clear up before I die, but I need help to do it, and I didn't know who to ask.

"Forty years ago my brother and I had a terrible fight, and we haven't met or spoken a word to each other since that day. I realize now that I was just too stubborn to give in, and I'm sorry all these years have passed without any contact. I wish I could see him before I die, to let him know I'm sorry and to ask his forgiveness. Could you help me find my brother?"

Mark was grateful there was something he could do, something which would help Joe face death peacefully. After some research, Mark finally located Joe's brother and explained why he was calling.

"I'm a hospice volunteer, assigned to your brother Joe and his family. Joe asked me to contact you, because he is close to dying now, and he would really like to see you and extend his apologies to you before he dies."

The brother's answer was stark: "I don't want to see Joe or have anything to do with him."

After the call, Mark wondered what to do. But soon he realized that the most important thing had already happened. Joe was truly sorry for his part in the fight, and through Mark he had communicated that to his brother. When he next went to visit Joe, Mark said, "I've contacted your brother, and although he will not be able to come and see you, he got your message."

On Joe's side, the unfinished business had been healed. Perhaps his brother was not yet ready to let go of his own bad feelings. Yet later, nearing the end of his own life, Joe's brother might also want to release this old burden, and if or when he does, he will know he has already received Joe's conciliatory message.

Healing Relationships: Completing Unfinished Business

Here are some of the common reasons we have "unfinished business" with people:

- We're afraid of being hurt again, or of being rejected.
- The other person has already refused to forgive us.
- We feel that what we've done is unforgivable.
- We want to punish the other person with our anger.
- We don't want to let go of our attachment to the person or the past.
- We're afraid to have our part of the problem revealed.
- The other person has gone from our life, or has already died.

These are natural fears or obstacles to speaking directly with someone about clearing up an old emotional problem, yet our unfinished business is our responsibility to resolve, and we can finish it *whether or not the other person is present or willing to communicate and forgive us*. The purpose of the method for completing unfinished business which follows is to release us from our own heavy baggage of anger, attachment, or guilt, and free us from our painful memories. Therefore, it is not necessary to meet with the other person to finish with our emotional burden and let go.

The Method for Completing Unfinished Business

First sit quietly and find in your heart the willingness to communicate your problem one last time *and let go of it*. Also establish your willingness to really feel heard and to listen to and hear the other person's perspective on this problem.

Now visualize the person with whom you have unfinished business. Imagine this person is sitting in front of you looking exactly the way you remember her; but now with one very important difference: *consider that she is more open and receptive than ever before, and this person can really hear everything you have to say.*

Reflect on what has been the main difficulty for you, without rekindling the emotions attached to it. Imagine that you are now telling this problem to the person in front of you, remembering that she is very receptive and genuinely able to hear you. Once again reflect and see if you have any other unexpressed problems, and imagine telling them to the other person.

Next, take a pen and paper and write down what you have just considered saying. Write out the problem, as responsibly as possible, without attacking or defending. Remember that you are speaking to the other person's open heart and that she is receptive and can truly hear you.

Now, allow the other person to express her side of the problem. Just begin writing and see what happens. Since you have been speaking to her "best side" and your feelings have been heard, her response probably won't be what you expect. Next, write down any other problems—old angers, regrets, attachments, or fears—you may have had with the person. Again, allow her to respond to you with her perspective.

Continue writing both parts of this dialogue and expressing all the layers of your difficulties with the other person, until you feel you are no longer harboring anything negative in your heart. If the other person had previously hurt you, see if you can now extend forgiveness to her. If you realize that you have hurt the other person, ask her forgiveness. You might reflect that *the best part* of the other person would understand your regret, and would not hesitate to extend her forgiveness to you. Allow yourself to receive the healing love of this forgiveness, and let go of any feelings of guilt or self-condemnation.

Finally, look into your heart once again and see if there is any appreciation and love for the other person—any positive feelings which you have been holding back. Communicate your love in writing, and, thanking the other person, say good-bye. You can even envision the person turning and leaving. As she leaves, ask yourself truthfully: Are you really letting go now and wishing her well?

If the person has already died, a good way to conclude this emotional healing is with a spiritual practice such as the Essential Phowa, a special visualization for healing and for the time of death, described in Chapter 9. Of course, you could do any practices—scriptural readings, prayers, or rituals—from your own tradition for giving spiritual support to the deceased.

When you conclude this practice, you can dedicate it with a strong wish that the other person and yourself may be healed of all emotional pain or past traumas, that your relationship, now and in the future, may be one of mutual benefit, and that all others with whom you have contact in your life may share in the healing power which comes from this resolution.

Later, try reading your dialogue aloud in front of a photo of the person, or to a friend. This may yield an even deeper sense of completion, as though you had actually said it to the person. If you like, you can also write: "I would like to hear from you." Many people have told me that if the person is still living, they do hear from her within days or weeks of concluding their unfinished business, and she often communicates a sense of resolution on her side as well.

Although we can complete our unfinished business by using the above method, once we have healed our own pain we may find we now possess the confidence and clarity to communicate directly with the other person.

The biggest unexamined baggage in Helen's life was her lack of relationship with her father. They were estranged when Helen was thirteen years old, and she was now thirty-four. Her parents' divorce was a bitter one, and Helen's memories of her father consisted solely of the judgments and recriminations she had heard constantly expressed by the rest of her family. Using the method for completing unfinished business, Helen worked through her old hurt and anger with her father, releasing her deep disappointments and fears. With much of her emotional tension dissipated, Helen was able to contact her father and renew the relationship. He was very grateful to her for making contact, as he had been recently diagnosed with cancer.

Helen's father lived another year and a half, and during that time they were able to establish a connection and deep communication, share their lives with each other, and dissolve any remaining problems from the past.

Helen's brother and sister never tried to reconnect with their father, and they imagined their emotional baggage would simply disappear once he had died. Yet after his death, they were aware that they continued to carry these burdens from the past.

If your unfinished business is connected to experiences of severe trauma or abuse, you can seek out a professional therapist to assist you in healing from the past, rather than trying to work on it alone. For greater inspiration in healing very painful memories, you can, as Sogyal Rinpoche describes:

> Visualize that all the buddhas and enlightened beings are in the sky above and around you, shining down their rays of compassionate light and giving you their support and blessing. In their presence grieve and say what you have to say, what is really in your heart and mind, to your loved one who has died.[1]

Having created this very powerful field of blessings and love, you may feel safer to face your memories and bring the healing power of compassion to everyone involved.

The Secret of Forgiveness

Sometimes we hold on to our righteous anger for years, believing that we are somehow punishing another person with it. Although we think our problem comes entirely from outside, an honest self-examination is likely to reveal an inner stubbornness, selfishness, or vindictiveness—negative qualities not unlike those we have been judging in the other person. Not forgiving hurts us, imprisoning us in past memories of pain or powerlessness. We can even become addicted to our pattern of suffering and our identity as victim; then our unspoken fear might be: If I let go of my suffering, won't "I" cease to exist?

Forgiving is a very powerful act, probably the most positive and transformative decision we are repeatedly called to make in this life. Forgiveness does not mean we condone or accept another person's hurtful acts; rather it releases our reactions of hurt, anger, or fear, taking the thorn out of an old wound so it can heal. A harmful pattern continues when everyone keeps playing the same part; thus when we let go of our reaction and finally respond with forgiveness and love, we are able to break the pattern and free ourselves of a painful memory. That's the secret: *forgiveness frees us.*

When you find yourself standing in judgment of others, turn inward and examine your own actions, your own motivations, the state of your own mind. When you clearly see your weaknesses and faults, your selfish patterns, when you become aware of a lifetime of secret and obvious transgressions you have committed against others through your actions, words, and even thoughts, how can you possibly hold a grudge against someone else? You'll realize that we're all in the same boat, acting and reacting most of the time with confusion and fear, rather than the clarity and compassion of our real nature.

Sometimes the one you're holding the biggest judgment against is yourself. You may secretly wonder if your actions are forgivable. One way to atone for the harm you have done is to confess it and find ways to benefit or bring joy to others; another way is to practice forgiving anyone you feel has ever harmed you.

The Buddhist teachings explain that, in truth, everything and everyone is interconnected and interdependent. Thus everything we do to others is actually being done to ourselves. Whether we immediately see it or not, there's a principle of cause and effect, called *karma,* operating in the universe. For example, those who relive all the events of their life during a near-death experience are surprised to find they are now on the receiving end of everything they did, thought, and said—for better or worse.

When we are not aware of this interconnectedness and the eventual consequence of our harmful actions, we hurt each other thoughtlessly. Could it be that the person you've been holding responsible for your pain is also unaware that by harming you, she is drawing more suffering onto herself? In fact, she is probably so deeply lost in her own pain and past conditioning that she doesn't even see you. The Tibetan word for ignorance is *marigpa,* which means *"not seeing."* She only sees her projections, through clouds of fear, and reacts blindly. You might consider that if the other person could really see you, she wouldn't hurt you.

When you observe a person doing harmful things, then, instead of judging him or her, remember that the real enemy is "ignorance." This understanding might awaken your compassion for the person who is mindlessly creating her own future suffering.

Another meditation that helps to arouse love and compassion when you feel blocked is to visualize someone you love in circumstances of great suffering or pain. As you feel the compassion rising in you toward your friend who suffers so greatly, put in the place of your friend a stranger, and generate the same powerful compassion toward her, with a strong wish: "May this person be free of suffering and the causes of suffering." Finally, imagine a person who has hurt you very badly also in these same dire circumstances, and extend this same tenderness and compassion toward him or her.

(You need not fear that your visualization will have a deleterious effect on your friend; since through this meditation you are arousing a very powerful and limitless compassion, your friend will also receive great benefit and merit from your doing this practice.)

With the practice of Tonglen, each of our experiences of hurt or trauma can be brought onto our spiritual path and purified. By facing our past suffering, learning to forgive and heal, we may find that the person who had seemed to be our enemy has now become a treasure in our life, helping us soften our heart and deepen our connection to the truths of our spiritual path. As Geshe Langri Thangpa wrote:

> When even my dearest friend, whom I had helped,
> Unexpectedly turns against me,
> May I view him as a great treasure, difficult to find.

Chapter 8

GIVING LOVE AND LETTING GO

ANGIE WAS FORTY-FOUR, AND HER MOTHER MEANT everything to her—more, she said, than her own husband and children. Angie's mother, Helen, had developed multiple metastases from advanced breast cancer, and her liver, spine, and hip all had new tumors. When I met Helen in the hospital, I observed how frail and weak she was. She revealed to me that she knew her life span was limited.

Angie was agitated and tense when we met soon thereafter. "Whenever we visit Helen's doctor, he says she is going to get better," Angie told me. "But the nurses in the hospital say her condition is terminal. So tell me: Is my mother dying or not?"

Now I began to feel tense. If I told her the truth, it would be like dropping a bomb in her life. I searched for a way out.

"I'm not a medical expert," I replied cautiously, "so I am not qualified to answer your question. Isn't there another doctor you can speak with?"

"I suppose I could ask her other doctor, the radiologist who treats her every week. But I still want to know your opinion, since you have been working with hospice for so long. Is my mother dying?"

"Do you want me to be frank with you?"

"Yes."

"All right," I ventured, "but you must promise me you will ask the doctor again for his assessment. Now, I know that people with cancer can go into remission or even be cured. But with the number of metastases and complications your mother has, and as frail and weak as she has become, it looks to me as though your mother is dying."

"HOW can you say my mother is dying! You have *no right* to say that!" Angie shouted. "What do *you* know about my mother?"

Oh no, this was a mistake, I thought, as she continued to blast me with indignation. Yet I knew her anger was not really meant for me. As I reflected on the love behind her painful outburst, I was able to let her pain wash past me. Finally, Angie broke down into deep, racking sobs. I stayed by her side, reassuring her that it was all right to cry and that she had every reason to feel sad. In ten minutes or so Angie was calmer, having broken through the resistance and denial which had shielded her from her grief. Then she asked me what she should do now.

"What do you feel you *want* to do?"

"I think it's time to speak openly with my mother, and tell her I know she is dying, and that I love her. I am going to stay with her and help her through this."

Angie and Helen were finally able to speak freely with each other, and openly share their grief and love. They made the deep, meaningful connection for which they had both been longing. Afterward, Helen's condition surprisingly improved, and she lived another eighteen months. During those months, when I apologized to Angie for having informed her that her mother was dying, she was actually grateful because facing the truth had sparked the breakthrough in their communication and brought them closer.

"Besides," she added, "I know my mother is going to die one day anyway. Facing this now helps me be more prepared for the inevitable."

It is extremely difficult to create a genuine connection if we're hiding from each other, trying to avoid facing the inevitability of death. Part of making a genuine connection is facing our present situation; another part is sharing our natural response to it. Yet sometimes our strong attachment to the dying person makes it difficult for us to communicate openly. This is why it is important for the family members closest to the dying person to have support in facing the reality of their loss, so they don't burden the dying person with their painful attachment. Once they have begun to face the truth and release some of their grief, family members can speak more peacefully with the dying person about the oncoming death. Finding the courage to speak about the inevitability of death early on establishes a valuable trust and connection which will facilitate authentic communication in subsequent crises.

Fears of Speaking About Death

When family members are resistant to letting their loved one know he is dying, we might ask what they imagine will happen if they do:

"If I tell my friend he is dying, then . . ."
        ". . . he'll feel hopeless and depressed."
        ". . . I might break down in front of him."
        ". . . he'll think I want him to die."
        ". . . he'll simply give up and die."

The avoidance of acknowledging death generally stems from one of two problems: either the family members view death as something very negative, hopeless and tragic, or they fear experiencing the sadness and grief which will be released when they first face the truth together.

Many people have a deep fear of grief. Especially since they may have never known how to finish and heal the grief from former losses, the family or the dying person himself may be carrying a burden of unresolved grief. Resistance to speaking about the oncoming death may stem from the awareness that doing so may bring them face to face with a deep pool of pain.

What we fail to realize is that by considering death to be tragic and hopeless we end up making it that way, because we let our fears inhibit us from genuinely connecting and sharing our life and our love. I often tell family members: "To be told you are dying is *not* the worst thing that can happen to you. *The worst thing is to feel abandoned in a time of crisis.*" When we avoid speaking about the coming death, we unknowingly isolate the dying person during the greatest physical and emotional pain of his life. Even if he is surrounded by friends, when they cannot share the truth together the dying person will feel alone and abandoned.

I cannot say this strongly enough: telling a dying person the truth does not cause the person to die. While it is true that some people die soon after being told that their condition is not curable, there is nothing wrong with this. They may have been valiantly hanging on for the sake of loved ones until they feel that their loved ones are finally willing to accept the inevitable. Hearing the news that they are dying may give them a long-awaited sense of permission to let go.

It can be helpful for family members to look at things from the dying person's point of view:

There you are, lying in the hospital bed all day, acutely aware of the sensations and changes in your body. Frequent tests are being taken but everyone is vague about the results. During her increasingly brief visits, the doctor stands closer to the doorway, speaking rapidly, her eyes trying to avoid yours. Your family and friends speak to you with a forced cheeriness in their voice, and sometimes you see their eyes are red, probably from crying. It's not hard to deduce that you are dying. Yet since your loved ones don't mention it, you conclude they are not ready to face the truth, so you avoid bringing up the subject as well. This is how the game of mutual pretense continues.

When the dying person is not clearly informed of his prognosis, he may end up making inappropriate choices about his medical care or unrealistic plans for the future that could have negative repercussions for the survivors. He will not be able to arrange and finish with the practical or financial details of his life; heal and conclude his significant relationships; or turn more deeply toward his spiritual beliefs and practices to prepare for the coming death.

How to Tell?

As Elisabeth Kübler-Ross says, the question is not *whether* to tell someone they are dying, but *how to tell*. First, establish an atmosphere of trust, by spending time together and extending a warm friendship and love to your friend. If the dying person, sensing your own attitude of ease and acceptance, feels emotionally safe, he may even reveal to you his awareness of the truth. And if you are the one to first share the news, it's very important to offer it with hope: reassure your friend that you love him and will continue to be with him through this process.

Creating a supportive atmosphere depends a great deal on our personal level of comfort with death, which the dying person can sense. If we view death as a tragedy and assiduously avoid grief, another person's dying will ignite our fear. If we have faced the truth of our own death and found a meaning to our life, then we will bring a peaceful presence to the discussion, understanding the larger perspective of life's meaning and potential.

WHEN CAREGIVERS BREAK THE NEWS

The best way for letting a person know he or she is dying is for the doctor to bring the patient and his family together in a quiet room. Giving the news bluntly—"There's nothing more I can do for you"—can induce shock and hopelessness. Instead, the doctor can say, "Since there are no more treatments we know of that might cure your illness, the focus of your medical care from this point forward will be to do everything we can to ensure the quality of your life, relieving your pain and discomfort as much as possible." Then the doctor can allow the family to be alone together to absorb the news and share their response. After ten minutes or so the doctor could return and respond to their questions and concerns, helping outline a practical plan for the immediate future.

What if the family and doctor are all withholding the truth, and a nurse or other caregiver is asked point-blank by the patient, "Am I dying?" I favor a response which is both appropriate and honest. You can tell him, "As your nurse, it is not my role to tell you if you are dying or not. But there is nothing stopping you if you want to tell me—or your doctor or family—what you think is going on. You can also let them know that you are open to hearing the truth." After listening to the patient's assessment of his condition, you can then speak with the family and let them know that the dying person is now ready to hear his prognosis.

Confronting the Dying Person's Denial

Judy was thirty-five years old when her father, Harry, was dying of cancer. Although the whole family had been informed together that Harry was close to death, he adamantly refused to let anyone speak about it. Continually tense and angry, Harry attacked everyone who tried to come near. After many unsuccessful attempts at making a connection, Judy and her family grew increasingly frustrated and distanced from him.

Harry was weakening and Judy realized that if nothing changed soon, all they would experience in the remaining weeks or days of her father's life would be distance, anger, and blame. Realizing she had nothing to lose, Judy got up the courage to speak forcefully to her father. "We all know you are dying, and we wish you weren't because we love you. But we cannot change the fact that you're going to leave us one day soon. You may not realize it, but when you are so tense and angry with us, we aren't able to get near you anymore. Time is so precious now, and we want to spend it by your side. Won't you let us be close with you, before it's too late?"

The loving motivation behind Judy's words and her courageous manner of speaking finally broke through Harry's shell of self-imposed isolation. He allowed his family to come close, and they were able to communicate and share their love, expressing all that was in their hearts, before he died.

Denial and anger arise from our fearful resistance to entering the process of mourning and letting go. *Even more than our fear of death, we have a deep fear of grief.* Under certain circumstances, a dying person's denial can be all right. Yet if the denial continues until the dying person's last weeks or days, often the loved ones are effectively blocked from expressing their love and concluding their relationship. In this case, our role is not so much to *confront* another person's denial as it is to consider how we can help him feel safe enough to express his fears or sadness. It is only appropriate to break through another person's denial when all the following conditions are met:

1. Our motivation is clear. Instead of judging the other person, we reflect on his suffering and the possible causes of his denial and distress. As his suffering touches our compassion, we are able to relate directly with the person with love, rather than fear.

2. We are willing to be vulnerable ourselves, experiencing with the dying person any painful feelings that the truth may open up. Instead of being in denial of our own eventual death, we speak with our friend as an equal, acknowledging and sharing the pain of our human condition.

3. We have no intent of abandoning the dying person. Offering our love and support includes a commitment to continue to be there for him over the long run.

4. We are free of expectations or conditions, willing to offer our love and acceptance *no matter what.* If the person reacts with anger or chooses to stay in denial, we clearly communicate that we love him and will continue to visit and support him throughout his illness.

THE BOTTOM LINE IS
TO MAKE A CONNECTION

In rare instances, telling a person a terminal prognosis could have adverse psychological consequences, so I am not proposing it is always good to tell the truth. However, we often err on the side of our own discomfort and fear, rather than making a decision appropriate for the person in front of us. We can ask the dying person if he would like us to fully disclose his prognosis, keeping in mind that even a negative reply may be related to who is offering to give the news or to his present level of readiness.

If the dying person or circumstances prevent us from speaking directly about death, there are other ways we can generate an authentic dialogue. We can ask our dying friend to tell us about his life and describe what he has accomplished; or we can ask him to share with us how he's coped with the setbacks and changes in his life; or what he's learned from being ill. We can gently let him know we are open to hearing any of his thoughts and feelings, whenever he is ready to talk about them. Sometimes our relationship is healed and concluded nonverbally, simply by offering to take care of the dying person, or in quietly sharing the last few days and nights together.

The Family's Journey Toward Death

Just before midnight, the call came. As she listened to the young woman's description of her mother's condition, Lee, a hospice nurse, assessed that the mother would probably die during that night. Lee gently informed the daughter that the physical changes she was witnessing were normal and no cause for alarm.

"Are you aware that your mother is very close to dying?"

"Yes. It's hard to hear it once again, but I knew deep down the end was near. She wanted to have a peaceful death, so I arranged everything I could to bring her home to die. We've only had one visit from the hospice nurse since then. I just didn't know the end would come so quickly. I feel so unprepared. Is there anything I can do for her now?"

With a few more questions, Lee learned that everything that could be done medically for the dying woman had been arranged. She was alert and relatively pain-free. On a personal level, Lee asked, "Have you and your mother spoken about her coming death? Have you expressed all that you wish to, and said a good good-bye?"

"Oh no," said the horrified young woman, "I couldn't bring that up. I wouldn't want her to think I was giving up on her!"

"You're not giving up on your mother. She is dying, and from what I can hear, you love her very much. Isn't it time you told her so? Look how lucky you are! Some people have a loved one die without any warning, or when they are not by the person's side. You've put off speaking openly with your mother, yet she is still alert and aware, so it's not too late. Please use this special time you have together—possibly her last few hours—to express all that is in your heart before she dies."

The next day, the daughter phoned Lee again. "You were right, my mother did die in the early hours of the morning." She paused. "And thank you for strongly encouraging me to speak openly with my mother. We were able to have a wonderful conversation before she died, and I will always cherish all that she said to me. In my heart I was yearning to do this, but I was so afraid to begin—I was worried about what she would think. Without your having pushed me a little, we probably would have missed the opportunity we had last night."

Giving support and encouragement to the family members is an essential part of helping the dying person to let go and die peacefully. During my years of hospice work, I've had the same scene repeat itself countless times: Speaking privately to the dying person in his room, I would describe how a hospice volunteer might be able to support him in preparing for his death. Many times I heard the following response: "I know I am dying, and I've made my peace with it. I don't know if I need any more help. *But would you please help my wife? She's having such a hard time with this!*"

The partner or closest family members experience a massive number of stresses in the prolonged process of dealing with a life-threatening illness or the debilitations of aging. They are often responsible for the financial aspects of that person's life, and may be helping with the daily physical care, or visiting regularly in the hospital. Primary caregivers must also continue with the myriad details of daily life: shopping, cooking, paying bills, going to work, raising children, and so on. The partner or caregivers of the dying person are always aware that one day their loved one will be gone, and they must continue life alone. And, in filling all their new responsibilities, they may have forfeited taking breaks or vacations, and lost their usual recreational or social contacts.

Since the ongoing responsibility for the dying person's care may become quite exhausting, it's not unusual for the primary caregiver to wish secretly that her partner would die (simultaneously judging herself harshly for having these thoughts, of course).

Like the dying person, close family members have entered a bardo, losing their security and references, and with complete uncertainty as to how the future will unfold. *Family members feel sometimes as though they are dying,* since their known world, much like the dying person's, is dissolving. Yet no one is validating the intensity of their situation.

Emotionally, each member of the family may be in a different place in his or her process of accepting the death. Some may be resisting with denial, anger, or withdrawal; others may be openly grieving and beginning to let go; while still others may have already released their attachment and arrived at a peaceful acceptance of the new reality. Just as dying does not happen in a straightforward way, our own vacillations between denial and acceptance of the coming death can follow upon each other in the same hour. Each individual may have difficulty accepting his or her own emotional vulnerability, and as a consequence, may be harshly judging other family members' reactions as well.

When the dragons of old griefs, guilts, or fears are awakened, people may lash out or blame each other, instead of facing their own unfinished business. Thus there is often stress and conflict between family members during the dying process. The dying person's most difficult struggle may emanate from his concern for the stress his illness is causing the family and fears for their ability to survive once he has died. Lacking other sources of support, family members may either burden the dying person with their troubles or attempt to suppress their difficult feelings each time they visit, making meaningful contact nearly impossible.

GIVING SUPPORT AND DIRECTION TO THE FAMILY

When professional caregivers intervene with the family, their assistance will likely be much appreciated, since in the family's view they are considered "experts" familiar with the territory. They can offer to meet with the family members as a group, or individually, in order to validate their suffering, enable them to understand each other better, and help them align themselves to one goal: how to best focus on the dying person's needs in preparing for the coming death. One need not be a professional caregiver, however, in order to establish an effective dialogue with the family. Before you attempt to intervene with them, please remember to:

- Be aware of your own issues, emotions, hopes, and fears, and find a way to minimize them so that you are clear and present.
- Be willing to meet the other person where he or she is.
- See your role as opening doors for the person, skillfully drawing out his own innate wisdom and inner resources.
- Reflect on your motivation—to relieve suffering— and let go of any attachment to a particular outcome.

In communicating with distressed family members, it's important to begin by building trust. Invite them to tell you what they feel is happening, what they need, and where they perceive difficulties, both personally and within the family context. Ask questions to draw them out further, listening without judgment to their experiences and perceptions. Remember, they have a long history together, and a unique way of relating which they may neither recognize nor be willing to change.

Family members may be relieved to hear you describe all the different stresses and emotional pains that are normal for families facing a death. People feel validated when they understand why they are suffering with such extreme emotions, and they may stop blaming themselves for not being "in control."

When they are lost and alone with their own pain, family members may not be aware of the needs or experiences of their loved one who is dying. Once they feel supported, however, we can help reorient the family toward the dying person's needs by encouraging them to consider exchanging places with him:

"Imagine that you are the one who is dying, as if you were standing on the deck of an ocean liner. The ocean liner is already beginning to depart from the dock, and you don't have a choice about it. As you gaze toward the shore, you see your family and friends saying good-bye to you. How do you want them to be saying good-bye? What will help you on your journey?"

The Four Tasks of Living and Dying

REASSURING FAMILY MEMBERS

Along with validating their experience of powerful stresses and emotions, give family members these important messages:

Whatever you are feeling is normal. You might at times be feeling out of control; extremely vulnerable, confused, or besieged by conflicting and unfamiliar emotions. Remember that these difficult feelings are not permanent and they will change eventually. There's nothing wrong with you; you are in a new situation.

Be kind to yourself. Don't constantly judge yourself and hold yourself to an old or impossible ideal. You're faced with very difficult circumstances, and you can't always do everything perfectly. When you see your mistakes or limitations, go easy on yourself; you are doing the best you can.

We're not designed to go through crises alone. When you're in crisis, it is important to find support beyond the circle of your immediate family. None of us can be totally independent all the time; now it's your turn to ask for—and be willing to receive—love and support from others.

LETTING GO WITH LOVE

Family members and the intimate partner of the dying person usually have great difficulty in letting go, and this is natural. Letting go can feel like the worst sort of betrayal—especially if the dying person has been through sequential health crises, and family members have previously seen their role as the forceful catalyst in helping the person rally and get better.

Most people tend to assume that "letting go" can be completed in one moment or conversation, a single rush of tears and sadness. Yet after one such intimate dialogue of grief and letting go, a loved one may find herself a few days later hanging on as tightly as ever. *Letting go is a process, and it takes time.*

Many people confuse accepting the death with *wishing for the death.* "If I let go, he'll think I don't love him; he'll think I want him to die." To assuage this unnecessary guilt, family members may subtly or overtly beseech their loved one in the final stages of dying to keep hanging on to life, without realizing the consequences will be prolonged pain and suffering.

If our attachment to the dying person is too strong, mixed with an intense fear that we couldn't survive without him, our grasping and insecurity will only intensify as death approaches, making it harder for him to let go with peace of mind.

In loving someone, it's normal to feel some attachment for him or her; at the same time, we must keep the wish in our heart for his "highest good." When impermanence or death heralds the loss of the form of our relationship, our task is to let go of our painful attachment. *We do not have to let go of our love or our wonderful memories.* Even while letting go then, our hearts can still be full of love.

Pat was very devoted to his partner dying of AIDS, and had committed to caring for him at home until the time of his death. Katie, the home-care nurse, asked Pat what was most important to him.

"I really want to be right beside John when he dies, and I have a terrible time going to bed in my own room each night. I'm afraid he'll die while I'm asleep."

Katie gently informed Pat that this could very well happen. The only choice he had was to prepare himself for that eventuality. This wasn't what he wanted to hear, but later Pat described the results.

"The nurse suggested that every night I say good-bye to him *as though it was the last time.* It was very, very hard to do, but after a few nights it got easier to say good-bye before I went to sleep. If John were to die while I was away from his side, I know now that it would be all right."

LANDMARKS ON THE JOURNEY

When we are facing death, or if we have a loved one dying, most of us are entering what seems to be a frightening and uncharted territory called "dying and death." A large part of the unnecessary suffering of dying comes from this lack of familiarity with where we are in the journey, and not knowing what is coming or how to prepare.

Since the professionals and volunteers who care for the dying are familiar with the territory, they have a vital responsibility to inform the family and the dying person what might happen during this process and to suggest ways in which they can best prepare themselves for the journey ahead.

Family members are usually aware they are holding back, waiting for the "right time" to speak, yet this heightens their anxiety each time they visit, and their opportunities may vanish as the reality of death unfolds. What they thought would be the right time never arrives, and they feel cheated. There are no guarantees about how or when the end will come. This is why family members need to have the journey of dying fully described to them, so they can identify the atmosphere they would like to create for the time of death, and begin to connect, share their love, and say their good-byes before it is too late.

Prepare the family for the major turning points where they will feel a new jolt of letting go, as the reality of death comes closer. Like dying itself, letting go is a process, stage by stage, where they will begin to acknowledge the coming loss in deeper and more tangible ways. Rehearsing letting go with each successive "little death" will help them feel more peaceful when the actual time of death arrives.

When the emphasis of the medical care necessarily shifts—from working toward curing the disease toward the palliation of any distressful symptoms—family members must also make a similar shift. Previously they may have seen their role as doing everything possible to help their loved one rally and get better. Now, when the person's illness is no longer curable, this is a signal for family members to begin letting go of their former role and show their love through listening to and unconditionally accepting the dying person.

Another marker in the journey of letting go is when the dying person loses the function of a major organ, or when he or she can no longer eat. A choice is made at this point whether to extend life by artificial means. Again, before this potential crisis is reached, the closest family members and a social worker or counselor need to meet together with the dying person and elicit his preferences and values so they know under which conditions he would either want to prolong his life or choose to discontinue medical intervention. They can also discuss together the dying person's wishes for the moment of death.

"What would you want to be happening in the room when you are close to death? How could we make this a peaceful atmosphere for you? Are there any prayers, inspiring readings, or meditations you would like us to be doing at the time of your death?"

This discussion may bring up sad feelings, as the family and dying person are sharing another poignant moment of facing the death and letting go. But we should not fear our natural sadness and let it keep us from entering this vital dialogue. Meeting and preparing thoroughly for the death will bear good fruit, as knowing and honoring the dying person's preferences will ease a lot of unnecessary suffering for everyone involved.

Especially when a person is dying at home, the family must be informed about and prepared for the physical and cognitive changes they might see when death is near, and be assured that they have round-the-clock support available from a home-care nurse and the doctor. Then, rather than panicking and rushing the person back to the hospital at the final signs of death, they will have a plan for responding instead with the support of their love and spiritual practice.

Family members need to know that the dying person could *at any time* lose the ability to communicate or fall into a comatose state. The dying person may become extremely weak or confused, and not have the energy or capacity to carry on a meaningful dialogue with loved ones. And even when family members wish to be at the side of their loved one in the final moments of life, those who are dying often feel more free to let go and die during the hours they are alone. Thus it is important to encourage the family and friends: *Don't hold something back for a later time, as later may never come.*

PREPARING FOR DEATH

Ask the doctor or home-care nurse to tell you their "best estimate" of when the person may die—whether it's a few weeks, days, or hours. It's all right if their assessment turns out to be wrong (there is no accurate way to gauge such an individual process); however, hearing such a warning will help you realize that there is no more time for procrastinating.

One of the most healing and reassuring things that can happen just before death is for the dying person and his loved ones to verbally express "I love you." Especially when a person had been reserved about saying it throughout life, his courage to verbalize his love one last time before dying can make all the difference in the world for those who survive him.

And when they are very close to death, the dying need to hear two reassurances from their loved ones. "It is all right for you to let go and die. You don't have to hang on and suffer any more. Know that you are loved, and we wish you well. *And please don't worry about us;* we are going to be fine." If family have really prepared for the death, if they have gracefully entered the process of letting go, and have allowed themselves to mourn together in anticipation of the coming death, then they will be able to give these two vital reassurances wholeheartedly.

When Time Is Running Out

Each afternoon when the father of a twenty-four-year-old son who was dying came to the hospital to visit, the nurse, Anne, observed a similar painful scene. The father entered his son's room slightly hunched, his face a mixture of sadness and feigned cheerfulness. He would move a chair to the side of the bed, hoping to look into his son's face, and every day as he started to speak, his son would turn his head toward the opposite wall.

A week passed with this continuing standoff, a week closer to the son's imminent death. Although she felt uncertain, Anne decided to intervene, reminding herself, "Time is running short for them and they may not realize it. If nothing changes, they will never connect or communicate before the young man dies, and both of them will lose out. Besides," she realized, "even if my intervening should backfire, I don't think things could get any worse."

The next day, before he entered his son's room, Anne brought the father into an empty room and spoke to him forcefully to break through his daze.

"WHY do you let your son treat you like that?" Anne implored. "You know you need to talk with him, in order to release you both from any hurt feelings or regrets. And you need to tell him you love him *before it is too late!* I don't know what happened between you, but now it is time to go beyond it. Your son's time is running out, and he might slip into a coma before he dies. Speak to him strongly, tell him what's in your heart—and do it now. There's no telling if or when you'll have another chance!"

Anne's strong words did break through the father's shell and he thanked her. Now he knew what to do. With determination, he walked into his son's room and as he began opening up and revealing his regrets and his love, his son slowly turned and looked into his father's face, tears in his eyes. The healing of their relationship, the love they both yearned to feel and express, was made possible by the father's willingness to take a risk, speak openly, and make a meaningful connection with his son.

Family members sometimes need strong encouragement to do what they are already yearning to do. If our motivation is loving and clear, free of expectations, it is appropriate to intervene, even to speak strongly, especially when time is running out. If loved ones fail to use the time of dying well, to heal their relationship and make a connection, after the death they will feel doubly bereft. After a loved one dies, *the pain that stays with us is the love we held back.*

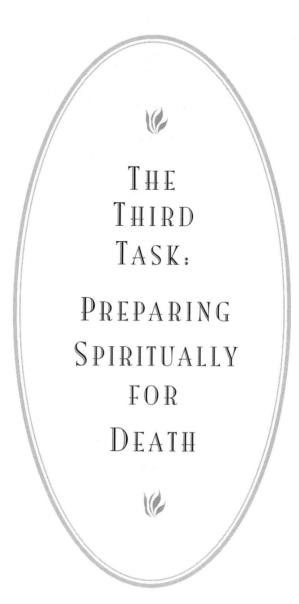

THE
THIRD
TASK:

PREPARING
SPIRITUALLY
FOR
DEATH

Chapter 9

SPIRITUAL PREPARATION FOR DEATH

Dying is not the end, it is just the beginning. Death is a continuation of life. This is the meaning of eternal life; it is where our soul goes to God, to be in the presence of God, to see God, to speak to God, to continue loving Him with greater love. We only surrender our body in death—our heart and our soul live forever.

Yesterday is gone and tomorrow has not yet come; we must live each day as if it were our last so that when God calls us we are ready, and prepared, to die with a clean heart.

MOTHER TERESA[1]

If we use our entire life and the time of dying to prepare meaningfully for death, our potential for freedom is heightened—as is our potential for magnified suffering if negative habits hold sway in our mind and heart. The Chinese character depicting the word "crisis" has two meanings: danger, and opportunity. Lacking an understanding of the opportunity in death, we may react only to our sense of danger.

The secret to traversing the bardo of dying is recognizing that we are in a crucial transition and deciding on the outcome we want, thereby giving ourselves a direction through the seemingly dangerous upheavals of dying. Yet this direction—our ultimate hope and highest spiritual potential—is the same hope that we must nurture in our heart and mind throughout life. Every religious tradition emphasizes that to prepare spiritually for death it is vital that we establish right now a daily spiritual practice, a practice so deeply ingrained that it becomes part of our flesh and bones, our reflexive response to every situation in life, including our experiences of suffering.

Principles of Spiritual Preparation

People often die the way they lived. Yet we can help the dying see that, even at the crossroads of death, it is possible to change their attitude and the course of their life. If they choose to, those facing death can use their last weeks or days to transform their habits, purify regrets, heal relationships, and deepen their compassion.

We must be willing to understand the dying person's spiritual beliefs, and offer reassurance with words and concepts that support her way of thinking, being careful not to impose our own beliefs. The key is to *listen* to the person facing death, and respect her wishes and needs. If she asks us to share our beliefs, we should find an appropriate way to express them, so that she feels free to accept or reject whatever we've offered.

People who have faith in their religion may view death positively, seeing it as an opportunity to become "one with God." Yet they may have difficulty while they are dying if they feel that God is very distant and unknowable. They might feel uncertain about how they could prepare to enter God's kingdom. Aware of her human weaknesses and foibles, the dying person might be wondering: Will God forgive me even though I feel unforgivable? Or, she simply may not know *how to let go and die,* to reach her desired goal: God's infinite love.

A person facing death might profess to believe in God, but she may have left her traditional religion owing to problems with its tenets or dogmas. We should encourage her to focus not on these problems, but on whatever constitutes for her the deepest part of her faith: her devotion, trust, or compassion. As one priest told me, "At the time of their death, I believe every person is given another chance to make their peace with God."

If the dying person has no formal prayers or rituals to rely on, we can encourage her to pray in her own words, with sincere and heartfelt devotion, a simple prayer such as the following: "Dear God, please be with me at the moment of death, guide me. Give me strength during the process of dying, give me the courage to let go. Please forgive all of my sins, and make me ready to be with You."

Everyone has a "spark," an inner source of hope. Even those who say they are not religious may in truth be deeply spiritual.

Our role is to draw out from the dying person this spark, or an empowering image of death that enables her to prepare meaningfully for it. Ask the dying person to tell you about her life. Help her identify the best human qualities she has observed in herself or others. If she speaks about compassion, a memory of love, a moment of forgiveness or reconciliation, encourage her to continue remembering and feeling one of these uplifting qualities while she is dying.

Throughout our life, it's important to establish a personal connection with and trust in God, speaking with God like a dear and trusted friend, and receiving God's limitless blessings of acceptance, forgiveness, and love. Having established such a relationship of trust and gratitude, then in times of suffering and while we are dying, we will feel that our best friend is always present to guide and protect us.

At the moment of death, our intimate relationship with God will give us strength. Opening our heart in prayer, we can ask God (or Christ, or whoever we feel a devotion to) to be present in our room at the hour of our death. As Christ himself promised: "If you shall ask anything in my name, I will do it."[2] Thus we can have confidence that God responds to our heartfelt prayer and is with us as soon as we invoke Him.

Part of our task in dying is to find a way to "make our peace with God," confessing our mistakes and clearing our soul, by asking for—and being willing to receive—God's unconditional forgiveness. If the dying person feels unforgivable, we can encourage her to meditate on God's mercy and love, reflecting on stories from the Bible—for example, the father who forgave his prodigal son and joyfully welcomed him home. *As soon as we feel remorse, as soon as we confess and ask forgiveness, God's forgiveness and love are already there.* As Ruth Hatch wrote: "There is no condemnation in God. He is not shocked by anything you have done. There is nothing human beings can do that He has not seen. He is not even interested in what you have done. He only wants your love."[3]

Above all, we can encourage our dying loved one to identify a spiritual practice—a special prayer, meditation, hymn, or scriptural reading—that inspires her with confidence and strength. Regularly doing an inspiring practice, especially if she is suffering, will focus the energy of her heart and mind in a positive way and help to rekindle her devotion and trust. The sacred inspiration of this continual prayer or meditation may begin to pervade her every waking and sleeping moment, and this is an excellent way to prepare for death. And, if her family, friends, or caregivers do this practice with her whenever they visit, they will feel more prepared at the moment of her death—more inspired to let her go, peacefully and with love.

Examples from the Christian Tradition

Sylvia, a hospice patient I had visited for over a year, said that for her the hardest part of dying was feeling "abandoned" by Christ. "All my life," she said, "I've had a devotion to Jesus Christ, gone to church regularly, and prayed. Yet now, with all my pain and difficulties, when I pray I feel no one is there. I feel totally alone in my suffering. What can I do?"

I had no answer for Sylvia at that moment. When I left her, I reflected on her dilemma. Some dying people I knew had offered prayer in the form of an expectation or demand: "I'll trust in you if you take away my pain or heal me." Yet God's role in our lives is not to rescue us from our problems. It is in "turning to God," filling our heart with devotion and trust, that we find a way through our difficulty and gain the strength to cope with seemingly unbearable pain. We can turn to God as our refuge and comforter as we go through the vicissitudes of illness, suffering, and death.

I started to remember as well the story of Christ's suffering and death. On the eve of his own capture, Jesus prayed to God to release him from the suffering which lay ahead. In the end, Christ's trust was expressed in his words: "Not my will, but Thine, be done." On the cross, suffering the last torments of pain and thirst, he cried out, "My God, my God, why hast thou forsaken me?"

Sylvia and I spoke together about the meaning of Christ's experience of dying. Even Christ prayed to have the cup of suffering, which he knew was coming, taken away from him. And, Sylvia mused, perhaps *everyone* feels forsaken during the painful process of dying. In reciting the opening lines of Psalm 22 on the cross, Christ revealed that he shared in the human experience of dying. Yet he turned to God during his last hour, and ultimately he was not forsaken.

With tremendous compassion, Christ dedicated and prayed that through his death he might be able to take on the suffering and purify the sins of all beings. Doing so, he transcended death altogether. The compassionate motivation Jesus Christ aroused in accepting his suffering and death *shows the way* for those who follow him to traverse their suffering in life and transcend their death.

Each of the Christian traditions offers a vast and rich array of teachings and prayers for dying and death. For example, the prayer a Catholic priest recites by the side of a person who has just died brings together the elements of devotion, trust, mercy, and love. Even though the following prayer is for the "moment of death," if a family were to read it again and again to their loved one as she is dying, this may help them prepare to let go in the highest way: offering her back to God.

> Saints of God, come to his (her) aid!
> Come to meet him (her), angels of the Lord!
> Receive his (her) soul and present him (her) to God the Most
>   High.
>
> May Christ, who called you, take you to himself;
> may angels lead you to Abraham's side.
> Receive his (her) soul and present him (her) to God the Most
>   High.
>
> Give him (her) eternal rest, O Lord,
> and may your light shine on him (her) forever.
> Receive his (her) soul and present him (her) to God the Most
>   High.
>
> Let us pray.
> All-powerful and merciful God,
> We commend to you, *(name)*, your servant.
> In your mercy and love,
> blot out the sins he (she) has committed through human
>   weakness.
> In this world he (she) has died:
> let him (her) live with you for ever.
> We ask this through Christ our Lord.
> Amen.[4]

Examples from the Jewish Tradition

In the Jewish tradition, the hope offered to a dying person is not that of a heavenly existence after death, but rather in the righteous

life he or she has lived on earth. Hope comes from being connected to a living spiritual tradition and its rituals, having lived
one's life in accordance with God's law, and from having used one's
life meaningfully, contributing to the community, and helping to
care for family and friends. Many of the prayers and psalms said
during the time of dying are in praise of God's goodness and
mercy. The prayers express both supplication and surrender to
God's will, taking refuge in God's protection to bring one through
the sufferings or temptations of dying.

A dying person is encouraged to accept the reality of her death
squarely and conclude her life well, putting all her affairs in order,
so that her partner or children are prepared to survive well after she
has died. While dying, she examines her life, acknowledging and
atoning for any harm she has done, and extending forgiveness to
anyone who has harmed her.

The dying person is encouraged to make a final confession to
God; one such confession is called *Viduy:* "I acknowledge before
You, Hashem, my God and God of my fathers, that my recovery
or death is in Your hands. May it be Your will that You heal me
completely; but if I die, may my death be an atonement for all the
mistakes, sins and rebellions I have erred, sinned, and rebelled
before You. May my portion be in Gan Eden, and may You allow
me to be in the World to Come, which lies in store for the righteous."[5]

A candle is lit at the moment of death, and a traditional prayer,
the Shema Yisrael, is recited then and regularly in the rituals afterward. The Shema may be the dying person's last words, or the last
thing he or she hears: "Hear O Israel, Hashem is our God,
Hashem, the One and Only. Blessed is the Name of His glorious
kingdom for all eternity."

Prayers for the person who has died are recited on a regular
basis, especially during the Shivah—a gathering for reflection and
prayer at the home of the deceased in the first seven days—and
prayers for the dead, especially the Kaddish, continue regularly
throughout the year, as those surviving the death are encouraged
to grieve and let go.

Preparation in the Tibetan Buddhist Tradition

Be free of attachment and aversion,
Keep your mind pure,
And unite your mind with the wisdom mind of the
    Buddha.

These are the crucial reminders the Tibetan masters would have us always remember as death approaches—the essence of how we should prepare for our death.

"BE FREE OF ATTACHMENT AND AVERSION"

When you are dying, you are in a powerful transition and you don't have a choice—the ship is already departing from the dock and you're on board. Your task is to create auspicious conditions for dying, and let go of all the bonds of responsibility and attachment that may hold you back. It is time to prepare spiritually for the journey ahead.

Rather than "giving up" you could imagine "offering up"—to all the Buddhas and enlightened beings—those things to which you are most attached: your body, health, physical appearance, and independence; your possessions and wealth; your jobs and talents; your friends and family and your feelings of responsibility for them. You could even offer up your aversions or fears—aversion to the deterioration and pain of dying, aversion to being confined to the hospital or subjected to medical tests or procedures, fear of being abandoned, or of losing physical or mental control.

You should get all your business and financial affairs in order, ensuring that those who survive you are as informed and prepared as possible. Before dying, make a thorough list and be sure to give away all your material possessions. In many religious traditions, it's considered virtuous and auspicious before dying to make an offering to the poor.

As I've described earlier, you must prepare emotionally by healing your relationships, expressing your love, and grieving with and saying a sincere good-bye to your loved ones. Doing this in advance ensures that the moment of your death is peaceful, free of attachment and aversion.

If you are leaving behind children, you'll naturally tend to feel anguish over your attachment to them and your sense of responsibility for their well-being. But holding on to your attachment only increases your suffering and theirs. The only real thing to do is prepare for your children's physical, emotional, and spiritual well-being as thoroughly as you can. For instance, you can make sure that a good friend or counselor is available to support them during their bereavement. You can offer up your feelings of responsibility, and pray that your children's lives will be happy, dedicating whatever spiritual practice you do to their benefit. Praying with such compassion for your children will help them far more than prolonging your yearning and attachment.

You should do everything possible to arrange that the environment at the time of your death is peaceful, with minimal distractions. Coming home from the hospital to die—even for the last few days of your life—is best, but if you *must* die in a hospital, ask to be moved to a private room. Clearly establish your directives regarding artificial life support or resuscitation in a Living Will. Name a legal representative in a "Durable Power of Attorney for Health Care" who can act as an advocate for you, and communicate your directives to the doctors and medical staff.[6]

As they get close to death, some people arrange to have their room kept quiet and imbued with peace. To lessen emotional entanglements they see fewer visitors as the end draws near, requesting the presence of only those friends or family members who can create an environment of sincerity and warmth, of peace and of letting go, through continuous, heartfelt spiritual practice.

"KEEP YOUR MIND PURE"

The Tibetan Buddhist teachings describe death as a very special opportunity to attain liberation. The supreme way of preparing spiritually for death is to take care of ourselves—by stabilizing our recognition of the true nature of mind through committed spiritual training and practice throughout life. Then, when we are dying, we simply remain, undistracted, in the luminosity and all-pervading space of our true nature.

A spiritual book much read in the West in the last few decades is *The Tibetan Book of the Dead,* a text from the Nyingma school of Tibetan Buddhism. The title of the text in Tibetan is *Bardo Tödrol Chenmo*—"Great Liberation upon Hearing in the Bardo" (referring here to the states of existence after death). The original author of the *Bardo Tödrol* is Padmasambhava (Guru Rinpoche), considered by people of the Himalayan regions to be a second, mystical Buddha. Padmasambhava gathered the teachings of the Buddha, including the more advanced wisdom practices, and presented them according to the six bardos: life, sleep and dream, meditation, dying, *dharmata* (intrinsic radiance), and becoming.

The *Bardo Tödrol* is but one small part of this larger cycle of teachings and practices given by Padmasambhava to help practitioners use each of the bardos to attain liberation. The *Bardo Tödrol* itself is a guide to the after-death states, designed to be read by a master or spiritual friend to a practitioner as he or she dies, and for some time after death. If we read *The Tibetan Book of the Dead* without having received the complete teachings and training in these practices, we can easily miss the point.

For example, some people conclude that reading *The Tibetan Book of the Dead* to a dying friend constitutes the "spiritual care" offered in this tradition, but the text itself tells us that the very best way to prepare for death is *to have gained a stability in resting in the nature of mind in this life*. For a person who has reached this confident stability in their meditation, nothing special is required when they are dying; they simply meditate and remain in the nature of mind, and die in the unbroken awareness of that state. The advice in the *Bardo Tödrol* for a practitioner of this caliber is only one line: "O Sir (or Madam), now the basic luminosity is shining before you; recognize it, and rest in the practice."[7]

If the practitioner's realization is not yet stable, or if she is distracted due to physical pain or mental confusion while dying, then her teacher or spiritual friends can give her vital support by meditating and practicing by her side.

When a master or confident practitioner remains in the nature of mind by the bedside of a dying person, he or she is literally "showing" it to the heart and mind of the other person. Since the ego's cloudy layers of thought and emotion dissolve at death, it is much easier at that time for the dying person to *experience directly* any spiritual practice being offered on her behalf. Being able to remain in the stable recognition of the true nature of mind not only prepares us in the best way possible for death; it is also the most profound spiritual support we can offer to those who are dying.

If we are not sure whether the person's meditation has reached this level of stability, the *Bardo Tödrol* advises us to rely on the practice of *phowa*—a spiritual practice for purifying and liberating a person's consciousness—when the person exhales their last breath and for some time after the death. And finally, if the spiritual friends practicing for the dying person are not sure the phowa practice was effected successfully, they are advised to begin reading the text of the *Bardo Tödrol* to the person who has died.

Tracy was a student of Sogyal Rinpoche, and she had received teachings and blessings from many great Buddhist masters. After dedicating many years to spiritual practice, Tracy learned she was dying from a brain tumor. Her biggest fear was that the increasing impairment of her brain functions would prevent her from doing her spiritual practice as she approached death. Since that indeed could happen, I suggested that Tracy imagine herself in this situation and then communicate her wishes to her husband and friends. She might consider, for example, how they could create an inspiring atmosphere in her room, perhaps making a small shrine with candles and offerings, or placing special pictures or sacred images within the range of her gaze.

She could prepare for death by inspiring her every moment with meditation and spiritual practice, for as long as possible. In the event that she lost her cognitive abilities, Tracy should write down in advance which taped teachings or sacred chants and prayers she would like to hear.

Sogyal Rinpoche advised Tracy: "If the time comes when you cannot practice actively any more, the only really important thing for you to do is to relax, as deeply as possible, in the confidence of the View, and rest in the nature of mind. It does not matter whether your body or your brain are still functioning; the nature of your mind is always there, sky-like, radiant, blissful, limitless and unchanging."[8]

Sogyal Rinpoche encouraged Tracy to remember with gratitude the blessings and wonderful teachings she had received from her spiritual masters; to remember her devotion to them and their compassion for her; and to invoke their presence, in the form of Guru Rinpoche, and trust that she would recognize her true nature at the time of death.

When she was dying, Tracy and her husband moved to an area of France where there are numerous Buddhist retreat centers. Just after she died, her husband brought a Tibetan lama who lived in the region to her side to do the practice of phowa. The lama stood there quietly a few minutes and told her husband, "There is no need to do the phowa. She has found her own way."

Spiritual Preparation for Death

"UNITE YOUR MIND WITH THE WISDOM MIND OF THE BUDDHA"

In the Tibetan Buddhist tradition, phowa is considered the most valuable and effective practice for death. The word *phowa* means the transference or ejection of consciousness into the state of truth. Its success relies on invoking the presence of a buddha (a fully enlightened being), combined with our receptivity and devotion, and the familiarity which comes from having done the practice repeatedly throughout our life. There are many types of phowa; the more traditional form is an elaborate, inner yogic practice that is only transmitted from a spiritual master to his or her student after years of committed practice, and thus it cannot be described in a book.

Sogyal Rinpoche has taught an Essential Phowa practice, which, unlike the traditional phowa, is not just for the moment of death. The practice also helps to purify our regrets and negative karma, and it can be used to assist in emotional or physical healing. The Essential Phowa is a practice for our whole life as well as for the time of dying, and it is the principal practice for offering spiritual support to others at the moment of death, and afterward.

If we practice the Essential Phowa again and again, our compassionate motivation and our confident devotion will grow even deeper, increasingly becoming part of our "flesh and bones." As we begin to embody the practice, our heart and mind are opened, made more free and limitless. If we prepare for our own death with this depth of familiarity, devotion, and trust, we'll reap other rewards. For instance, our fear of death will diminish. And even if we should be in a sudden accident, facing death without warning, we'll know how to let go in the best way, because this profound practice has become like a reflex.

Also, by practicing the Essential Phowa regularly and as strongly as possible, we'll find that when a loved one is in great distress or is dying, we can respond with all our love and compassion and offer this rich spiritual practice for him or her. When we hear of a great tragedy or natural disaster we will realize that we can counter our feelings of helplessness by offering a practice to spiritually benefit those who are suffering.

The Four Tasks of Living and Dying

First sit quietly and settle yourself, bringing all the energies of your mind and body back home. As far as possible, relax into the deep presence and spacious awareness of your being. Before you begin, arouse a strong compassionate aspiration such as that described in *The Tibetan Book of the Dead:* "By means of this death, I will adopt only the attitude of the enlightened state of mind, loving kindness, and compassion, and attain perfect enlightenment for the sake of all sentient beings who are as limitless as space."[9]

With all your heart, invoke in the sky before you the presence of a buddha or a Divine Being for whom you feel a devotion. See the form of this Presence, not as flesh and blood, but as radiant light. Recognize that this being's qualities of perfect wisdom, boundless compassion, and limitless power to benefit beings are no different from the qualities of your own wisdom nature. Consider the Divine Presence you have invoked is *actually present*—alive, breathing, and gazing toward you with kindness and love. If you cannot clearly visualize a buddha or Divine Being, then simply imagine that a brilliant and loving Presence, who is *the embodiment of truth,* is in the sky in front of you in the form of light. Allow yourself to relax deeply and establish a personal connection with this Presence you have invoked.

Open yourself now, and acknowledge the aspects of your being that need purification, forgiveness, and blessing. Acknowledge any regrets, negative karma, or destructive emotions that you want to release and purify. Become aware of any places in your body where there is disease, weakness, or even a fear of illness. And recognize any doubts, fears, or old wounds in your heart that need healing and love. Then call out sincerely to the Divine Presence in front of you and ask for help.

Immediately this buddha or Divine Presence responds, sending love and compassion from his or her heart in a stream of tremendous rays of light directly into your being. Allow these powerful rays to penetrate you and purify you—filling you with forgiveness, healing energy, confidence, and unconditional love. Consider that these brilliant light rays of compassion and love dissolve all of your fears and defenses, so that you are totally immersed in light. To make yourself more receptive, you may want to recite a short prayer or mantra during this part of the practice.[10]

Visualize that this profound blessing streaming toward you purifies and transforms every aspect of your body and mind—even your painful memories, regrets, and negative karma. Then, after some time, consider that the purification has been completely effected, so much so that your whole being—body and mind—is entirely transformed into light. Now your being in the form of light rises up and dissolves into the heart of this Divine Presence—completely mixing with it, like light mixing with light.

Remain in this peaceful state as long as you can. This nondual, natural simplicity and inspired openness *is* your being. If thoughts rise or a "sense of self" begins to form, simply allow them to dissolve back into emptiness. Letting go, naturally remain.

At the conclusion, consider that your awareness is once again centered within your body. Resolve to continue the presence of *pure, clear awareness* as you enter into daily activities. And when you notice that you have lost it, gently bring your mind home to its true nature, again and again.

Dedicate your practice as you conclude, sharing the merit of blessings and wisdom with all beings, praying that, in whatever ways you can, you may be able to relieve their suffering, bring them happiness, and, ultimately, help them to realize the abiding peace of their deathless, true nature of mind.

PHOWA FOR OTHERS
AT THE MOMENT OF DEATH

You can do the Essential Phowa for someone who is ill or dying, in exactly the same way, except that you visualize a buddha or Divine Presence above the head of the other person. Call out on behalf of her, and visualize the Presence pouring down rays of light onto her, purifying and transforming her whole being. Then visualize that the other person, now fully purified, dissolves into light and merges indistinguishably with the enlightened Presence.

If the ill or dying person is interested, you can share the Essential Phowa practice with her, finding ways to adapt it to her own spiritual beliefs. Even though you can do the Essential Phowa throughout life, its special power becomes apparent when you practice it just at the moment of death. You may want to practice the Essential Phowa each time you visit the dying person. The most important time to practice is right at the moment of death, or as soon as you are informed of her death. If you cannot be physically present when your loved one dies, then visualize yourself practicing by her side at the place of her death.

As people come very near death, I have observed that their mind and heart become less contained by their body and more atmospheric; it feels as if their mind is filling the entire room. Thus any strong thoughts or emotions we bring into the space surrounding a dying person have a powerful effect on her state of mind, for better or worse. Thus, it is clear that if we have inspired ourselves with meditation before entering a dying person's room, or if we have strongly invoked the presence of a buddha or Divine Being to whom we continue to pray, this can have a tremendously positive influence on the dying person's state of mind.

When someone has just died suddenly and you do not have much time at his or her side, then you can do an abbreviated form of the Essential Phowa. As you stay by her side, invoke strongly the radiant presence of a buddha or Divine Being. Visualize the compassionate radiance emanating from this Presence filling the space surrounding both of you with protection and blessings.

Consider that the consciousness of the newly deceased person takes the form of a small sphere of light, and visualize it quickly flying out from her body, like a shooting star, and dissolving into the heart of the Divine Presence. In dedicating the practice, pray that the person may be freed from any of the sufferings or turmoil of her death, and released into the luminosity and all-pervading space of the true nature of her mind, in order to benefit all beings, especially those she is leaving behind. Afterward, you can do the complete Essential Phowa practice again for the person over the following days and weeks.

When I first learned the Essential Phowa, I questioned whether a beginner could effectively do the practice for a dying person. How could I possibly offer spiritual support for another person? What if I did it wrong? Sogyal Rinpoche responded to my doubts with these valuable insights:

First, just at the moment of death, after the consciousness of the dying person "faints into darkness," he or she will awaken into the luminous expanse of the truth. Thus our practice of Essential Phowa for the dying person is simply a skillful guidance to help her unite with the true nature of mind which will be dawning in her awareness at that time.

Second, in doing the phowa, we are invoking and relying on the limitless enlightened qualities of a buddha, a fully awakened being, which include an unbiased, boundless compassion and love, and the unlimited power to benefit and help all beings by responding to their needs, especially in the direst of circumstances. As soon as we invoke the presence of God, Christ, the Buddha, Padmasambhava, or another saint or Divine Being, their blessings and presence are spontaneously there. They will be present with the dying person in his or her hour of need, and *they will know what to do!*[11]

If done repeatedly, with strong compassion and devotion, the Essential Phowa practice can help the dying person on her journey toward liberation. Any practice or prayers we do for the dying person will help, at the very least, to purify negative karma or release her from the suffering and turmoil of her death and enable her to die peacefully.

Even if you are not an advanced practitioner, your practicing the Essential Phowa cannot in any way harm an ill or dying person. On a spiritual level, it will help her, even if you can't see or measure the benefit tangibly. I encourage those of you who are professional caregivers to do the Essential Phowa when your patients are dying, and observe the results for yourself. Sometimes after doing the practice, I have had a sense or a sign that the phowa has truly benefited the dying person, and I allow this to inspire my confidence that the practice does bring spiritual support, even on occasions when I don't perceive an immediate result. *Remember, nothing we do is ever lost.*

Supporting Those Who Are Nonreligious

How can we help someone prepare meaningfully for death if they profess not to believe in anything spiritual and are not even interested in talking about it? The bottom line in offering spiritual care is to help the dying face death with their heart and mind pure and at peace, free of troubling emotions such as yearning, attachment, frustration, or anger. Thus we can support the nonreligious by giving them our love, quietly inspiring ourselves with spiritual practice whenever we visit, and helping them to meet death without feeling empty-handed.

Even if the dying person has no spiritual practice to rely on, she can prepare for death by giving up her attachment, for it is attachment and grasping which really plunge us into suffering in life and after death. Yearning and attachment grow stronger when we feel a lack of love, and this might have been the dying person's experience throughout life. When a loved one is dying, it's crucial to not hold back anymore: give your love fully. If the dying person is filled with love at the end of her life, she will finally feel satisfied. The future—death itself—will loom less fearfully when she feels fulfilled and secure in the present.

And offer your love unconditionally. Give up hoping that your loved one will dramatically change, thank you, then smile and die happily. Even if there is no visible response, shower the dying person with your love, trusting that it is getting through. Because whether or not the person ever shows it, *your love is getting through*.

Before going to visit someone who is suffering or facing death, practice the Essential Phowa very strongly. Then, when you bring this atmosphere of heartfelt devotion, clear presence, and fearless love into the room of the dying person, she can draw strength from your whole way of being. She will feel the deep peace and profound compassion of this sacred environment you have generated through your practice. Without any words or philosophical exchanges, your confidence and strength can disarm any negativity or fear and inspire a confidence and peace in the dying person's heart and mind.

Paul's mother, Isabelle, did not have any religious faith and clearly told her family she didn't want to speak about spiritual matters. Near the end of her life, Isabelle became quite agitated and anxious, and required frequent doses of pain medication. Whenever Paul visited her, he spent part of the time silently continuing his practice of the Essential Phowa while she rested. After a few such visits, Isabelle confessed to her daughter that whenever Paul was with her, she felt much more peaceful and was able to skip her next dose of pain medication. Overcome with curiosity, his sister asked Paul what he was doing, and eventually she also began practicing the Essential Phowa for her mother while sitting by her bedside.

Now, whenever her daughter came to visit her, Isabelle felt a deep peace and relaxation, so she asked what they were doing that was helping her so much. Learning that her children were offering this spiritual practice to help her with the suffering of dying, and having already found one benefit from it, Isabelle asked them to continue practicing for her, and she became more and more peaceful and content as her death approached.

Above all, help the dying person face death without feeling empty-handed by reassuring her that her life was meaningful. Help her remember her accomplishments and focus on her positive qualities rather than dwelling on her failures. This can bring peace to her mind as she is dying. Even if she feels that there has not been any meaning or purpose to her life, you can encourage her to use the time of her dying to imbue her life and her death with meaning. (Insights for how to do this are described in the next chapter.)

Compassion and Dedication

> There is a Tibetan saying that "everything rests on the tip of one's motivation." This indicates the significance in every moment, of cultivating altruistic, selfless intention—bodhicitta. Endowed with such a luminous heart, even the smallest words, deeds, and actions that one accomplishes have vast and beneficial implications. This is the transforming magic of bodhicitta, a veritable wish-fulfilling jewel . . .
>
> NYOSHUL KHENPO RINPOCHE[12]

Generating a deep compassion through reflection and prayer is another meaningful way to prepare for death, and it heightens the effect of any practice we do for others. We can suggest that the dying person spend time each day reflecting on the suffering of others, especially all those who are experiencing the same illness or pain. As their suffering touches her heart, she may want to do the Tonglen practice (described in Chapter 6), breathing in the suffering of those who are ill or dying, and giving them, with each exhalation, all of her love and well-being in the form of light. Or, she could do the Tonglen in the form of a prayer: "May I give all beings my happiness; may I take the suffering of all beings onto me."

If the dying person is experiencing severe pain or strong emotional suffering or fear, she could recite the mantra of Avalokiteshvara, the Lord of Compassion, bringing this buddha's blessings of compassion and protection to fill the atmosphere of her heart and mind: *Om Mani Padme Hum Hrih.*[13]

Dedicating our dying and death to benefit others is another powerful way to transcend our suffering and imbue it with a sacred meaning. We can also dedicate our suffering in dying to atone for any of the harm we have done in our life.

Jean, a close friend, called me in distress. She would be visiting her dying father-in-law soon, probably for the last time. Ed was comatose, so Jean wouldn't be able to have a normal conversation with him. Her feelings were mixed—she knew it would be good if she could help him let go and die peacefully. Yet because of his alcoholism, he had brought considerable emotional suffering to his entire family, including his son, Jean's husband. Over the twenty-five years she'd been part of the family, the family members were always distant from each other, uncommunicative and nonsupportive.

Together we acknowledged that Jean's anger was normal. We discussed a way for her to communicate her frustration to him, while at the same time releasing herself from it. I suggested that before communicating with Ed, she could sit and meditate quietly by his side, reflecting on how much she would have liked to know the real man, not the alcoholic.

Together we found a way she could view the situation from a new perspective. We reflected together how much Ed must have suffered in his own childhood to be re-creating this same anguish in his own family now. And I proposed that Jean consider what it was going to be like for him to undergo the review of his entire life that is said to be a part of the death experience. At that time he would be acutely aware of all the pain he brought onto his loved ones; he would experience all of their suffering, together with his painful remorse.

As Jean reflected on Ed's past, future, and present suffering, her anger melted into understanding and compassion. "Is there anything I can do to help him now?" she asked.

"When you're with him," I suggested, "remember that although Ed appears to be comatose and unresponsive, the pure awareness of his true nature is still there, and this aspect of him can always hear you. Let him know that if he feels any regret for how he's lived, he can dedicate his suffering and his death to benefit his family, radiating his love and blessings to each person he cares about, with a strong prayer that they be healed of any hurt or pain he might have caused them."

When Jean began speaking to Ed, she kept thinking: "This is crazy. He can't possibly hear me. And if he was awake and knew what I was doing, he would kick me out of this room!" Still, when she first sat and meditated, sending her understanding and compassion to Ed, she sensed that it was gratefully received by the unconscious man. Jean went on to suggest to Ed that he use the moment of his death to heal his relationships and generate a strong healing love toward his family. Then Jean said her last good-bye.

Later that evening Jean was driving home, while her husband slept in the passenger seat. Suddenly he woke with a start, saying, "This is so much easier now. The bitterness I felt earlier is simply gone." Later they learned that this had been the moment of Ed's death. Jean wondered if Ed had in fact dedicated his death to atone for his life. A different kind of confirmation came the next day. Jean witnessed something she had not seen in her years with the family: After the funeral, Ed's family gathered together at their father's home, and the conversation and sense of connection between them was loving and affectionate, very caring and genuine.

Relying on Prayer and Devotion

The sincerity and depth of our devotion can increase the potency of our spiritual practice and prayers. By deepening our devotion and making it more fervent, and by praying with a deep sense of renunciation—acknowledging we cannot solve all of life's problems alone—*we open ourselves to receiving help.* By transforming our ordinary love into a limitless and sacred love, we purify the stubbornness and negativity in our heart, and come closer to recognizing the inherent perfection and purity of our original, divine nature.

Devotion can be misunderstood as blind faith, a submission of our will and intelligence to an external person or divinity. Yet most of us already exercise a blind faith in our own ego, heedlessly submitting to its selfish demands, which keeps us trapped in cycles of suffering. No matter how profound our inspiration, or how many glimpses we have of our true nature of mind, our ego, like the force of gravity, drags us back down. Devotion really means finding our will to become free of the ego and awaken to a greater power, the awareness of our wisdom nature.

The Divine Being or buddha to whom we offer devotion has no need of it. Inspiring ourselves with gratitude and devotion helps us progress along the path, so that we develop a pure heart and a heightened receptivity. Devotion makes it possible for the blessings of wisdom to enter and illuminate us. For example, at the conclusion of the Essential Phowa practice, we mix our mind with the wisdom mind of the buddhas or saints. Generating a strong devotion while we practice opens our heart and enables us to reach that nongrasping, nonconceptual state effortlessly. In the warmth of devotion we discover the best side of our being. Every religious tradition describes the lives of saints who had perfected their being through the practice of devotion and prayer.

Devotion also connotes a sense of respect and of longing. Many beautiful psalms praise the wondrous qualities of God, combined with a longing to see or be with God. "I yearn for the Lord, my soul doth yearn, more than they who yearn for the dawn" (Psalm 130). Devotion is awakened through gratitude, a recognition of our being blessed and unconditionally accepted.

Blessings are coming toward us continually. Yet we don't feel them because we experience ourselves as separate, unloved, unworthy, and disconnected. It's as though we've retreated into a dark house of the ego, closed every door, window, and curtain, and then gone to hide in the basement. When we call out and pray with heartfelt devotion, we are throwing open the doors and windows and curtains in our heart and mind, allowing the blessings of wisdom and compassion to come streaming in. As soon as we have devotion, blessings are spontaneously and naturally present.

The constant internal flow of grasping and selfish thoughts, judgments, and negative emotions that trouble us in life will continue to distract us from the peace of our true nature at the time of death. As death approaches, the dying person can train herself to "keep her mind pure" by transforming her mindstream and her entire life into a continuous flow of meditation or prayer, a constant reflection on devotion or compassion. She may choose to recite a brief phrase or prayer from her spiritual tradition that evokes her deepest devotion and trust.

Repeating a mantra or a short prayer with devotion opens our heart, transforms our mindstream in a positive way, and protects us from negativity. In the Nyingma tradition, a practitioner might focus her whole heart and mind on Padmasambhava and recite his mantra, which powerfully invokes his presence and blessing: *Om Ah Hum Vajra Guru Padma Siddhi Hum.* These Sanskrit words mean: "I invoke you, the Vajra Guru, Padmasambhava, by your blessing may you grant us ordinary and supreme accomplishments."

The Russian Orthodox tradition describes a devotional practice called the "continuous prayer of the heart," in which we visualize the presence of Jesus Christ in our heart, and train ourselves to sustain that presence, while reciting verbally or mentally a short, inspiring prayer in every waking moment. Although any prayer can be selected, the most common one is: "Lord, Jesus Christ, have mercy on me, a sinner." The practice of continual internal prayer deepens our devotion, confidence, and trust, so that our heart and mind are turned toward God in every activity. This integration of devotion, contemplation, and prayer with everyday life will support us when we are dying or bring us the inspiration and strength to support others who are suffering or dying.[14]

When we are in great distress, calling out for help and praying fervently from the heart have a special power. Even if the dying person does not pray, our sincere prayer and devotion can invoke divine help, and make a positive imprint on the dying person's mind and heart at the time of death.

Gregory was thirty-eight and dying from cancer. He and his wife, Rachel, were determined to do everything possible for him to be cured of his illness, and so they did not speculate much about the possibility of his dying. During that year, however, Rachel's friend gave her a copy of *The Tibetan Book of Living and Dying,* which she read and used to train herself in the practices of Tonglen, Guru Yoga, and Essential Phowa, invoking Padmasambhava as she did so. Doing the practices for Gregory helped focus her troubled mind during the months of his increasing pain and debilitation.

Gregory's final hours came rather unexpectedly, and when Rachel woke and heard his labored breathing, she knew the end was near. Sitting by his side, she gave him all her love, reassuring him that he could let go. Throughout the night while Gregory was near death, she practiced the Essential Phowa for him.

A few hours later Gregory had still not died, and Rachel went to lie down in the next room to rest. Feeling overwhelmed, she begged Padmasambhava to help Gregory. Immediately she heard a change in his breathing. She got up again and continued the phowa until he breathed out his last. Rachel writes of that moment: "I sat a few moments overwhelmed and astounded at the look in my beloved's eyes. They were wide open and his gaze was upward, as if he had seen something wonderful. Just looking at him gave me a feeling of such extraordinary peace."

Soon after, a friend came to be with Rachel, and after practicing the phowa again for Gregory, they went outside to watch the morning sky, standing together in silent comfort. Returning after a few minutes to his side, they were both startled at the change they observed: his mouth had closed into a peaceful, radiant smile. That look of joy in his face filled Rachel with confidence, confirming for her that Padmasambhava had come to his aid at the moment of death. For the next twenty-four hours, while Gregory's body remained in their home, his face sustained this joyful expression.

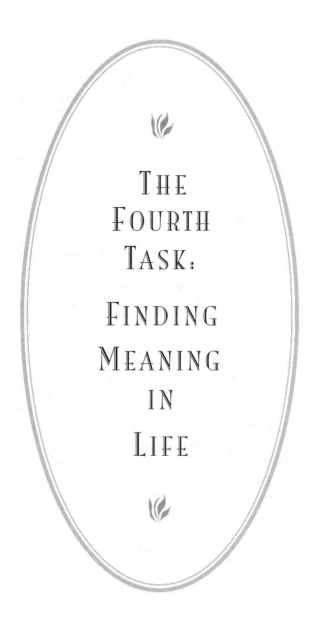

THE
FOURTH
TASK:

FINDING
MEANING
IN
LIFE

Chapter 10

FINDING MEANING IN LIFE

In *The Death of Ivan Ilych*, Leo Tolstoy wrote:

> *Ivan Ilych's physical sufferings were terrible, but worse than the physical sufferings were his mental sufferings, which were his chief torture.*
>
> *His mental sufferings were due to the fact that that night, as he looked as Gerasim's sleepy, good-natured face with its prominent cheekbones, the question suddenly occurred to him: "What if my whole life has really been wrong?"*
>
> *It occurred to him that what had appeared perfectly impossible before, namely that he had not spent his life as he should have done, might after all be true. . . .*
>
> *"But if that is so," he said to himself, "and I am leaving this life with the consciousness that I have lost all that was given me and it is impossible to rectify it—what then?"*
>
> *He lay on his back and began to pass his life in review in quite a new way. In the morning when he saw first his footman, then his wife, then his daughter, and then the doctor, their every word and movement confirmed to him the awful truth that had been revealed to him during the night. In them he saw himself—all that for which he had lived—and saw clearly that it was not real at all, but a terrible and huge deception which had hidden both life and death. This consciousness intensified his physical suffering tenfold. He groaned and tossed about, and pulled at his clothing which choked and stifled him. And he hated them on that account.*
>
> *. . . This occurred at the end of the third day, two hours before his death. Just then his schoolboy son had crept softly in and gone up to the bedside. The dying man was still screaming desperately and waving his arms. His hand fell on the boy's head, and the boy caught it, pressed it to his lips, and began to cry.*
>
> *At that very moment Ivan Ilych fell through and caught sight of*

the light, and it was revealed to him that though his life had not been what it should have been, this could still be rectified. He asked himself, "What is the right thing?" and grew still, listening. Then he felt that someone was kissing his hand. He opened his eyes, looked at his son, and felt sorry for him. His wife came up to him and he glanced at her. She was gazing at him open-mouthed, with undried tears on her nose and cheek and a despairing look on her face. He felt sorry for her too.

"Yes, I am making them wretched," he thought. "They are sorry, but it will be better for them when I die." He wished to say this but had not the strength to utter it. "Besides, why speak? I must act," he thought. With a look at his wife he indicated his son and said: "Take him away . . . sorry for him . . . sorry for you too . . ." He tried to add, "forgive me," but said "forego" and waved his hand, knowing that He whose understanding mattered would understand.

And suddenly it grew clear to him that what had been oppressing him and would not leave him was all dropping away at once from two sides, from ten sides, and from all sides. He was sorry for them, he must act so as not to hurt them: release them and free himself from these sufferings. "How good and how simple!" he thought. "And the pain?" he asked himself. "What has become of it? Where are you, pain?" [1]

As we review significant scenes and moments from our past with the potent awareness that life is drawing to a close, we might well wonder: What was the point? What difference did my life make? What did I accomplish? Like Ivan Ilych, we might revisit painful memories: choices we regret making, things we failed to do, or things we did that were selfish or unkind. Or we may realize that we were so preoccupied with material gain or personal ambition that we could never "find the time" for those activities, people, and values which we most cherished. The realization that our "whole life was not as it should have been" can magnify our physical pain and our fear as we are dying, making it harder for us to let go.

Most of us put off finding meaning in our life, hoping that somehow it will be divinely revealed to us. If we imagine life is meaningful only if we go to work in Dr. Schweitzer's hospitals in Africa or in Mother Teresa's Home for the Dying in Calcutta, we may conclude that the daily life we have—going to work or school or raising children—is devoid of meaning. Or we may hope that, after years of wasting our time, we'll be warned. Perhaps a nicely embossed card will come in the mail, saying, "You have only five years left. Get your act together now." No one I know ever gets such a conveniently timed message. But I will give it to you here: *Get your act together now.*

Believing that we and those we love will live forever, we give our attention to the transitory ups and downs of daily existence, letting them sap all our energy and time. When we forget to regard our life as finite and therefore precious, we fail to commit to any purpose or meaning beyond our immediate needs and personal gratification. Grasping after the wrong things, we waste our potential and journey toward death empty-handed. We may feel cheated when we learn we are dying, realizing that we had never really lived. We put off enjoying our life for some anticipated future, only to discover that the future is suddenly foreclosed.

Fourteen years ago, I met Dr. Ben Weiniger, a renowned psychiatrist and pioneer in the field of community counseling (training nonprofessionals to offer counseling). He was in his seventies and seemed very frail, yet his mind was sharp, sparkling with wit. I told him my dream of building a hospice based on the spiritual principles outlined in Buddhist teachings, and he encouraged me to develop the idea. "But," he warned me, "don't call it a home for the dying. I won't come. Call it a home for the living, *then I'll come.*" Six years later, when I met him again, he was even more frail than before. I told him I had always remembered the advice he had given me. With a smile, he leaned over to confide something, which I sensed was the summation of his life's work: "I'll tell you something else. People are not afraid of dying. *They are afraid of living.*"

Ironically, it is because we avoid the reality that our life will end someday that we take life for granted. Living halfheartedly, we hide from ourselves, from our loved ones, and ultimately from life itself. As management specialist Stephen Covey queries: "How many people on their deathbed wish they'd spent more time in the office?"[2] Yet some, even in dying, never leave their "office"—a metaphor for the blanket of busyness we wrap tighter around our lives to avoid facing ourselves and healing our pain.

Society conditions us to believe that our life has meaning and value only when we are productive, able to pay the bills, provide for loved ones, and take care of our own needs. Whether we face the gradual debilitation of aging or the increasing limitations on our strength due to illness, each of us will one day lose the independent or productive "role" with which we've identified ourselves, and will become increasingly dependent on others for help with the most intimate aspects of our existence. The stronger our identification with that former role, the more we'll suffer as we are dying, seeing ourselves as only a useless burden and imagining that the remainder of our life is meaningless.

Like Ivan Ilych, if we are haunted by the fear that we did not use well all that we were given in life, we may struggle against letting go when we are dying and wonder: Here I am weak and confined to a bed. *What can I possibly do about how I have lived?*

Messages from the Threshold of Death

We never face ourselves until death unequivocally faces us. If rather than running the other way, we gazed into the mirror of our death today, we might be motivated to find a purposeful direction for our life. Those who know their time is limited sometimes discover just how askew their priorities have been, and consequently rearrange their time and activities—and their spiritual commitment—to reflect their true values. They actually use the time of dying as a final opportunity to face themselves honestly and to grow, personally and spiritually.

Many who have clinically "died" and then reported a near-death experience feel challenged afterward to reevaluate their priorities in life and their ways of relating to others. The near-death accounts provide valuable insights into how each of us can find our purpose in life. While witnessing a review of every single event of their life, those who clinically died describe feeling as if they were being asked two questions: *What have you accomplished in your life?* and *What have you learned in the way of love and wisdom?*

A young man told Kenneth Ring that he developed "a total awareness of not just the material and how much we can buy—in the way of cars and stuff, or food or anything. There's more than just consuming life. There's a point where you have to *give* to it and that's real important. And there was an awareness at that point that I had to give more of myself *out* of life."[3]

Those who have reviewed their life on death's threshold realized that what counts at death isn't their grand or impressive actions, but rather the awareness and compassion they bring to the most simple acts of daily life. How willing have we been to truly care for others, to hear and respond when they needed help? How much respect and understanding have we brought to our relationships? How often have we been willing to stretch beyond our limits and change, finding the courage to heal our old wounds and become more authentically alive?

Researchers have asked those who returned from death how they now understand the meaning of life. Another person told Kenneth Ring, "Fulfilling yourself with love by *giving*. As much as by getting. And . . . recognizing that we're all in the same boat and we all have weaknesses and we all have strengths, and to help is where it's at."[4]

Margot Grey reported another response: "I felt as if I had emerged from darkness into light. I felt reborn. I know that I am here for a purpose, which is part of God's plan. I feel I am here to learn God's law and to love unconditionally. Since my experience I am no longer content to live life for myself. My sense of fulfillment comes from developing my potential for the benefit of service to others. . . . Material possessions are no longer important. The real riches lie within."[5]

What do these insights from the threshold of death suggest about supporting someone who is suffering or presently facing death? The purpose of this task is to show how we can respond when the ill or dying person feels his life is meaningless, or has no spiritual belief or hope in afterlife. The bottom line in offering spiritual care is to help the dying person not face death empty-handed. To do this, we help him to find a meaning in the life he has lived, or find a way to conclude his life well, making his process of dying meaningful.

Recognizing Accomplishments, Releasing Regrets

The Buddhist teachings remind us that at the time of death we should "prolong the results of good karma"; in other words, dwell on the good we have done in our life so that our heart is infused with positive feelings such as compassion, acceptance, forgiveness, or love when we die. Whether a person is facing death at eighteen or eighty-two, we can help him review his life and find meaning in it. Left to himself, the dying person may become obsessed with his failures, and his mind and heart may be clouded with feelings of remorse, fear, unresolved angers or hurts. It is vital to help him remember and take solace in what he accomplished in his life—the experiences of growth; courageous moments of self-confrontation and change; his having overcome challenges or limitations; and moments of extending kindness or forgiveness.

If the dying person is our relative or friend, we can help him to die feeling fulfilled by telling him how he has contributed to our life. If we are caregivers and thus do not share a past history with our dying patients, we can let the dying person know how he is contributing to our life now. *We should view our relationship with the dying as one of mutual healing, one of giving and receiving.* In a sense, we are both facing death together and have something important to learn from each other. Sometimes we can ask him to help us work through a problem or difficulty. We can invite the dying person to give us his last gifts of wisdom or courage as he goes through the suffering of dying and deepens his understanding of life.

If the person facing death feels his life is a virtual string of regrets, encourage him to see that he can use the time of dying to confess and heal any of the harm or suffering he had created. Acknowledging his regrets and being willing to atone for past mistakes can make the end of his life meaningful. As Sogyal Rinpoche writes: "Through forgiving and being forgiven, we purify ourselves of the darkness of what we have done, and prepare ourselves most completely for the journey through death."[6]

George clung to life for weeks after everyone expected him to die, and he was suffering greatly. His nurse asked, "George, is there something holding you back, something keeping you here?"

George looked at her with pain on his face, speaking slowly: "Yes. When I look back on my life, all I see are the selfish things I did and said, and the times I hurt my ex-wife and children. I can't let go and die, knowing this is what I've done with my life."

At George's request, the nurse phoned his ex-wife, Sheila, and explained why he wanted to see her. Sheila was troubled when she spoke to a friend about going to the hospital: "I don't think I can help him die peacefully. I am still angry with him. George was an alcoholic during most of our marriage. He hurt me and our children so much, I've never been able to forgive him or to forget. If I go see him, I'll probably just blow up and start shouting at him."

Carol helped Sheila to see that what she'd been yearning for all these years had finally happened: George now understood the hurt he had brought onto others. He wanted to acknowledge his remorse and ask her forgiveness. Aware now of the pain he'd brought to his family, George was suffering tremendously in his process of dying.

Carol encouraged Sheila to help George remember some positive aspects of their relationship, some contributions he made, so that he wouldn't die feeling his life was a complete failure. And she described to Sheila the Essential Phowa practice, explaining how this profound meditation might help George to heal and release himself from this life. Sheila felt more secure when she went to visit her ex-husband that night, realizing she now understood George's situation and had some insights into how she could help him.

When Sheila came in the room, George himself was surprised that she didn't start shouting at him. She sat by his side, taking in the vision of his emaciated body and seeing George from a new perspective. He spoke first.

"Sheila, I know how much I hurt you and the kids, and I feel terrible. I am haunted every night with the terrible memories of what I've done to you. And I am so, so sorry. Could you ever find it possible to forgive me?"

"George, I have been hurt and angry for so many years. I felt you never knew or understood the hurt you had brought on us. I'm sorry for all the years we've stayed angry and bitter. But I want to put the past behind us now. Yes, George, I forgive you."

They sat together in silence for some time, sharing their grief in this atmosphere of understanding. Finally Sheila spoke: "George, I know these painful memories are part of our history, but don't forget the good that you've done too. Remember the time you worked extra hours so Tim could have braces? And remember how you took the kids on a short vacation just to play, when I was recovering from surgery? You helped us too—don't forget that. And you and I had some good times at the beginning, where we had fun and shared our love easily."

As they spoke together, George's face and body were beginning to soften and relax, because as he felt Sheila's acceptance and understanding, he finally could begin to accept himself. Sheila felt a new ease in herself as well. Making this connection and extending forgiveness wasn't just something she was doing for George. Sheila realized it was also releasing her from the painful store of angry feelings that she had carried through the years.

After some time, Sheila added, "The nurse told me you have had difficulty letting go. I've learned a meditation for dying which might help to ease your mind and help you let go. If you are interested, I could describe it to you."

"I feel too weak to concentrate or learn anything new right now. But I would be grateful if you would do this meditation for me," George said. So Sheila sat quietly by his side and did the Essential Phowa practice for him, before saying good-bye.

The next morning the hospital nurse phoned to tell her that during the night George had died peacefully.

Three Commitments for a Meaningful Life

How can we help a person find meaning in his life and death when he is dying young, when he is bedridden in pain, or immobilized from a stroke? Elisabeth Kübler-Ross described five stages, or responses, to dying or loss; yet not everyone moves through those stages smoothly, as some get stuck in their denial, bargaining, or anger. Is there a way we can assist the dying to move out of their emotional resistance and fear toward a peaceful acceptance of their coming death?

The Reverend Mwalimu Imara, an early colleague of Elisabeth Kübler-Ross, found that the dying will not be able to accept their death unless they feel their life is meaningful. He enumerates three commitments we must make if we are to find meaning in dying or at any stage of life:

- To become aware of and accept ourselves
- To invest ourselves in authentic dialogue with others
- To decide on a positive direction of growth

AWARENESS AND SELF-ACCEPTANCE

In order to feel our life is meaningful, we must be willing to *feel alive,* which means being fully aware of and accepting our present experience. Instead, most of us go through life trying to live up to the "roles" we've been cast into by others—our parents, partner, boss, or children—or we constrain ourselves in a self-imposed image. Suppressing our natural feelings while trying to fit into these restrictive molds, we gradually lose touch with who we are and what we really feel.

Then, when we are suffering or dying, we're suddenly brought face to face with aspects of ourselves which were long buried, feelings we didn't know existed, yearnings and deep fears never given voice to. Worried about "losing control," judging harshly our painful emotions, fearing we will lose others' respect if we appear vulnerable, we don't know how to begin accepting these unfamiliar parts of ourselves now rising to awareness.

When we cannot find a way through our suffering, we often retreat into a shell of isolation. Attempting to filter from awareness any threatening, uncomfortable feelings, we also limit our ability to experience all that makes life meaningful—a sense of aliveness and joy, inner peace, genuine compassion, playfulness and curiosity, the openness and trust to give and receive love.

For a dying person to feel his life is meaningful, he must break out of these old constraints, be open to experiencing his authentic feelings, whatever they are, and accept himself with understanding and compassion. *The dying person will not be able to move beyond his fear, resistance, or anger and begin to mourn and accept his losses until and unless he feels safe.* And to feel safe, he needs to know that if he lets his defenses down, he will be accepted in spite of his painful emotions, exactly as he is. No matter what he reveals, he trusts he can be natural and risk being real.

Elisabeth Kübler-Ross has said that the dying need our "unconditional love." This phrase might seem like a tall order for us if we haven't learned how to love ourselves, let alone others, unconditionally. What we *can* offer others, however, is our unconditional *acceptance,* the willingness to be understanding, nonjudgmental, and compassionate, regardless of what they might feel or say. As Mwalimu Imara writes:

> Going through the five stages of a terminal person's grief is a process moving toward a blessing, "acceptance." But we are able to journey fully through the process only when we feel the "acceptance" of another person. Our "acceptance" of our own being, that is, our sensing that we are significant as

a person, depends on *knowing* that we are accepted by someone or something larger than our individual self. . . .
Acceptance is the beginning of growth.[7]

Margaret's cancer had weakened her considerably, and for two
weeks I'd been visiting her in the convalescent hospital, where she
seemed to be in good spirits. One day, before going directly into
her room, I asked the nurse how she was doing.

"She's not doing well at all," the nurse replied. "In fact, she's
extremely depressed. Margaret acts very cheerful and strong when
anyone comes to visit, but when her visitors leave she is depressed
and crying all the time."

Margaret's grieving was a sign she was beginning to mourn and
accept her death. Yet she obviously did not feel safe sharing her
grief with others, and my heart went out to her in her fear and
loneliness. As I entered her room, I realized with some anxiety that
I didn't have any ideas about how I might deepen our communication beyond its superficial level. Margaret greeted me cheerfully,
yet her brow was furrowed under her soft gray hair. The first
relaxed stage of our conversation allowed me to observe her mood
and the tension in her voice. But how could I break through this
polite and guarded communication?

"Margaret, you seem a little worried today. Is anything troubling
you?"

"No," she answered, "nothing at all."

I tried another approach. "Sometimes I consider that I may get
cancer one day myself, and I wonder how I would handle it. And
you have already faced this illness and gone through different treatments. Would you mind sharing with me what it's been like for
you, and what has helped you?"

Margaret's reply surprised me, as it seemed unrelated to my
question.

"You know, I hate taking my friend Jenny out with me in the
evenings. It's so much trouble to take her anywhere since her husband died. Jenny has a hard time living alone in her trailer, and
when she comes home at night, she's afraid. She's so much trouble
to take anywhere. Every time I bring her home in my car, she
makes me go in the trailer with her, and we have to go into every
room and turn the lights on. I wish she'd get over her fear, because
I am getting tired of this routine we go through every time she
comes home."

Every story someone tells us is a snapshot of their inner world. Stories are symbolic language—a deep communication given in a roundabout way, to test the waters of the listener's receptivity. While I listened, I imagined changing places with Margaret, and I realized that her story was revealing what she didn't feel safe saying directly to me.

"Margaret, you have entered what is probably the most difficult and frightening journey of your life. Maybe you think it would be asking too much to expect my support. But we're sharing this together, and I don't mind entering each dark room with you and relieving your concerns. In one way, it looks like I am here to help you. *Yet you are also helping me,* giving me a chance to explore this journey with you, and this is a tremendous gift. I don't have all the answers for everything you're going through, but I want you to know you are not alone. Whatever you are feeling, I am not going to give up on you."

From listening deeply and putting myself in her place, I was able to understand and respond directly to what Margaret was communicating. After this dialogue, she and I could grieve together openly, and over the next weeks she felt safe to express her losses, her fears and doubts with me, making her journey toward death a little easier.

INVESTING IN AUTHENTIC DIALOGUE

The second commitment necessary to experiencing life as meaningful is to invest ourselves in authentic relationships and creative dialogue with others. We must take the risk of opening and revealing ourselves to at least one other person, establishing a true and heartfelt communication. In committing to engage in real dialogue, we must also be willing to listen to and accept the other person and his experience.

What makes us feel hopeless is not our difficult situation; it's being isolated in our suffering, fear, or grief, and not being able to connect with others. Sooner or later, we need to let go of our pride and fear, and tell the truth. We must begin reaching out and asking for the help we need. Making a genuine and heartfelt connection with at least one other person gives us a ray of hope in the darkest periods of our lives. One young man told me this story:

"After my mother died, the hardest thing was reaching out to my dad. Each time, he responded by getting angry and criticizing me. I didn't understand him, and I didn't know how to cope with his response. Then I withdrew, blaming him for not helping me. I realized, though, that I couldn't face this grief alone—I felt trapped with all my feelings and my sorrow. I knew that I needed love and support, but there wasn't anyone in my life who could give it to me. So, I reasoned, if I can't receive love maybe I can find a way to give love. But I wasn't sure if I knew how to give love. I knew how to be friendly, so I figured I could start there.

"I spent an afternoon on the streets of my town, running into a few people I knew who started to pour out all their troubles to me. I was glad to be able to take the time to listen to them and give them support. When I went home that night, I felt better. I felt as though I had been supported too."

The most satisfying relationships are those in which we feel safe to be ourselves, willing to get to know and meet the other person where he is and being willing to be "met." Real communication, and our finest experience of love, is this true "meeting" of two people. As Suzuki Roshi wrote:

When you listen to someone, you should give up all your preconceived ideas and your subjective opinions; you should just listen to him, just observe what his way is. We put very little emphasis on right and wrong or good and bad. We just see things as they are with him, and accept them. This is how we communicate with each other. Usually when you listen to some statement, you hear it as a kind of echo of yourself. You are actually listening to your own opinion. If it agrees with your opinion you may accept it, but if it does not, you will reject it or you may not even really hear it. That is one danger when you listen to someone. The other danger is to be caught by the statement . . . without understanding the spirit behind the words.

We should be concentrated with our full mind and body on what we do; and we should be faithful, subjectively and objectively, to ourselves, and especially to our feelings. Even when you do not feel so well, it is better to express how you feel without any particular attachment or intention. So you may say, "Oh, I am sorry, I do not feel well." That is enough. You should not say, "You made me so!" That is too much. You may say, "Oh, I am sorry, I am so angry with you." There is no need to say that you are not angry when you are

angry. You should just say, "I am angry." That is enough. . . .
True communication depends on our being straightforward
with one another.[8]

The first commitment really means "coming out of hiding"
from ourselves. In the second commitment, we are challenged to
come out of hiding from others and make a significant human
connection, valuing others as we begin to value and accept ourselves. The open and genuine relationships we have cultivated
throughout life are invaluable resources for helping us face the
inevitable suffering and losses of dying.

DECIDING ON A POSITIVE DIRECTION

If we have no direction or purpose, we're not really living, we're
just existing. And then when we face life's inevitable losses, our
existence may seem nothing more than meaningless suffering, and
we are left feeling helplessness and despair.

The psychiatrist Viktor Frankl noticed that some elderly or
frail people survived in Nazi concentration camps while younger
and stronger people died. He discovered that the survivors had
given themselves a goal—something to live for—or they had
found a meaning in their existence, a meaning that transcended
their external conditions. Frankl personally observed the truth of
Nietzsche's words: "If you have a *why* to live for, you can bear
with any *how.*"

Frankl spoke to his fellow prisoners one night when they were
in a particularly low mood, encouraging them to find meaning in
what they had accomplished and experienced in the past, and hope
in their future, which had a veil of uncertainty drawn over it. He
went on to say:

Human life, under any circumstances, never ceases to have a
meaning, and this infinite meaning of life includes suffering
and dying, privation and death. I asked the poor creatures
who listened to me attentively in the darkness of the hut to
face up to the seriousness of our position. They must not lose
hope but should keep their courage in the certainty that the
hopelessness of our struggle did not detract from its meaning. I said that someone looks down on each of us in difficult
hours—a friend, a wife, somebody alive or dead, or a God,
and he would not expect us to disappoint him. He would

hope to find us suffering proudly—not miserably—knowing how to die.

And finally I spoke of our sacrifice, which had meaning in every case. It was in the nature of this sacrifice that it should appear to be pointless in the normal world, the world of material success. But in reality our sacrifice did have meaning. Those of us who had any religious faith, I said frankly, could understand this without difficulty. I told them of a comrade who on his arrival in camp had tried to make a pact with Heaven that his suffering and death should save the human being he loved from a painful end. For this man, suffering and death were meaningful; his was a sacrifice of the deepest significance. He did not want to die for nothing. None of us wanted that.[9]

We must commit to a purpose in life greater than the fulfillment of our personal mundane desires, and find a way that we can *give* to life. Then we will know what the most important thing is for us. Then, although our life may have its pleasures, changes, suffering, or pain, nothing will divert us from our primary purpose. Painful circumstances and suffering will not cast us as victims of tragedy, but rather we understand them as part of our life's path, opportunities for transformation and growth. By choosing a creative response to every situation or difficulty we encounter, we define daily and hourly the meaning of our life.

To respond to circumstances in a transformative way, we must find a direction through our transition, asking ourselves: "What would I like to consciously let go of, since I have to let go anyway, and what would I like to create, or become? How would I like my new existence to be?" Whatever we understand as the *best part of our being* is that to which we must commit during the remainder of our life.

If we are a caregiver or friend of someone dying, we can help him identify a direction by exploring with him these themes:

Can you use this suffering as a catalyst for changing those parts of your life which you know needed changing anyway?

How would you describe the best part of your being—the highest potential you could reach? What steps could you take that will enable you to fulfill that potential?

.   .   .

Every spiritual tradition offers the means for working toward the actualization of our sacred potential. The dying person may realize that he has never prayed meaningfully or taken the spiritual teachings of his religion to heart. For some people, then, their commitment might be to enter their own spiritual tradition in a deeper and more meaningful way.

From the Buddhist perspective, our highest potential is to completely realize our true nature and attain enlightenment for the benefit of all beings. Yet whether or not death brings a final and lasting freedom is up to us. Everything depends on our appreciation of the preciousness of life's potential and the extent of our commitment to train and prepare *before* we come to die, so that at the crucial bardo of death we are able to release our self-grasping and surrender into the radiant and vast expanse of the truth. The period of dying, then, is a meaningful opportunity to heal our lives, free ourselves of old patterns, and deepen our compassion and wisdom.

Those who are not connected to a formal religion may want only to make the first two commitments—becoming more accepting of themselves and more willing to communicate and relate to others with genuine acceptance and respect. Engaging in only these two commitments is still reflective of spiritual growth, because they enable us to become better human beings.

Sandol Stoddard, author of *The Hospice Movement,* recounts the insights of Lillian Preston, a young woman with a troubled history, dying of stomach cancer at St. Christopher's Hospice in London:

> The temptation for me, I am sure now, has been to believe that I would be perfect from now on, and that all the people around me, being so kind as they are, would be perfect saints. They are only human beings, though. And they will do things that make me cross, and things that I do not like. They even make mistakes, sometimes. Love is the thing I have been learning. Love that accepts people the way they are. I have to do it now and it is a terrific struggle. But you know, I think it is the reason why I am still here. It is something I have to know about, or else my whole life has been wasted. And the only way I can really know it is to do it myself, no matter how weak my body is, just care for people and love them the way that they are.[10]

Everyone yearns to do "one noble act" before they die, something that brings a sense of fulfillment in life and a meaning to their dying. Since young people facing death will not have had much opportunity to discover a greater purpose in their life, they might need suggestions about how to use their remaining time meaningfully. As Rabbi Pesach Krauss writes:

> Too many people make the mistake of judging life by its length rather than by its depth, by its problems rather than its promises. One is never too old or too ill to grow. Life is a series of peak moments. Such cherished moments—when we bring dignity upon ourselves, when we take a stand, when we experience love, when we open ourselves to others and to the world—give meaning to our lives.[11]

Here are some examples of a "noble act" that any dying person might consider:

- Preparing your loved ones to survive your death
- Donating an organ or a retina
- Asking forgiveness or extending forgiveness
- Appreciating the goodness and beauty in life
- Dedicating your suffering and death to benefit others or to atone for your mistakes
- Expressing your gratitude and love to others
- Making offerings—to atone for past harm to others, to express appreciation, or to assist religious or charitable organizations in their work
- Changing even one negative or selfish pattern
- Writing or taping messages of courage, wisdom, and love for those you are leaving

Adults who lost a parent when they were children and had messages—letters, audiotapes, or videotapes—left for them have told me that they never felt abandoned in their bereavement, as they could always return to this living testimony of their parent's love and encouragement.

Finding Meaning When the Dying Are Cognitively Impaired

It's extremely difficult to relate to someone who is comatose or suffers from brain disease or dementia. Normal dialogue is impossible, and most of us have no experience with other means of communication.

Two common temptations are to treat the person condescendingly, like an infant, or to speak as if he is no longer in the room—already dead, for all intents and purposes. *We must, in all circumstances, treat the dying or cognitively impaired person with respect and kindness, the same way we would wish to be treated in his place.* Whether or not the confused or comatose person can speak with any clarity, or even speak at all, he is nonetheless aware and present in the room.

When a person has severe brain damage due to disease or aging, close family members experience that on one level they have "lost" this person, for the personality they've long known is disintegrating. Loved ones will naturally grieve this loss, as they let go of their attachment to the old form of the relationship. Even so, they don't have to let go of their love, or abandon him as though he were already dead. By continuing to give the cognitively impaired person their love, speaking to him genuinely and sharing their lives with him, loved ones are giving his life meaning.

So how can we communicate with a confused or unresponsive person? First, we should never let his condition keep us from seeing who he really is. Remember, the fundamental nature of every being is a pure awareness and "good heart." This innermost essence or wisdom nature is the indestructible ground of our being; therefore it's always present, irrespective of the functions of the brain or sense organs. Since the confused or comatose person never loses this deepest level of awareness, we can always communicate and connect with him on that level. And this is why we must always treat him as a living person, respecting him in the same way we would if we were meeting him at the prime of life.

Our next task is to acknowledge and release our own fear of or aversion to the person's condition, and for this the meditations on compassion may be useful (described in Chapters 6 and 7). Then we can connect with the person through deeper types of communication:

- Touch
- Eye contact
- Humor and play
- Music or singing
- Offering prayers or spiritual practice
- Sending loving, positive thoughts
- Resolving our side of any unfinished business

If communication is both giving and receiving, how can we "hear" from those who are noncommunicative and understand them? Through meditation we can empty our mind of concepts, and inspire ourselves by connecting with our clear awareness and loving receptivity. Then, after we express what is in our heart with sincerity and kindness, we can listen in silence and learn to intuitively sense the other person's experience and needs. Coleman Barks translates a poem by the Sufi mystic Rumi in which a judge asks, to determine which of three sons will inherit his father's fortune:

> "What if a man cannot be made to say anything?
> How do you learn his hidden nature?"

And the third son replies:

> "I sit in front of him in silence,
> and set up a ladder made of patience,
> and if in his presence a language from beyond joy
> and beyond grief begins to pour from my chest,
> I know that his soul is as deep and bright
> as the star Canopus rising over Yemen.
> And so when I start speaking a powerful right arm
> of words sweeping down, I know him from what *I* say,
> and how I say it, because there's a window open
> between us, mixing the night air of our beings."[12]

When we speak genuinely to the dying person, even if he cannot respond verbally, he will respond to us in his heart and mind. We must find creative ways to "open a window between us" which can help ease the noncommunicative person's suffering and loneliness.

Alex's friend Tony had been unconscious for close to two weeks. Tony was dying from complications of AIDS, and his parents stayed by his side in the hospital for long hours, loving their son yet feeling rather helpless. In the past week, Tony's face had grown into a tight grimace and his body had constricted in a fetal position, hands and legs curled close to his body. Medical caregivers, concerned that these were indications of pain, administered higher doses of narcotic, but there was no change in Tony's appearance.

One day Alex heard the frustrated nurse mumble, "Tony needs to *relax!*" as she walked past him, and Alex got an idea. Tony's parents had gone to have a meal, and Alex had some uninterrupted time with his friend.

"Tony, you need to relax now. I don't know if you can hear me, but if so, try to imagine the following scene. Imagine you are climbing to the top of a small grassy hill on a spring day. As you lie down on the top of the hill, you can feel the soft grass underneath you and the warm sun shining on your body. Just allow yourself to drop any cares or concerns, and relax in the warm sunlight."

As he spoke, Alex could see Tony's limbs beginning to uncurl and soften. "Now imagine gazing into the clear blue sky above you. Consider that your mind is a little bit like that vast blue sky—completely open, radiant with love, and expansive. Each time you breathe, feel your mind and heart becoming more open, more relaxed, more and more free."

As the meditation progressed, Tony's face began to soften and ease, until finally his entire body relaxed. When Tony's parents returned, they were very grateful to Alex. "Whatever you have done for Tony just now, please keep doing it!" Tony remained in this open, relaxed state until his death a few days later.

There is another practical reason why we should treat those in a coma as though they are consciously present. Many people who come out of a short- or long-term coma report they were indeed fully aware of what others in the room did and said, sometimes even what they were thinking. Thus besides offering the best we can in terms of medical care, the greatest comfort and relief we can give is our respect, friendship, and love.

If the person is nearing death but seems unable to let go, we can reassure him of our love, and that it is all right for him to die. Since we aren't sure what may be holding the unconscious person back, we can help him prepare for death by verbalizing for him the Four Tasks of Living and Dying.

My second grandmother, my father's mother, was a widow well into her eighties. She had become very frail in her last few years and had begun to prepare for her death. Before going into surgery for a bowel obstruction, she'd made out a Living Will, requesting to dispense with any artificial means of life support if she were dying. During the surgery she did die, and was eventually resuscitated, but she came out, in the specialist's assessment, with severe, irreparable brain damage. She lay in an unresponsive coma for days, connected to every possible means of life support, with a respirator going constantly and a monitor tracking each heartbeat. My father had pleaded with the doctor to discontinue the life support, showing the written evidence of her wishes, but to no avail. Besides the new machinery supporting her life, my grandmother had a pacemaker, so my father and I wondered if it would even be possible for her to die.

When I went into her Intensive Care room, I meditated quietly for a few moments and realized that I did not know how fully she had prepared to die, or if anything might be holding her back.

"Grandma, even though we wish you would get better and come back to being with us, it doesn't look like that is what's happening. It looks like you are dying. We love you, and we won't leave you alone. We'll continue to visit you, no matter what happens. And whenever you are ready, you can let go. You don't need to worry about the rest of us, we'll be all right. You can release any feelings of responsibility for those you are leaving behind. We love you; and we don't want you to suffer any more.

"You gave a lot to others in your life, raising a family and helping others who were in trouble or alone, even helping the other old people in your retirement home, and that inspires me in my own life to do the same. Your life had meaning, and you contributed to others and taught us how to live. We will always cherish that.

"If there is anything we have done to hurt you, we are very sorry and ask your forgiveness. If there's anything you have done to harm anyone, please know that we forgive you and release you of those memories."

Stroking the side of her face as I spoke, I could hear the respirator rhythm alter every so often, as though she had sighed deeply. The line on the heart monitor would sometimes go flat and, gazing into her face, I could see my grandmother's eyes moving beneath her closed eyelids!

"Grandma, you kept all the commitments of your religion and had a devotion to Jesus Christ throughout your life, and this will help you now as you face your death. You can trust in God's mercy and love, knowing that any remaining sins which might be troubling you are forgiven as soon as you acknowledge them. . . . I am not sure, but perhaps you simply don't know how to let go at the time of death, so now I will meditate with you and show one way that might help you.

"Consider that above your head is the radiant, loving presence of Jesus Christ, and imagine tremendous rays of light streaming from him onto your body and soul, purifying any regrets and feelings of unworthiness, and releasing you from any attachment to this life. Feel the compassion and love of Christ fill your being as these rays of light come into you, and let them transform your whole being into light.

"With all the devotion in your heart, keep this presence of Christ here in the room with you from now on. And at the time of your death, consider that your entire being, purified into light, rises up and dissolves into the loving heart of Jesus. And in that blessed union, remain."

After a few moments of sharing this meditation with her in silence, I took my leave. "Grandma, I have to leave you now. Know that you have all my love. Remember, you are not alone. And I will remember you and pray for you. Good-bye."

That night, before going to sleep, I practiced the Essential Phowa for my grandmother once again. In the morning, we were grateful to learn that she had died peacefully during the night.

Completing the Four Tasks of Living and Dying

Facing death is an especially profound opportunity to undertake the tasks of personal and spiritual growth. Yet we don't have to wait until the end of life to begin to face ourselves and grow. Imagining ourselves on our future deathbed when we contemplate our present choices, we can free ourselves from the regret and shame Ivan Ilych suffered as he realized "all that for which he had lived . . . was not real at all, but a terrible and huge deception which had hidden both life and death."

Each task contains the seeds of all the others. Applying ourselves to beginning any one of them can bring us closer to the fundamental goodness of our nature. We will reap the rewards the next time suffering or grief comes into our life; and without a doubt, by having begun to heal our relationship with life and prepared for our own death, we will know how to compassionately support others going through crises or facing death.

Dying is never a "hopeless" state—even when our body and energies are fading, we can still use our mind and heart in a positive way, deepening in wisdom, extending compassion toward our own and others' suffering, and sharing forgiveness, appreciation, and love with those around us. In so doing, we will not face death empty-handed, but richer from having found a way through our suffering. As Brother David Steindl-Rast said:

> The finality of death is meant to challenge us to decision, the decision to be fully present here now, and so begin eternal life. For eternity rightly understood is not the perpetuation of time, on and on, but rather the overcoming of time by the now that does not pass away.
>
> The turning point of the spiritual life is the moment when time running out is turned into time being fulfilled. It rests with us whether death will be a fizzling out when our time runs out or an explosion of the fullness of time into the now of eternity. In the book of Deuteronomy God says: "I place before you today life and death: choose life." Choose life! Life is something we have to choose. One isn't alive simply vegetating; it is by choosing, making a decision, that you become alive. In every spiritual tradition life is not something that you automatically have, it is something that you must choose, and what makes you choose life is the challenge of death—learning to die not eventually, but here and now.[13]

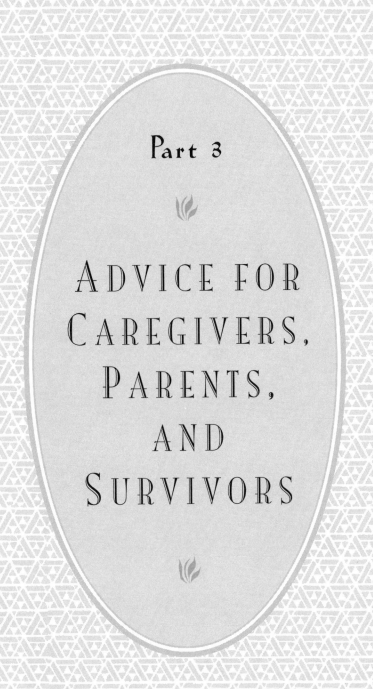

Part 3

Advice for Caregivers, Parents, and Survivors

Chapter 11

HEALING BEREAVEMENT

DURING THE YEAR MY HUSBAND WAS ILL WITH LEU-
kemia, I assumed that his illness and dying would be the hardest
period of my life. I was wrong. Nothing compared to the extreme
pain and bewilderment of my bereavement *after* Lyttle's death,
which was compounded by the struggle of going through it alone.

Many of us suffer needlessly when we do not understand the
normal process of bereavement, and when we do not know how
to heal and finish our grief. If we have a deep aversion to entering
this vulnerable state, we may suppress our grief for years and leave
it unresolved. Any subsequent losses are added to our burden of
unfinished grief, and our hearts grow heavier—or worse, become
numb.

Due to medical advances, a large proportion of the population
in developed countries now lives seventy years or more. Many of
us have reached middle age without ever experiencing the death
of someone close. No wonder death and bereavement seem so
unnatural! Having little personal exposure to bereavement, we may
have mistaken assumptions about the natural process of mourning.

For instance, if we have experienced the death of someone to
whom we were not especially close, our mourning was probably
not very intense and finished within a few weeks or months. After
this experience, we will very likely consider that every process of
mourning should be this easy to finish. Then, if our friend's partner should die suddenly, we might encourage him to "get over it"
quickly, only realizing our error years later when we ourselves are
faced with a more personal and profound loss.

If we fear experiencing the deep pain of our own grief, we will
fear witnessing such pain in others. When we meet a friend or co-
worker who has lost someone close, we may hesitate to bring up
the subject for fear of triggering the other person's grief. In doing

so, we are actually discouraging his or her process of grieving and healing. The bereaved need to talk about their loss and have it acknowledged by those around them; otherwise they may feel desperately isolated in their grief.

Bereavement refers to the emotional state of being *bereft,* a word whose root means "to be shorn" or "torn open." At no time do we feel more torn open than when we experience what is known as a "high grief" death: a sudden or violent death, a suicide, or the loss of a child. A "low grief" death is one which has been expected for a long time, such as that of an extremely elderly person; or a loss for which we have already grieved, such as our former relationship with a person suffering organic brain disease; or the death of someone to whom we are not especially attached. The depth of pain we experience in grief is connected to our degree of attachment to the person and how much he or she was integral to our sense of well-being.

For example, the death of an elderly aunt to whom you were close many years ago may cause you to feel sad, yet your grief is not exceptionally painful. But you may be confused at the depth of your response when, a month later, your aged family dog dies. Your grief is deep and sharp and constant, yet everyone encourages you to get over it, saying, "It's only a dog." And you find yourself wondering why this loss feels so profound.

Whether our bereavement is for the loss of a partner or a significant friend through divorce or death, for a miscarried baby, for the loss of an integral part of our health or even a favorite pet, *any grief we feel is valid.* When the person or situation we have lost is intimately connected to our day-to-day experience of well-being and feeling loved, then our sadness will be more painful and prolonged. And it will take time to heal.

When we seem to overreact to a loss which we know is actually not significant, it's probably because this fresh loss has uncovered an older, unresolved grief. However painful, we must give ourselves permission to mourn and heal our emotional unfinished business. *We will only be able to mourn and finish our grief when we feel safe to do so.* If we feel safe now—even if our sadness seems disproportionate to our current loss—we need to extend compassion to ourselves by expressing and healing our grief, whatever its source.

The Normal Process of Mourning

Mourning is experienced over time in a repeating cycle composed of three phases: shock and disbelief, full awareness of the loss, and recovery or rebalance. Immediately following the loss, the experience of shock and disbelief may be quite prolonged, lasting anywhere from a few weeks to a few months.

Two weeks after my husband, Lyttle, died, I began the fall quarter at UCLA. I felt vibrantly alive and aware, attuned to nature and very connected with people; I felt grateful to be alive. Once in a while, a recognition would seep through: *my husband has died.* This thought did not arouse intense pain, but rather a "poetic sadness," as if I were watching someone else's story. Quietly I congratulated myself: "This is much easier than I had imagined. It must be because I truly let go of Lyttle when he died."

This relatively painless disbelief cracked open unexpectedly four months after Lyttle's death. I will never forget the mid-January evening when "full awareness" of my loss finally dawned. It felt as though someone had knocked on my door and announced, "I'm sorry, your husband has just died."

My pain was deep and wrenching, and I felt as though my heart was being torn in two. For the next week, all I could feel was deep agony, and I wept continuously, an unwilling subject to utter despair and aloneness. I felt as though my whole world was shattering and disintegrating.

Then, like the end of a violent storm, the pain and despair of my grief seemed to abate. I could breathe again! I felt as if I was recovering from a disaster and getting back on my feet, back in the world of the living. After a while, this feeling of recovery and rebalance drifted unnoticeably back into shock and disbelief—a sense that Lyttle's death was illusory, a bad dream from which I would yet awaken.

Within a few weeks, the "full awareness" of my loss cycled around again, and the heart-wrenching pain and despair were just as intense as they had been the previous month. I was shocked. Why had the pain returned, as fresh and deep as before?

"All right," I bargained, "maybe I didn't fully experience and express all my grief, so this time I will, *and then it will be finished.*" Once again, the disruptive storm of excruciating sadness, loneliness, and yearning took over my life, and I allowed myself to cry, moan, sob, and express every feeling that arose. After a week or so, feeling like a shipwrecked survivor regaining consciousness on a beach, I was able to pick myself up and reenter the world of the living again. Yet unobtrusively this feeling of recovery once more drifted back into a subtle state of disbelief.

A month later, the intense life-disrupting pain returned, along with my "full awareness" of the death. The following month, again. And the next month, again, with the same depth of intensity as the very first time. Now a distinct fear crept into my thoughts: What is going on? Why do I feel so out of control? What if I am going crazy? Why doesn't this horrible pain ever go away? Finally I remembered a warning I'd been given two months after my husband's death. A family friend who had experienced the unexpected death of her husband two years previously was babysitting my son. During those first months of prolonged shock, I hadn't understood her warning: "Christine, don't expect the intensity to go away for some time." When I heard her words, I wondered: *What intensity?* Now, seven months later, I understood.

People often wonder if grief can be finished, or exactly what it means to "finish" our grief. In finding a way through my own grief, I eventually learned that the process of mourning does finish. Under normal conditions, mourning a death takes about two years to complete; after a high grief death, it will take longer, yet we *can* recover fully and finish our grief. As Judy Tatelbaum, author of *The Courage to Grieve,* writes: "To recover fully from a loss means to finish or completely let go. Finishing with a dead loved one does not erase the love or the memories, but it does mean that we have accepted the death, that the pain and sorrow have lessened, and that we feel free to reinvest in our lives."[1]

The bereaved person needs to hear this strong reassurance more than once: *You will survive; grief can be finished.*

Grief's Side Effects

Another normal but unsettling aspect of bereavement is the eruption of intense physical and cognitive symptoms. Although transitory, these symptoms can be frightening and may seem to presage a permanent loss of control. Some of the temporary physical changes that may be associated with grief include: shortness of breath, dizziness, irregular heartbeat, hot or cold flashes, disruption of normal sleep patterns, difficulty eating, manic energy, or sensations of heaviness or aching muscles. (Severe or chronic physical symptoms should be checked by one's physician.)

Possible cognitive and perceptual changes include disorientation, short-term memory loss, difficulty concentrating, or a sense that the normal world is now "unreal." When she sees people in the market carefully choosing melons, the survivor may wonder: "What is the point? My loved one has died. Why is everyone behaving as though nothing has changed?"

The bereaved person may also feel as though she sometimes hears or sees the deceased, or has contact with him in dreams. These are all normal phenomena, based on old mental patterning, which continues for some time after a major change. However, they do eventually diminish. At times, very disturbing violent or irrational thoughts or images—such as driving one's car over a cliff—may surface. Unless such thoughts become obsessive or chronic, they should be considered normal side effects of bereavement.

Barriers to Finishing Grief

There are many obstacles that might prevent us from accepting the death and completing our mourning. Understanding the attitudes that stand in our way enables us to change them, so that we can heal our hearts and reinvest in life. The most common barrier is what I have just described: either we ourselves or our family and friends fail to understand what is normal in the process of bereavement, and judge our grieving process or encourage its suppression.

FEAR OF FACING THE PAIN ALONE

In the experience of mourning we lose some of our normal sense of "control"; thus the intensity of grief can dramatically heighten our fears and vulnerability. Whether we are facing an exceptionally painful loss in the present or the accumulated unfinished grief of a lifetime, we may fear that opening ourselves to our pain will cause us to "explode" or go crazy.

For those who experience a high grief death, those feelings and symptoms that are considered part of the normal process of mourning will be magnified greatly. No words are adequate to describe the total disruption and pain such a loss may precipitate in one's life. (Special issues related to sudden death and suicide are described in Chapter 12.)

When bereaved, we are thrust into a bardo similar to the bardo of dying. In this transition, we are suspended between the past and the future. We may feel extreme anxiety and loss of control as we experience the ground of our "known world" dissolving beneath our feet. The new shape of our life has not yet manifested, so we find no reassurance in the future. No wonder we find bereavement so difficult! Grieving challenges us to eventually die to our old way of life, letting go of our former expectations, identity, and all the associations we had with the deceased person.

If our family and friends encourage us to stifle our tears, telling us to pull ourselves together and be strong, then we may withdraw from them and become isolated, not trusting that we can face the depth of our pain alone. Yet I believe that, as human beings, we are not designed to go through crises alone. And bereavement is certainly one of the most powerful life crises we can ever face— an experience that can be as emotionally powerful as dying itself.

More than anything, we need friends who can extend to us a life raft of understanding, love, and support, if we are going to survive this death-within-life and complete our journey through mourning.

UNRESOLVED FEELINGS OF GUILT

After the death of a loved one, we often feel guilty. It's normal to feel this way. Our minds go back to the past and find lost opportunities for connecting, showing patience, or resolving misunderstandings. We may even search our memory for a "cause" of our loved one's illness or death, often imagining ourselves culpable. We start with one thing we feel guilty about—not getting him to the right doctor, loaning her the car, that last fight—and soon we've accumulated a long list that makes us feel unreasonably guilty and unforgivable. While feeling some guilt is natural, the danger is that we'll get stuck in it, becoming trapped in the past. Unresolved guilt prevents us from mourning and letting go of our loved one, and moving on in our life.

It's important to redefine our guilt feelings as "regret." While guilt traps us in the past, regret is a way of bringing us to the present, in order to take responsibility for our mistakes and begin to *do something* about them. It is up to us to heal and conclude the relationship. To do so, we can use the Method for Completing Unfinished Business (described in Chapter 7), combined with spiritual practice to help us purify ourselves and our deceased loved one from any painful memories or regrets. Once we take responsibility and clear up the past, we can resolve to live in a more caring and loving way from now on. We must develop a sense of perspective: no one is perfect. Life is a continuous process of making mistakes, taking responsibility for them, and then learning to be more aware and compassionate so that we don't accumulate new regrets.

CHRONIC FRUSTRATION AND ANGER

Like guilt, anger and frustration are normal feelings after a death, as we are forced to accept that we have no control over what has happened. Against death we feel powerless; this is especially true for parents who believed they could shield their child from suffering and death. After a loved one's death there are many possible sources of frustration, from our assessment of lapses in the person's medical care to our being left unprepared to cope with financial and practical matters.

Especially in the case of sudden death, we may project our anger and blame onto whoever we believe caused the death and our painful grief. Our feelings of frustration and anger are normal; it is getting stuck in anger which creates problems. If our angry thoughts are acknowledged and then let go of, we will have the emotional space to begin accepting our loss and feeling our sadness. If, however, we continually feed our angry thoughts and feelings over months or years, we will have bound ourselves to the past and created a wall around our heart. We need to find a responsible way to release our frustration and anger, if we want to finish our grief and be free to love once again.

INCREASED GRASPING AND ATTACHMENT

Instead of letting go of our attachment as we grieve, we can make the mistake of grasping on to the deceased person even more strongly. Halfway through the second year after my husband's death, the cycles of intense pain and sadness were continuing, and I felt a fresh fear that my grief would never finish. Part of me wanted to ignore this intense pain returning month after month, to push it down and avoid it altogether. Yet I suspected that repressing my pain would not help in the long run either, so I decided to bring more awareness to my situation. I asked myself if I was doing anything that might be prolonging the mourning process.

Then I uncovered the secret thoughts I was generating each time I felt deep sadness and pain: *I can't live without you. I hate being alone. I want you back.* There was so much grasping in my mind, so many wishes that could never be satisfied! If I continued to think and feel this way, I realized, there would be no end to my grief and despair. It was clear that I needed to replace my grasping with a new way of thinking: *I am letting you go and wishing you well. I am going to survive and be strong. I am going to make a new life for myself.* When I felt the deep sadness and pain rising again, I began practicing letting go in this way. After a few months of taking this approach, my process of mourning finished.

SELF-JUDGMENT ABOUT SADNESS AND GRIEF

Some people may suppress their grief with the thought: *It's a sign of weakness to cry, and I must be strong.* Or: *I'm just feeling sorry for myself.* When we grieve, we are mourning our loss of the person and our relationship to him or her. Rather than judging ourselves, we can translate our emotional experience into: *I am simply feeling sorrow.* Sorrow, like the joy we had felt previously, is an inescapable part of our experience of loving another person.

Most of us have been conditioned from childhood to be strong and not to cry, although women generally find it easier than men to weep. Men often need permission and encouragement to grieve and cry, as they may be judging themselves or fear the loss of other people's respect. Our fear and suppression of grief prevents us from living fully. It's vitally important to find a healthy outlet for our painful feelings, so they don't back up like a river blocked by debris and deadwood. Rather than weakness, it is actually a sign of strength to grieve and let go of people who have left our life; it is a sign of our vitality and desire for wholeness. As Judy Tatelbaum writes:

> Grief is a wound that needs attention in order to heal. To work through and complete grief means to face our feelings openly and honestly, to express or release our feelings fully,

and to tolerate and accept our feelings for however long it takes for the wound to heal. For most of us, that is a big order.

Therefore, it takes courage to grieve. It takes courage to feel our pain and to face the unfamiliar. It also takes courage to grieve in a society that mistakenly values restraint, where we risk the rejection of others by being open or different.[2]

RETREATING INTO A SHELL OF ISOLATION

When we are in pain, we often retreat into a shell of isolation—hiding from our feelings and also from the world. In this state, our loneliness is sealed, leading to feelings of utter hopelessness and despair. At a certain point in my own grieving process, I considered ending my life to escape from this deep pain. I felt as though I were at the bottom of a very deep and dark well, and that no one could possibly help me out. Even though I was an atheist at the time and I didn't know if anyone was listening, I began to pray for help.

After a few days of praying, in the midst of my despair, an image suddenly appeared in my mind, a photograph that was taken during the Vietnam War. The image was of a young mother holding her dead child in her arms and looking up to the sky in anguish. This vivid image broke my shell of isolation, as I understood that *we all grieve*. We all lose the people we love, and all of us experience the pain of grief. So I was not alone. This experience must be as hard for everyone else as it is for me, I realized, and others might not know how to heal their grief either. I resolved to find a way to go through and finish my grief, so I could help others do the same.

This was an important turning point for me. Part of the task of mourning is to let go of our former relationship and then consciously decide to create a new life, with meaning and purpose. This decision helps us summon the courage to finish our grief. Failing this, mourners can end up living halfheartedly in a shadow world, neither finished with the past nor connected to the present. Everyone who grieves needs to find their own personal answer to the question: *For what purpose will I continue to live?*

Finishing Grief: The Four Tasks of Bereavement

The survivor's experience of bereavement parallels the process of dying, and the tasks of bereavement similarly reflect the Four Tasks of Living and Dying:

- Accepting the reality of the death
- Healing and concluding the relationship
- Releasing our emotional pain and letting go
- Finding meaning in our new life

ACCEPTING THE REALITY OF THE DEATH

Mourning will never finish if it has never commenced. We must first come to accept the fact that the death has happened. When we do not have a physical, tangible experience of the reality of death, we may suppress our grief by denying the death for years. If we do not actually witness a death, then viewing the body afterward at home, in the hospital, or at the mortuary will help us begin to accept and get used to the reality of our loss.

When viewing the body of the deceased, we can arrange to have private time alone, enabling us to communicate what is unfinished, say our good-byes, and begin offering spiritual practice for him or her. All too often people who die in hospitals are whisked away before survivors arrive. If our loved one dies in a distant city, we may get the news through a phone call. In the case of sudden death, the inability to see or connect with the physical fact of death may lead to an even stronger denial or sense of unreality.

Early one morning I was called to help at the hospital with a young couple whose baby had died during the night. The officials needed to do an autopsy, but the parents were adamantly refusing permission. I sat down with them and asked a few questions, giving them time to tell me what had happened and how they felt about the death. Finally I reminded the parents that they would need to think about releasing the baby's body for an autopsy to be done. The mother responded strongly: "They're not going to cut my baby!"

I searched inside for what this young mother might be feeling, and realized that part of her still felt her baby was alive. I proposed then to the mother and father that they could go into the next room and hold their baby's body once again, in order to say good-bye. At first the mother looked at me in horror. With trepidation, I offered to go into the room with them.

Once the parents saw and touched their baby again, once they began to say good-bye in their hearts and allow the tears to come, they were then able to release the body for the autopsy. For this young couple, making a tangible connection to the fact of their baby's death initiated their process of mourning.

We need to be free to speak about the person who died, and not conceal the dynamic change already taking place within the family. Speaking about our memories is a way of "purifying" the past and helping us to let it go. Families who openly talk about the death have a much easier time supporting each other in their bereavement. We must learn not to be afraid of feeling our natural sadness, as this is what will eventually lead to our healing.

Shortly after a death, it's not uncommon for a large circle of friends and family to gather together, offering their practical and emotional support for a few days surrounding the funeral. During this time, though, we are likely in shock and can easily feel overwhelmed by dealing with so many visitors. Months later, when the painful cycles of grief begin, we will find ourselves alone. When our family gathers for the next holiday or birthday, they often avoid speaking about the recent death in a misguided attempt to spare us pain.

Many survivors have found great solace in arranging a memorial or celebration of the person's life a few months after the death or when their family comes together again for the next holiday. Instead of steeling themselves to avoid speaking about the death and their sad feelings, we could ask each family member to bring a memento, photograph, letter, or story to share about the person who died. They can also bring ideas for creating a simple and personal ritual—prayer, meditation, candle lighting, readings, or singing—in memory of the deceased. Perhaps there will be some sad moments during this memorial, yet afterward everyone will be able to laugh and celebrate because they have openly mourned together. (Spiritual practices for the deceased are described in Chapter 12.)

It's not easy to pack up and distribute the deceased person's belongings, and it may take a few months before we feel strong enough to do it. Yet doing so is another sign we have accepted the fact of the death and that we have begun the process of letting go.

Going to visit the grave can also help us begin to accept the reality of death. (Conversely, when the dying person has given instructions to have his ashes scattered by plane over the ocean, we may feel even more disconnected from the physical reality of the death.) Many survivors describe their wish to have a significant place to go, a place which marks their loved one's death in a physical way, and where they can continue their process of letting go.

HEALING AND CONCLUDING
THE RELATIONSHIP

Getting stuck in any kind of emotional unfinished business prevents us from completing our mourning. We may sustain an unbalanced image of the deceased, seeing him either as our lifelong nemesis or as a saint who could do no wrong. To generate a more balanced view of the deceased, we should reflect on what we will miss about the deceased person and also on what we will *not* miss.

After a death, whether expected or sudden, we are challenged to communicate all of our conflicting emotions, frustrations, and unexpressed regrets. If we didn't do so previously, we will also need to conclude our relationship and say good-bye. Some people start a journal or write letters to the deceased. Although helpful, these methods can remain somewhat open-ended, because we may only partially vent our problems and feelings and never actually let them go. The Method for Completing Unfinished Business is exceptionally effective in helping us express and release our emotional pain, and bring closure to the relationship. In the case of a high grief death, it is vital we seek out the support of a trained grief counselor to assist us in releasing our powerfully charged emotions or unfinished business.

Jenny, an old friend of mine, showed me her "Deathography," an account of her personal encounters with death, which she'd written for a college class. In two pages she described in great detail her father's illness and death, which had occurred three years earlier. I was startled to see one sentence standing alone at the end of the story: "Six weeks after my father's death, my mother died."

When I asked Jenny about this, she said she felt so guilty about her mother's death, she couldn't even think about it. Jenny had remained in the family home to support her mother for a few weeks after her father's death, but she and her mother had always had a difficult relationship and this recent death strained it even further. Finally Jenny had flown back to her own home and returned to work. Her mother died alone a few weeks later, after suffering a bad fall.

Because of our long friendship, and Jenny's willingness to heal the past, she agreed to work with me on resolving her unfinished business with her mother. I asked Jenny to imagine that her mother was in front of her once more. "See her as very open and receptive, willing to hear what you have to say. What do you want to tell your mother?"

Jenny finally said out loud all the things about which she felt guilty. I invited her to express as well any other old angers, regrets, or hurts from their long relationship. Finally, Jenny was able to express her love to her mother.

"Jenny, if you were speaking to the 'best part' of your mother, and if she were able to really hear your pain and remorse, would she forgive you now?"

"Yes."

"Allow yourself to receive and feel your mother's forgiveness coming toward you," I suggested. "And, Jenny, if your mother felt a similar remorse for any times she hurt you, would you forgive her?"

"Yes, I would."

"Tell your mother you forgive her, and really let go of these past memories now."

Throughout our work together, Jenny's unexpressed pain and tears flowed freely, enabling her to forgive, to accept forgiveness, to grieve and let go of her mother.

RELEASING OUR EMOTIONAL PAIN AND LETTING GO

To feel safe to grieve, we need the support of others who can validate the many layers of our suffering and emotional pain and who can extend to us their love and unconditional acceptance. Following a death, each spouse—or the teenagers within the same family—often expect support from each other, and are disappointed and angry when they don't receive it. Within a nuclear family, it is not possible to get the support we need, since each family member is in the midst of his or her own crisis. We need to look outside our immediate family and *find the right kind of sup-*

port—from friends, counselors, or members of a grief support group who are not afraid of hearing our memories and thoughts, or of sharing our pain.

We may be tempted to judge those friends who do not know how to extend the kind of emotional support we need. If they have never lived through such a powerful grief, our friends will feel extremely uncertain about how to offer support, or they may fear witnessing our pain. Sometimes our friends just don't have the skill or awareness to be there for us in extreme circumstances. Still, we can ask for their company at times, to enjoy a meal or a concert together, or to help with the gardening or other simple tasks. Even if they are not great comforters, our friends may be grateful if we suggest simple, practical things they can do to help and support us.

We must keep our eyes open for support from unexpected places—perhaps a neighbor down the street, a co-worker, or a member of our church or synagogue who has gone through a process of mourning and has recovered well. Those who are familiar with bereavement are often happy to offer support, for they remember how much the support of others helped them.

We might receive support from our hospice team after a death, or turn to self-help support groups composed of people who have experienced a similar loss, such as a Compassionate Friends group for parents who have lost a child.[3] Men and women alike have described the vital solace such groups provide: here are people who know how bad it is; they have lived through the yearly markers of birthdays and anniversaries; they aren't shocked by expressions of anger or guilt; and to newly bereaved parents the group members are "beacons of hope," proving that it is possible to survive a painful loss and find a way back to life itself.

We need to find ways to release our sadness and tears. Men have told me that when tears don't come easily, it helps them to find an activity to express their grief: planting a tree, dedicating one's daily run to the memory of their loved one, creating something with their hands, or going into nature for solace. Listening to music, painting, or writing have been viable emotional expressions of grief for others. Whatever helps us express and release our pain, we will need to return to it again and again while on the journey toward fully letting go.

We need to give ourselves permission to grieve. And we need to take time out for healing. Part of our life has been dramatically altered, and we can't just bounce back as though nothing has changed. Even if we have to return to work soon after a death, we can create a private space and time in each day to allow our natural feelings to surface. Perhaps at work we have to stop the flow of emotions, but we can set aside a period of time to be alone after we come home—even a half hour—for sorting out our feelings and giving ourselves permission to grieve freely. Then, when we take the rest of the evening to relax or join our family, we can be fully present within ourselves and with our loved ones.

One technique I found to be effective for releasing emotionally charged memories from the last year of Lyttle's life was to deliberately review each potent memory again. As I relived the moment in my memory, I mentally "finished" that experience in the way I would like to have done at the time. Summoning a different memory each day, gradually I managed to untangle the emotional knots that kept me from accepting Lyttle's death and from accepting and forgiving myself. Besides healing my memory of the past, this process of imagining what I wished I had done or said also allowed me to rehearse a different way of responding to future life challenges.

While the process of mourning includes facing our dragons and moving through our pain, we must also find ways to comfort and take care of ourselves. It is not a testament to our loved one if we neglect our own well-being or become self-destructive, if we neglect other family members, or if we avoid laughter or activities that connect us to the pleasure of being alive. One useful technique is to imagine what our deceased loved one might wish for us now.

A man in his mid-seventies spoke quite glowingly of how he made his peace with the death of his wife two years before. "At first I felt like I wanted to die too, and I started neglecting myself, just staying at home and letting the four walls close in on me. I secretly wondered how long it would take me to become terminally ill so I could join her. Then I reflected on what had made my wife happy, and I asked myself: Is there anything I can do even now that would please her?

"I realized that my wife was most happy when I was happy. She would want me to still take care of myself, go out into the world and do things I enjoyed, or even learn new things. Now, by enjoying my life, I feel every day I am telling my wife that I love her."

Advice for Caregivers, Parents, and Survivors

FINDING MEANING IN OUR NEW LIFE

Judy Tatelbaum writes:

Just as we know that loss is inevitable, we know now that recovering from our sorrow can also be inevitable. We can even use our loss in loving testimonial to the deceased as a step in our own growth, as a positive turning point in our lives.

As we journey through these painful experiences of living, we must never forget that we have an amazing resilience and capacity to survive. Just as whole forests burn to the ground and eventually grow anew, just as spring follows winter, so it is nature's way that through it all, whatever we suffer, we can keep on growing. It takes courage to believe we can survive, that we will grow. It takes courage, too, to live now and not postpone living until some vague tomorrow.[4]

In letting go of someone we dearly love, each of us faces the same conscious commitment—to mourn and let go of the past so that we can give shape to our new life. We remain aware of the uncompromising reality of impermanence and death, but we must resist the temptation to close our heart, to decide never to love or trust another person again. If we succumb to that temptation, we will freeze our life in the past, and end up bringing untold suffering to those who still love us, especially our intimate partner and children. Trying to defend ourselves from pain, we lose contact with the source of love in our heart and inadvertently bring further pain to ourselves.

Poignantly aware that we will eventually lose everyone we love, we can decide instead to learn to appreciate the people in our lives even more. Awareness of impermanence can become a catalyst for helping us realize that in the light of death, many of our troubles are not so big after all. Then it becomes easier to forgive and let go, easier to tell another person how grateful we are for what he or she brings to our life. We can allow the truth of impermanence to remind us to be more patient, more attentive, and more willing to be present for others.

The process of recovering from our grief can help us to live more fully and appreciate each day, and each person, as an irreplaceable gift. In grieving, *we must eventually let go of our attachment to the person who is gone, yet we can keep their love with us.* We are not abandoned in bereavement; we can nurture our memories of love, and allow love to keep flowing toward us.

Even if the person we've lost was the central person in our life, we can broaden our expression of love after he or she has died. One widow told me, "The hardest part isn't losing my husband's love, because wherever he is now, I can still feel his love for me. The hard part is feeling cut off from any ways of expressing my love. This is why I'd like to become a hospice volunteer."

While our grief is finishing we need to find a way to contribute to the world, a means of dedicating our life to something greater than our personal desires and needs. We can even dedicate our work to the memory of the deceased. A word of caution, though, as it is important to maintain a balance. Some people take refuge in their new, meaningful activity and allow this to consume all their energy and time, thereby avoiding their journey through grief and neglecting those loved ones who are still alive.

The realization of the reality of impermanence and death can also help us recognize that we will be at the mercy of our ego-centered attachments and fears until we commit to a spiritual path.

Krisha Gotami was a young mother who lived at the time of the Buddha. After her only child died, she desperately searched for someone who could bring him back to life. Finally she turned to the Buddha for help, and he instructed her to bring him a mustard seed from a household that had never experienced a death. After going from door to door throughout the local village, Krisha Gotami finally realized the truth: everyone experiences the death of a loved one, and thus no one is truly alone in grief. She realized that everything in life was subject to impermanence and death, and that she could find no lasting happiness in imperfect, changing circumstances or people. She then asked the Buddha for the teachings which could bring her out of this endless cycle of suffering and help her realize her inherent, deathless nature. The Buddha accepted her as his disciple, and she followed the spiritual path he taught with diligence. And before she died, Krisha Gotami attained enlightenment.

Supporting a Bereaved Person

What helps someone going through bereavement is our friendship and presence, simply *being with them in their pain,* even when there is nothing we can say or do to ease it. In the section "Responding to the Suffering of Others" in Chapter 5, I described how we can be most effectively present for someone who is suffering. The following list includes additional points especially relevant to supporting the bereaved.

1. Offer your continued presence and friendship.

2. Validate the person's mourning, and give her permission to grieve. Reassure her that her intense feelings and sense of losing control are normal in bereavement.

3. Accept the person unconditionally, regardless of any thoughts or emotions she might express.

4. Inform the bereaved and her closest family members about the normal process and duration of mourning. Reassure them that grief can be finished.

5. Invite her to speak about her memories of the deceased person, even repeatedly.

6. Encourage her to complete any unfinished business.

7. Consider what practical support she might need and offer your help in specific ways: shopping or cooking, spending time with children, maintaining the apartment or garden, working through bills or the paperwork related to the death.

8. Assist her in identifying friends, professionals, or other resources in the community she could turn to for support.

9. Encourage her to take care of herself, and to take the time she needs to nurture herself and allow this deep wound to heal.

10. Identify activities she had formerly enjoyed, and invite her to join you in doing some of them, especially outdoor activities which entail some physical movement or contact with the beauty of nature.

11. Share comforting hugs and affection. Relate stories from life and cultivate a sense of humor where appropriate, knowing that uncomfortable moments will be inevitable.

12. Let the survivor know all the ways she has contributed to your life. Allow her to lend emotional or practical support to you sometimes.

Friends often make the mistake of leaving the bereaved alone, thinking they would prefer to have solitude. While all of us wish for some solitude when we experience pain, most bereaved people have too much of it. Single people need to have their long solitude interrupted by those friends who can sometimes nurture, sometimes listen in silence, and sometimes just play. Alternatively, parents with children need encouragement and perhaps an offer of weekly child care so they can enjoy some solitude for mourning and taking care of their own needs.

The bereaved person can easily make the mistake of not letting anyone in, particularly by responding dishonestly when friends call to ask how she is or to offer their love. After some time she may find herself totally alone. Most friends are well-intentioned and would be happy to learn how to help and support a bereaved friend. Yet they may not know what they can do. If we are to survive our grief, we must swallow our fear and pride and learn to ask others for their presence and help, even verbalizing what it is we most need from them.

During the first year of bereavement, one's rational thinking process often seems to be crystal clear and very convincing. Dramatic plans can be quickly formulated and acted on: selling the house and moving to a different part of the country, entering into a commitment in a new relationship, or making some other sudden lifestyle or career change. As a result, the survivor can unwittingly stop the natural process of grief and effectively cut off dependable sources of love and support. What appears to be rational mental clarity spurring these impulsive decisions is called the "first-year crazies." We can encourage the bereaved to put off any major, life-changing decisions until at least the first anniversary of the death has passed.

If we are able to intervene, we can refer the survivor to professional help when we see signs of an abnormal grief response—behaviors that may threaten her own or her family's well-being. These signs include prolonged dejection and depression, hints dropped regarding suicide, new or increased phobias, neglect of her own health or of her children's health, excessive withdrawal, or continued denial of the death. Not all counselors or psychologists have training in grief therapy, but a local hospice or community counseling center can make an appropriate referral.

Above all, remind the grieving person that she is more than her suffering. We must keep our heart open with love and support her in her pain, yet never lose sight of the big picture. We are all living in a world of suffering; loss, illness, death, and grief are not unusual. They are very powerful transitions, however, opportunities for us to wake up from our self-centered, materialistic approach to life.

Bereavement can be a time of despair and disintegration, as well as a time for a surprising renewal of faith, as C. S. Lewis discovered and wrote about in *A Grief Observed*.[5] For much of his life Lewis had been an inspiring author and sought-after lecturer on Christian faith. After his wife died of cancer, he chronicled his anger and sadness over the ensuing months, and experienced a despair and aloneness so profound that everything he had formerly believed now seemed to be empty, hollow words. He felt abandoned by God and lost his faith. Yet as Lewis continued to question and search and slowly heal his painful grief, he gradually rebuilt, from the ashes of his suffering and despair, a potent and living faith.

As Lewis observed, when we lose that which we hold most dear, we have no choice but to mourn and let go. In the end, we must land on the ground again—what better ground to land on than the truth? We can encourage the grieving person to combine her mourning with her spiritual life. Finding an ultimate refuge in the midst of our deepest pain can be like throwing open the shutters on the windows of a long-abandoned house.

Most of all, we must never give up on the bereaved. With kindness and patience, we continue to offer our love and support over the many months it will take for her to complete the most painful part of her mourning. And we mustn't wait for the bereaved person to call us and ask for help. As a rule, she will find it very, very hard to admit, even when we contact her, that she is intensely lonely and afraid. She is afraid to admit she feels like hell; afraid she is going crazy. She is afraid we wouldn't want to be with her in her pain. And she is afraid to make those first steps back into life.

Thus it is left to us to be dynamic, caring, and honest so that she feels safe to let down her guard and allow herself to receive love and support.

The following story is one both Sogyal Rinpoche and I like to tell because of its special message for those supporting the bereaved. One widow was asked, a year after her husband's death, "Is there anything special which helped you during this year of your bereavement?"

"Yes," she said. "It was the people who kept calling and coming by *even though I had said 'No.'*"

The widow's answer is significant for two reasons. First, when we call the bereaved person during the week she is experiencing the "disbelief" or "recovery" part of her grieving cycle, she may genuinely not need our presence or help. Yet if we keep calling or stopping by to see her, we will eventually make contact—and be able to lend meaningful support—during the most painful and despairing periods, when she will feel unable to pick up the phone and ask anyone for help.

Second, we usually have a slight aversion to witnessing another person's pain. Although we might be willing to spend time with the bereaved person in spite of our fear, when she says, "No, don't come," we are tempted to hang up the phone with relief, and not try again! What helps the most, then, is to continue calling and offering to vigil with the bereaved person through her "dark night of the soul." With the love and continued presence offered by dedicated friends, the bereaved feel their life has new meaning and the future offers hope.

Chapter 12

THE SPIRITUAL DIMENSION OF BEREAVEMENT

Whil e the major religious traditions of the world all affirm that there is some form of existence after the death of the physical body, Tibetan Buddhism describes in great detail the possible forms of this existence and the myriad experiences which are part of the journey through the bardos after death. These teachings increase our understanding of what the person who has died might be experiencing, and how family and friends can offer him invaluable spiritual support.

Like the bardo of dying, the bardo after death is a period which can be fraught with great uncertainty and suffering, or a time of extraordinary opportunity—if we understand what is happening and know how to choose our direction wisely at this "crossroads" between death and the next life.

As you read this information about the survival of consciousness after death, please bring the finest part of you to this discussion— and know that you can be of real benefit to a loved one who has died. We often think only of our own needs in bereavement, and not of the needs of the deceased. These teachings reveal the crucial role you may have in helping your loved one toward attaining complete freedom from suffering, or at least a rebirth with greater potential for his happiness and spiritual evolution.

Even if you do not believe in rebirth, I hope the teachings presented here will help you realize that you are capable of bringing your loved one who has died valuable spiritual support. If some aspect of the teaching does not fit with your own religious beliefs, please do not worry about it. Simply use whichever insights help you understand and appreciate the teachings and practices for death from your own spiritual tradition.

The Tibetan Buddhist teachings underscore this point: the moment of death and the period afterward are of enormous spiritual significance. When you engage in religious practice or prayer for someone who has died, do it with deliberate awareness and the intent to help. Don't take rituals or prayers for granted or merely go through the motions out of a sense of obligation.

As you read this chapter, you may become aware that what you did after a loved one died might have inadvertently brought him suffering. When I first heard these teachings, I deeply regretted what I had done, and failed to do, in the months after my husband's death. Always remember that you did the best you could with what you knew at the time. If you didn't offer spiritual support before your loved one died, you can still do something for him even now. Remember: *It is never too late to help and benefit your loved one, no matter how long ago he or she died.*

Entering the Bardos After Death

What happens to us after we die is not like a random throw of the dice. In the same way that every present moment unfolds from what we have done in the previous moment, our existence after death—for better or worse—will be a complete unfolding of the patterns we have sown in our mind and heart during life.

Our experience after death can fall within a wide range of possibilities, depending on how we lived and the state of mind at the moment of death. Sogyal Rinpoche describes the complete outer and inner dissolution of the dying process in *The Tibetan Book of Living and Dying;* I will summarize here some relevant points. After breathing out our last breath, our life force and energy begin dissolving and moving inward, toward the heart center. After twenty minutes or so, we will experience a sensation of "fainting" into utter darkness and peace. This is the actual moment of death, the conclusion of the "painful bardo of dying," when our body dies, along with our ego, or "self-grasping."

Coming out of this faint, we awaken into the vastness and luminosity of our true nature. Now we are poised at the threshold between life and the bardo states after death. Since all conscious life has this essential nature, everyone who dies will experience this infinite luminosity. Yet what unfolds afterward will depend on how spiritually prepared we are.

At one end of the scale, an experienced practitioner can recognize the luminosity of death, the dawning of the "Ground Luminosity," and unite with it effortlessly. By remaining in that state, he is liberated. Great practitioners may even rest in this state for a number of days after death. At the other end of the scale are the majority of people, who, lacking any familiarity with the innermost nature of mind, will not recognize the luminosity of death at all. Instead they simply faint into an unconscious state, which is said to last for as long as three and a half days. As Sogyal Rinpoche writes:

> When the Ground Luminosity dawns, the crucial issue will be how much we have been able to rest in the nature of mind, how much we have been able to unite our absolute nature and our everyday life, and how much we have been able to purify our ordinary condition into the state of primordial purity.[1]

When the vastness of our true nature dawns we find ourselves in a pure experience of nonduality, a limitless state with no boundaries or references. There is nothing to hold on to, nothing to relate to, not even an "I." Now it's as if we are presented with a choice: to surrender into the essence of our enlightened nature (becoming "one with God") or to react and respond with grasping, aggression, or fear. If we react, we separate from that pure essence and begin progressively to reincarnate our former "sense of self" with its conditioned mental suffering.

If we compare the luminosity at death to the bright morning sky just before dawn, then what follows is like the rising of the sun in all its splendor. This next bardo of death is called "the luminous bardo of dharmata"—*dharmata* means "the intrinsic nature of reality." In this bardo the raw energy or inherent radiance of the essential nature of mind blazes out. Brilliant lights and colors, piercing rays of light, and thunderous sounds manifest, affording us another opportunity for liberation if we can recognize these unfolding "pure appearances" as emanating from our wisdom nature. Yet without spiritual training, this bardo will simply flash by, as we fail to recognize it. Just as we do in everyday life, we'll react to our mind's seemingly real projections by taking refuge in our emotions once again, thereby generating the causes of our next birth.

The teachings on the third bardo of death, "the karmic bardo of becoming," might be difficult to contemplate. They explain not only that our existence continues after death but that we might be thrust into even more suffering than we had in life, and feel more helpless to free ourselves from it. Our karma unfolds unequivocally; our mental habits can automatically propel us from one mental reality to the next. Thus it is said that we are blown helplessly by the "winds of karma" and experience no resting place.

Most people prefer the descriptions of positive near-death experiences (NDEs) in which people report being immersed in a brilliant loving light, deep bliss, and unbroken peace. But actual death goes on much longer than a few moments. If we read further into these NDEs we will find hints of the sufferings to come in the ongoing experiences after death. For example, as those who clinically died witness their loved ones' deep grief and anguish on learning of their apparent "death," they feel a heightened sense of responsibility and worry for them. Dr. Michael Sabom recounts a young woman's strongest impression during her NDE: "I was sitting way up there looking at myself convulsing and my mother and my maid screaming and yelling because they thought I was dead. I felt so sorry for them . . . deep, deep sadness. But I felt I was free up there and there was no reason for suffering."[2]

During the review of their entire life that occurs during their near-death experience, many survivors felt tormented by shame and guilt for the harm they had brought onto others, and wished they could rectify their mistakes. Harshly judging their own actions, some felt unworthy of the unconditional love streaming toward them.

Rarely do we read accounts of the more frightening near-death experiences. Those who have hellish or frightening experiences are reluctant to report them, fearing what others would think, and they try to quickly wipe them from memory. Still, some published near-death experiences describe desolate landscapes, terrifying experiences of being chased or harmed, or of witnessing entire worlds filled with beings in various states of suffering.

Similar experiences are depicted in the descriptions of the "karmic bardo of becoming." In this bardo, the consequences of our actions in life begin to ripen as seemingly real and vivid experiences of either pleasure or suffering. Even though we lack a physical body in the bardo, we still believe we exist, and therefore fear that we can be harmed.

When consciousness floats free of the body, it is very impressionable, very sensitive and open—so open that any thought or feeling we have immediately becomes our whole reality. A similar state was dramatized in an episode of the television program *Star Trek: The Next Generation* when the starship *Enterprise* entered a strange force field in which the crew members' thoughts or emotions manifested spontaneously as their reality. The chaos aboard the *Enterprise* was spectacular! Fires broke out, old lovers appeared, aggressions became intense.

When he finally realized what was happening, Captain Picard broadcast to all the crew a message which parallels the instruction in *The Tibetan Book of the Dead* for someone going through the bardo of becoming: *Everything that is appearing to you is a result of your own mind. It does not actually exist, so do not react to it. What you are experiencing is your own projection.*

To prepare fully for death, we must begin training and taming our mind and emotions while we are alive, a discipline which progressively frees us from suffering in life, and especially after we die. As the teachings for the bardos say: "In an instant, complete enlightenment; in an instant, complete confusion."

Why We Can Help the Deceased

Once consciousness separates from the body, it takes the form of an extremely light and lucid "mental body," said to be a youthful and healthy form completely free of limitations or disabilities. Freed of the constraints of the gross physical body, the consciousness is seven times clearer than in life, and has some supernatural powers—including a rudimentary clairvoyance, the ability to travel instantaneously by thought, the capacity to penetrate or pass through physical objects, and extreme sensitivity.

Likewise, the literature of near-death experiences suggests the availability of certain of the powers attributed to this "mental body" even on the threshold of death: temporary separation from the physical body, with awareness of resuscitation attempts; direct apprehension of the family's emotions and thoughts; observation of remote events; the ability to travel anywhere just by thinking of a destination; and the ability to see and communicate with others who have died previously.

All of these abilities are described in the Tibetan teachings in the context of the bardo of becoming. Those who work with the dying have noted that some of these experiences may even begin while the person is nearing death.[3] Because of these special abilities and sensitivities, those who are still living can affect the person who has died—for better or worse—by the things they think, say, and do.

When the consciousness of the deceased reawakens on separating from the body, he will feel as though he's just awakened from a bad dream. Thinking he is still alive, he may return home and attempt to communicate with loved ones. Seeing them weeping, disposing of his belongings, and planning a funeral, he will realize—with some anguish and fear—that he is dead. Being very sensitive to other people's thoughts, he'll know the true feelings and motivations of his family and friends, and even the minister performing his funeral. His emotional reactions to what he witnesses may generate strong experiences of hurt or anger.

According to the habits of mind we have generated in life, we can literally create a heavenly or hellish existence after our death.

Dr. George Ritchie, himself a Christian, had a prolonged near-death experience when he was a nineteen-year-old army recruit in 1943.[4] In the extraordinary experience he reports, Ritchie describes how Jesus Christ appeared to him and traveled with him, revealing different realms of existence where beings were trapped in suffering after death. The form of their existence and suffering was determined by their strongest attachments and addictions, or their greatest negative emotional propensities which had been carried over from their life. Ritchie understood then the vital message and connection between life and death in Jesus' words from the Sermon on the Mount: "Lay not up for yourselves treasures on earth. *For where your treasure is, there will your heart be also!*" Where our heart lies—that to which we are most attached—is the source of suffering in this life, and of untold continued suffering after we die.

In the more dramatic and sometimes terrifying experiences of this bardo, the consciousness of the person who has died will be desperately wishing for help, and thus be more receptive to whatever support we may offer.

Imagine waking up in a completely dark cave with frightening sounds all around you. Now someone lights a match. Wouldn't your mind be attracted at once to that refuge of light? Similarly, when we summon up all our love and pray or practice for our loved one who has died, his mind will be attracted to our meditation and sincere prayers. The truth and goodness of this practice can then become his new reality.

The teachings say that it is relatively easy to lend spiritual support to a loved one who has died. Since the mind is no longer associated with the body, the person's consciousness is more malleable. A huge tree trunk on the ground is very difficult to move, yet floating in water it becomes much easier to guide. Whatever spiritual practice we do after someone has died has a powerful influence, because the person's consciousness is now more receptive and clear. This receptivity is present even if a person was not interested in spirituality during life or if he died in a confused state.

One friend told me of a near-death experience connected to a massive car accident on a major highway. A man in this accident sustained multiple fractures and major damage to internal organs, and clinically died. He felt his consciousness rise above his body and was able to survey the accident scene below. Traffic had come to a complete stop behind the accident, while emergency vehicles with their lights and sirens whizzed past.

Unable to see the accident, but surmising that it must have been quite serious, a woman whose car was now at a standstill down the freeway began to pray. The consciousness of the man who had clinically died was immediately attracted to her prayer, and found it gave him strength. Eventually, the emergency crews were able to resuscitate him; upon reentering his body he experienced unimaginable pain. After many months of surgery and rehabilitation, he was finally able to leave the hospital.

Soon after, grateful for her prayers and thankful that he was still alive, he went to the woman's home to thank her. She was surprised, as she didn't remember doing anything special. Besides, how did he know she prayed for him? And how did he find her again? Feeling the love and positive power of her prayer when his consciousness was above the accident scene, he was so grateful for her compassion that in order to thank her later, he had noticed and remembered her license plate number!

The teachings make us realize that if we love and sincerely desire to help someone who has died, there is much we can do. Every thought or spiritual practice we offer can influence the person's consciousness in a positive way. It can release him from potential suffering in the bardo, or help him on his path toward liberation. The point, then, isn't to wonder and worry—"Is my loved one suffering?"—but to realize that *we are uniquely positioned to help the person who died with our spiritual practice right now.*

Spiritual Care After Death

The supreme support for a person who has just died is the depth of our own spiritual practice and the strength of our positive, compassionate intention. If through our practice we are familiar with the nature of mind and can rest undistractedly in that state, then meditating on behalf of our deceased friend will "show" him the truth of his own nature. As Padmasambhava said:

As soon as our body has separated into mind and matter, in the gap before it has been encased once again in the net of a future body, the mind along with its magical display has no concrete material support. For as long as it lacks such a material basis we are independent and we can recognize. This power to attain stability by just recognizing the nature of mind is like a torch which in one instant can clear away the darkness of eons.[5]

The next most powerful spiritual care we can offer a person who has recently died is our concentrated practice of the Essential Phowa. The Essential Phowa practice has the potential to heal the spirit of a dying person, to help purify the regrets of his life and the suffering of his death, to guide him on his path toward liberation or lead him toward a better rebirth. Therefore, we should do the Essential Phowa practice with deep compassion and devotion, again and again, after a loved one has died:

After arousing your motivation of compassion, visualize your loved one sitting in front of you, and invoke with all your heart the radiant presence of a buddha or Divine Being above his head. On behalf of the other person, ask this Presence to purify the traces of any negative actions, and to release him from any distress or suffering connected with his death.

Visualize that this Presence lovingly sends out tremendous rays of light toward the deceased, blessing and purifying him. Reciting a mantra or short prayer will help effect the purification, which eventually transforms the other person completely into light. His being—body and mind—now rises up and dissolves into the heart of the Divine Presence.

In dedicating this practice or any prayers you offer on behalf of your loved one, think not only of the person you know but of all who have died alone or in great fear, during traumatic circumstances such as famines, disasters, or wars. Extend your compassion to all beings, praying that they all may be purified of the suffering of their life and death, experience happiness and peace, and ultimately attain complete liberation from suffering.

Sharing the Teachings

Someone who has just died may be confused and not know what to do. To share inspiring teachings which introduce the nature of mind or which generate feelings of compassion or devotion can influence his mind in a wholesome way. Even hearing one or two lines of the teachings could change the destiny of or even liberate a person wandering through the bardo states after death.

This is why *The Tibetan Book of the Dead,* or *Bardo Tödrol Chenmo,* means "Great Liberation upon Hearing in the Bardo." Hearing in the bardo a reminder—a teaching or practice which wakes us up to the truth—could clarify everything, could cut through our confusion and suffering the same way a loud bell can awaken us out of a horrific nightmare. If a practitioner is simultaneously resting in the true nature of mind as he or she reads the instruction, the person who has died can read the practitioner's mind and, directly experiencing this profound meditation, be liberated.

The principal instructions in the *Bardo Tödrol* for after death include:

- Remember everything is emptiness—"you" don't exist and therefore cannot be hurt. All phenomena you experience, both tempting and frightening, are only projections of mind. Since "emptiness cannot hurt emptiness," there is nothing to fear.
- Remember your principal spiritual practice and do it fervently now.
- Take refuge in the "Three Jewels"—a Buddhist practice reminding us to rely completely on the Buddha (the guide to liberation), the Dharma (the spiritual path), and the Sangha (spiritual friends and those in the lineage who have attained enlightenment). Tak-

ing refuge in another faith would be to direct our heart and mind toward God, Christ, the Virgin Mary, or whatever for us represents the ultimate source of blessings and protection.

- Call out to the Lord of Compassion, Avalokiteshvara, whose presence and blessing will be there as soon as we think of him. Invoke his name or recite his mantra: *Om Mani Padme Hum Hrih.*
- And above all: "Do not be distracted."

The main body of the text of the *Bardo Tödrol* describes the visions of the Hundred Peaceful and Wrathful Deities, which appear to the consciousness in the second bardo of death, called *dharmata*, the inherent radiance of the nature of mind. These instructions are intended for someone who has trained in this tradition. They serve as a reminder, so that upon hearing the instructions again after death, the consciousness of the practitioner will understand what is happening and will remember what to do to attain liberation. Although it is a profound teaching, I don't recommend reading *The Tibetan Book of the Dead* to a person who lacks a basis of previous training and study in this tradition, as hearing the text might only confuse or irritate him while he is dying.

Dedicating Positive Actions

We can dedicate the merit of positive, life-affirming actions to our loved one who has died. By helping others in trouble, visiting the sick, imprisoned, or dying, offering food, clothing, or shelter, saving the lives of animals about to be killed, taking part in or sponsoring a retreat—whatever positive actions we dedicate for a loved one will actually benefit his karma in that moment, whether he is still in the bardo or has taken a new birth. We become like a proxy for the person who has died.

We can make a donation, or offer part of our inheritance, to a charity or spiritual project in the name of the person who has died, and he or she will receive the benefit of this. A beautiful traditional practice for the dead in all major religions is the offering of light. When you light the candle or lamp, you might say a prayer or have an aspiration: "May this light guide my loved one to the luminous nature of his mind; may it be a guide for him through the bardo."

Doing something actively to benefit others can also relieve a lot of the helplessness the bereaved normally feel, especially after a sudden death.

An American family was vacationing in Italy when tragedy struck: on the roadside, robbers took their money and killed their youngest son. When the boy's body was brought to the local hospital, the parents gave permission for any of their son's organs to be donated to whoever needed them. Even amidst their painful bereavement, they allowed the press to interview them and describe the motivation behind their action. Their son could not be brought back, but maybe his death could have meaning if it could help others to live. Across Italy, many who watched or read these interviews with the parents were touched by their compassion. Since this event, an unprecedented number of Italian people have begun donating organs in response to this courageous gesture of love.

Not only did this compassionate gesture enable the parents to feel that their son did not die in vain, but the positive power of their loving action has also benefited their son. The benefit of their compassion continues to grow as so many others are now inspired to give and receive life at the threshold of death.

Healing the Relationship

Since the deceased can be easily influenced by the actions, words, and thoughts of their family and friends, it is important that survivors be aware of their thoughts and quickly transform any negative emotions with compassion and love. This is also why it is vital that the survivors acknowledge and be willing to heal any past negative feelings they have been carrying in their relationship with the person who has died.

If we reflect on what our loved one needs after death, we realize that any attempts to stay in regular contact with him may only increase his attachment to this life and make it harder for him to go on. Yet if there are old or fresh negative emotions clouding our relationship with him, it is vital that we heal and release this unfinished business, for his sake and ours. When using the Method for Completing Unfinished Business (described in Chapter 7), we imagine the person is once again sitting in front of us, not to hold on to him but with the intention of fully forgiving and letting go of the past. We can conclude the method with the Essential Phowa practice, guiding our loved one toward the ultimate freedom of his true nature.

The Best Time to Practice

The best time to do spiritual practice for someone who has died is right at the moment he exhales his last breath, and regularly afterward. For three and a half days following death, the consciousness may still be within the body. In the Tibetan Buddhist tradition we are encouraged to leave the body undisturbed as much as possible during that period, repeatedly doing the practice of phowa until we have signs that it was effected or that the consciousness has separated from the body.

At the time of death, our spiritual practice can affect the person's mind and heart in an extraordinary way. When we are resting in the vivid presence of the true nature of mind, or invoking the radiant, loving presence of a buddha or Divine Being, we are literally creating a sacred environment for him to die within. Our devoted spiritual practice may become his actual experience at the moment of death. It will make a strong imprint on his mind—and this last imprint is what he will wake up to after death.

Since we may not be by the person's side at the time of death, we can practice each time we visit him as though it were our last visit, and practice again regularly when we learn of his death. For three to four days following the death, do the Essential Phowa intensively (or whatever practice and prayers are recommended for the dead in your spiritual tradition). Whatever you do, practice with a strong intention that the deceased may be released from any attachment to his life, and from any suffering of his death, and that he may unite with the luminosity and all-pervading space of his true nature.

We should also pray and practice for the person in the first forty-nine days after his death, to help liberate his consciousness before he journeys toward rebirth in a new realm of existence. (Rebirth is not always into a human realm; there are six potential realms of existence in which we can be born according to the emotional and mental patterning we have habitually generated.)

Yet the time to concentrate our spiritual practice is in the first twenty-one days, while the consciousness is more associated with this life and is thus easier to guide. We should especially remember to do the Essential Phowa each week following the death, on the same day of the week and hour of the day the person died, as he will briefly reexperience the death at these times, and thus our practice has more potential to help him.

During the period the partner or closest friends of the deceased are still in shock and not feeling the full force of their grief, they can be encouraged to do intensive spiritual practice. This turning toward spiritual practice early on in the bereavement will give them a ground to land on when the deeper pain of their grief begins to surface.

Even if our loved one died a long time ago, he is not beyond help. His karma continues to unfold and can be affected by our sincere practice and through dedicating the merit of our positive actions to him. If he has already been reborn, whatever we dedicate on his behalf will benefit him wherever he is. Our spiritual practice can affect his karma, remove obstacles in his life, and help him progress spiritually. If the person for whom we are practicing has already attained enlightenment, our prayers and practice can assist him in his work of helping others. *Our close connection to those who have been part of our life does not dissolve at death.*

Sometimes the friends or family of a person who died can't relate to a term such as *prayer.* We can encourage them instead to send the deceased person their love, and with their best wishes, to let him go. And even if the person who died had no spiritual beliefs, we will not be offending him when we pray or do spiritual practice for him. Unless it's mixed with grasping—a desire to hold on to him—prayer is not experienced by the deceased as an imposition, but as love.

Karen, a young Englishwoman in extremely critical condition, was scheduled to be rushed into surgery. The surgeon warned Karen's family that she might not survive, and the family in turn contacted other family members to let them know of the crisis. During the surgery Karen clinically died and was resuscitated after a few minutes. She recovered well, and once her strength improved, she traveled to Canada to visit her sister, Jane.

Karen told Jane about her surgery and clinical death, and Jane asked her if she had experienced anything unusual during her few moments of death.

"Yes, and it was very positive and healing for me," Karen said. "I rose up above my body, and felt myself surrounded by a circle of beings who were sending me love in the form of light. When I came back into my body, even though my health was still critical for a while, I felt a deep peace inside whenever I remembered this experience. It was very real, and it stayed with me."

Jane had a flash of recognition. "I don't know if this is related to your experience, but during the hours of your surgery I asked a group of my church members to sit in a circle with me and we prayed together for you during that time."

Sincere prayers which are offered for the "highest good" for our loved one can bring him protection, blessings, and grace, whether he lives or dies.

Practice Strongly and Meaningfully

We don't really know if our loved one is suffering or not after he has died, so just to be sure, we can practice regularly and intensively for him or her, as though everything depended on it. In a sense, our potent and committed practice is like a "spiritual 911," which has the potential to rescue someone in the bardo from great distress. The teachings say that at such times the buddhas or enlightened beings come even more quickly. As soon as we invoke them, their presence is there, and our loved one in need immediately receives their help.

When they think of the dead or pass by a place where someone died, Tibetans immediately recite the mantra of the Lord of Compassion, Avalokiteshvara: *Om Mani Padme Hum Hrih*. The mantra actually invokes the presence of this Buddha, and the radiance of his wisdom and compassion. When we say the mantra we are bringing this very sacred and compassionate presence into the mind and heart of the person for whom we are practicing, which can help to dissolve his suffering.

The traditional teachings say that our crying and weeping, especially right at the time of death, may cause anguish for the person who is dying and may hold him back. This is why it is crucial for families to come to terms with the death, share their tears and good-byes, so that the moment of death is peaceful. During bereavement, however, it is natural and even important that we feel our grief and allow ourselves to weep. *The problem is our attachment, not our tears.* As we grieve, then, it is important to continue letting go with love. As the poet Mary Oliver wrote:

> . . . To live in this world
>
> you must be able
> to do three things:
> to love what is mortal;
> to hold it
>
> against your bones knowing
> your own life depends on it;
> and, when the time comes to let it go,
> to let it go.[6]

Sudden Death and Suicide

When a loved one dies in a sudden or violent way, or through taking his or her own life, our own suffering afterward is immense. We feel cut off from any possibility of healing or concluding our relationship. We imagine the person dying in great pain or emotional distress, without support or love, and we feel helpless to do anything about it now. Sometimes we have intense feelings of guilt and panic, as if we should have somehow prevented the death.

Even if someone experienced pain before a violent or sudden end, all physical pain is finished at death. Many who have had near-death experiences survived a sudden or accidental death, and although their body appeared to be in a painful state, their consciousness, floating free of the body at death, experienced no physical pain.

After a three-year-old boy was killed by a car, his parents stayed with his body in the emergency room, holding him and adjusting to their shock, even bathing his body. Before the body was to be cremated three days later, friends encouraged the parents to go to the mortuary and see their son's body one more time. Meg, the mother, said, "I cannot tell you how important it was for us to see the body a few days after our son's death. I could only remember his body at the time of his death, and I kept imagining that he was still suffering and in pain. But when I saw his body three days later, it was very clear that this was an empty shell, and my son was no longer there. He was free of the pain of his death, so my mind could be free of that memory also."

The Spiritual Dimension of Bereavement

One of the most disrupting and painful types of sudden death we can experience is the suicide of a friend or family member. Words cannot describe the intensity and total upheaval that survivors of suicide experience. Survivors may feel a wide range of intense and conflicted emotions: frustration, rejection, guilt, sadness, hopelessness, and anger. While all of these feelings are natural after a suicide, they are compounded by the survivors' fear—or experience—of the judgment of others, or of their own feelings of self-blame.

Thus it will take a lot of time and compassionate understanding to face and work through these intense responses to the death. Express your painful feelings with the support of good friends or a therapist. As you begin to acknowledge and release your pain, keep in your heart a motivation that, by doing so, both you and your deceased loved one may be completely freed of all past patterns of suffering. The practices of Tonglen and Essential Phowa can be especially effective in gradually purifying the suffering and pain for everyone connected with a suicide.

We must never judge someone who committed suicide; we simply cannot fathom the depth of suffering, loneliness, and despair he must have felt to take his own life. Still, by reflecting on our loved one's potential past and present suffering, we open our heart to him with great compassion, forgiveness, and love—*because that is what he needs from us now.*

Someone taking his or her life wants to be free of intense suffering, an understandable intention. He may not have found any other way out. The teachings say that the suffering in our mind and heart does not cease after we die, and in fact may intensify in the bardo, leaving us even more helpless to become free of it. So suicide does not automatically free a person from the suffering in life he was hoping to escape.

Although the person who took his life may have felt trapped and without options, we who survive him are not trapped. We may not have been able to reach or even allowed to help our loved one before he committed suicide; yet we can turn the depth of our regret and the energy of our compassion into committed spiritual practice on his behalf. Instead of dwelling on the past, or getting stuck in destructive emotions, we can concentrate all the energy of our mind and heart into what we can do now for our loved one.

EMOTIONAL SUFFERING AFTER DEATH

Although physical pain ends at death, a person's emotional pain may still continue, and he may feel as much anguish at being suddenly pulled out of his life as we feel in losing him. And, like us who survive him, the person who died unexpectedly may be keenly aware of his unfinished business or regrets, which he feels helpless to communicate or resolve. No matter how difficult our former relationship was, we can reflect that our loved one may be in extreme circumstances now, and will be intensely interested in dissolving old misunderstandings and grudges. Thus the "best part" of that person will be looking toward us for forgiveness and reconciliation.

Whatever we couldn't express before our loved one died, we can still express after his death: asking for forgiveness for that last fight, expressing our gratitude and our love one more time, saying good-bye and wishing him well. Some bereaved people verbalize these final messages when they privately view the body, or at the graveside, or while looking at a photo of the deceased. Expressing our forgiveness and love out loud can have a very healing effect.

If our unfinished business after a sudden death is especially heavy, we can and should seek out help. We don't have the resources to cope with such extreme suffering, which may far exceed anything we have learned to cope with previously. Now is not the kind of situation in which we can "go it alone." I believe it is possible to heal and finish with any pain in our former relationships, and it is vital to seek out the right kind of support—from support groups or counselors trained in grief therapy—so that we feel safe to do so.

Survivors of a sudden death can torment themselves with a belief that they could have prevented the death, an experience depicted well in the book and film *Ordinary People,* in which two teenage brothers had a boating accident and only one survived. Like the surviving brother, many of us think unrealistically that we could have circumvented tragedy or death for our loved ones. Our intense experience of helplessness after a sudden death may be projected as anger and blame toward whoever we think is responsible. Parents especially suffer when their child dies, often secretly blaming each other for the child's death. This sort of anger is misplaced and can become very destructive; in fact, many marriages fall apart after such a high grief death.

Other survivors may turn this piercing blame inward, and consequently suffer from chronic depression, increased ill health, or suicidal feelings. Thus it is vital that survivors of a sudden death seek out the right kind of support.

PURIFYING THE SUFFERING
OF A SUDDEN DEATH

After a sudden death, we should bring every ounce of our will and compassion into our meditation or prayers to purify the person of any possible suffering at the time of his death, enabling him to release his attachment to this life and help him in his journey toward attaining liberation. If possible, we can do the Essential Phowa at the place where the person died, or visualize the person at that place when we practice. We should consider that the buddha or Divine Being we've invoked is actually present, and then fervently request his or her compassion and blessing on behalf of our loved one.

Along with our own intensive practice after a loved one dies suddenly, in the Tibetan Buddhist tradition we often ask an accomplished spiritual master to practice for our loved one as well. Through the compassion and power of their spiritual realization, the master can do specific meditations and rituals to help purify, bless, and liberate the person's consciousness.

Yet our own practice for the dying person should not be discounted. Since we who are friends or family have a close bond with the person who died, the intensity of our love and the strength and sincerity of our intention give our practice and prayers an added power.

The best bereavement, then, is when loved ones are doing spiritual practice. This is the finest expression of our love for the person who died, and it will also help us to release our painful attachment and heal our grief more swiftly. As we do the Essential Phowa or any other prayer or practice for the person who died, we can also pray for ourselves, that we might become more and more free of suffering and open to the wisdom and compassion of our true nature.

By generating deeper levels of compassion, extending forgiveness toward ourselves and others, and engaging in positive actions and spiritual practice after a loved one dies, we will find that our bereavement can set us firmly on a spiritual path and enable us to connect more confidently and deeply with the innermost essence of our being—that fundamental goodness which illuminates and pervades our entire life. Experiencing loss in this way can purify and transform our entire relationship to life.

Never Lose Heart

Having a child disappear or die; surviving the horrors of war; being struck down in the middle of life by a serious illness; hearing about the violent death of a friend; losing many people we love in a short period of time—if you are in the midst of any such catastrophe, you may wonder if God has completely abandoned you. Faced with utter desolation and great pain, you may feel bereft of love or hope. There are three things I have learned that can help us get through such a "dark night of the soul." First, find an anchor—at least one memory of love to connect with again and again; second, have the humility and courage to ask one other person to help you; and finally, pray for grace.

To help you nurture the seeds of love and joy within, you can turn to the Loving Kindness Meditation and the compassion practices described in Chapter 6, or explore the following meditation practice for healing your heart:

Invoke in the sky in front of you the radiant presence of a buddha or Divine Being for whom you feel a devotion. Consider that this Presence embodies the wisdom and infinite compassion and love of all enlightened beings, saints, and masters. Feel this presence is *truly there,* in the space in front of you.

Opening yourself, acknowledge to this Presence all your suffering, pain, loneliness, and despair, and really ask for help from the depth of your heart. If tears come, let them flow—allow your sadness its natural expression.

Consider that this loving Presence is truly there for you, listening and understanding you completely, like a trustworthy friend. Imagine this enlightened being responding and sending tremendous rays of light toward you, filling you with his or her love, compassion, and wisdom. Visualize that this light flows into you in the form of golden nectar, filling your heart and transforming all your suffering into bliss. As you visualize this nectar coming into you, recite a mantra or prayer to help you feel even more receptive to the blessings and love filling your heart.

Feel this nectar dissolving your loneliness, tension, fears, and attachments, bringing you unconditional acceptance and love, and filling you with protective blessings and grace. Let your tears flow and wash away any harsh self-judgment, any feelings of isolation or unworthiness.

You are connected, you are loved. The radiant heart and mind within you is always good, always whole, always capable of giving and receiving love. As your sorrow is transformed into bliss, allow the source of wisdom and love—your bodhicitta—to shine out even more brilliantly as a universal and infinite compassion toward all beings.

Another image for the transformation of suffering is to meditate on the sacred heart of Jesus, which is surrounded by thorns and yet radiates brilliant light rays of compassion and wisdom toward all beings.

We don't know how or when grace will arrive. Keep nurturing any memory of love you have, pray for courage and wisdom to grow within you, and open yourself fully, asking for blessings and love to fill your heart. Slowly, surprisingly, you will find in ways small or large that the universe supports you even in your deepest grief. As we pass through the challenge of one of life's "big deaths" we have the opportunity to let go of all our ego's baggage and become lighter and more free. As Rabbi Pesach Krauss wrote:

On Yom Kippur, services are completed with a prayer: "Open to us a gate even as the gates are closing." There is always a gate. We just have to find it and never lose heart. We need courage and the insight that life is a gift. We must be grateful for every moment and for blessings, past and present. We must also realize that losses are an integral part of life. We must use these inevitable losses creatively, like rungs on a ladder, to achieve a higher awareness of our perceptions, feelings, emotions, and our humanity.[7]

Chapter 13

UNDERSTANDING CHILDREN'S
VIEWS OF DEATH

As they grow and develop, children encounter death in many guises—the death of an animal by the side of the road, a death they learn of in the news, the loss of a pet, the death of a grandparent—and these afford us opportunities to help them come to understand death as a natural part of life. We do children an invaluable service by helping them understand death, and—from the time they are very young—giving them permission to grieve.

If we have done so, then when someone in their immediate family is dying, our children will not feel there is anything unnatural about death. We can include children in the family's process of facing the death, and find ways they can participate in the day-to-day life of the dying person. Most children fear abandonment far more than death. When they feel part of a loving and supportive family who treat the dying naturally, and share laughter as well as tears, then death will not provoke great fear.

If we attempt to shield a child from death or grief, our attempts will only backfire. When the subject of death is taboo in a home, or when the family refuses to grieve openly, the child nonetheless experiences her own inner grief, as well as a painful emotional distance from parents and siblings who are hiding their natural feelings of sadness. She will then learn to view death as something unnatural and bad, and grief as something to suppress.

If a child carries into adulthood her unresolved grief (often mixed with a child's irrational feelings of guilt after a death), she is likely to have difficulty loving or trusting in future relationships. Subsequent losses will only compound her grief. Many adults who experienced a death in the family during their childhood or teen years are still carrying a burden of unfinished grief and unresolved guilt in their heart.

The Source of Misunderstandings

When a death occurs, children begin to learn and assimilate their parents' understanding of death. Whether parents view death negatively, as something to be avoided at all costs, or naturally, as a necessary aspect of the process of living and loving others, the family's *context* for death will have an impact on the child's *response,* for better or worse.

It's important to be aware of the words we choose when we speak about illness, its treatments, dying, and death. Many words and concepts are new to a child, and if we don't explain them fully, she may panic over what she thinks is happening. When a child sees her aunt laid out in a casket, with fresh cosmetics making her appear as if she were only sleeping, imagine the child's terror when she hears that her aunt will be cremated or buried the next day!

If they don't take time to consider their answers, adults may describe death or its causes in simplistic and inaccurate terms, precipitating strong reactions in a child. When we say that a person "died in his sleep," or died because "God wanted him in heaven," the child may fear that sleep causes death, or become resentful toward God for taking her daddy. Even when adults are honest and expressive about some aspect of illness, dying, or death, they may use words or images that are completely new for the child. Unless explained, this language can also lead to misunderstandings and unnecessary fear.

When my son Donovan was five years old, I brought him to the mortuary with me to view my grandfather's body. My grandfather was peacefully laid out in the casket, but my son refused to look at him. Thinking I understood his fear, I tried to describe how the body of my grandfather did not look hurt or bad, but peaceful. Still he refused to look. I offered to go to the opposite side of the room and hold him on my hip so he could view the body from a distance, but he still said no. Children at that age are naturally curious about death, so I was mystified by his reaction. When we got in the car to leave, I learned what the problem was. Donovan asked, "Did Grandpa have any clothes on?"

UNNECESSARY GUILT

Children are prone to "magical thinking" whenever a death in the family occurs, especially following a sudden death. Perhaps a younger sister is so angry at her brother, she shouts one day that she wishes he would "drop dead." If her brother suddenly falls ill or has an accident, the little girl will hold herself responsible, tormenting herself with guilt and never revealing her imagined culpability.

Prolonged guilt is one of the most painful and unnecessary aspects of a child's unexpressed grief. Young children live in a world which seems a bit magical—circumstances and people appear and disappear all the time without explanation. Life and death must seem to them like starting to assemble a giant jigsaw puzzle. They collect many little pieces each day, trying to fit them into a coherent picture, but instead getting some parts of the puzzle mismatched or incomplete. It could take years before a child gets a certain new piece of the puzzle which corrects an old misunderstanding.

After a child does something wrong, she may be scolded for being "bad," and when punished, she feels pain and sadness, rejection and isolation. Later, when someone in her immediate family dies, a child may experience similar feelings. Yet if family members refuse to speak about the death or express their grief, the child is even more isolated with her feelings and fears. She can easily conclude she is being "punished" and that the death occurred because she did something bad.

Clear and Honest Communication

When someone in the family is facing death, children are very aware of the changed and emotionally charged environment. We need to sit down and spend time with the children, explaining, in a manner that's appropriate to their capacity to understand, what dying and death means. Children need to feel safe to ask questions and to express their fears and feelings again and again.

Since even after our clearest explanations there is room for misunderstanding, we can check how our communication is received by asking a child to repeat back to us what she's heard. When a child seems afraid or distressed, we should always ask directly what she is thinking or feeling, rather than assume that her difficulties are the same as ours.

Children need to learn how others understand death, and that other family members also have confused and sad feelings. We can let children know that they are not alone in having negative thoughts or expressing angry words, while reassuring them that negative thoughts do not have the power to *cause* a person's death.

If a child confesses to feelings of guilt or regret, she can be encouraged to ask forgiveness, to write a letter, or to express her love to someone who is dying or who has died. One five-year-old dictated a letter for her grandfather five days after his death:

"I love you, Grandpa. I wish you didn't die. I have an orange doggie and I brought him to school. His name is Orangey. I love you, Grandpa, and I wish you didn't die. I love you, Grandpa. I got you pretty orange flowers, orange daylilies. I know your grandma's lonely, Grandpa, and, Grandpa, that's too bad you died and I wish you didn't. Grandpa, every single day I'm gonna get you some flowers 'cause I love you. I'm gonna draw you a happy face."

Include Children in the Life of the Dying Person

When a family member is dying, allow children to participate in his life or his care. They can bring a meal to the room, give a painting they have made, rub lotion on his hands, or just sit on the bed and tell a story. When a child visits someone who is very ill, pick the right time of day when the child's energy is calmer. Children love to feel they can *do* something, so when they are allowed to make gifts for the dying, are encouraged to write or dictate letters, or offer their prayers each night to him, they feel connected and useful.

Dying and death are not so difficult for children; they suffer most when they feel excluded from the family's process. A young boy was run over by a car while his father and older brother looked on helplessly. The parents rushed to the hospital, but their grievously injured son could not be revived. Weeks later, a grief therapist met with Tommy, the surviving brother. Tommy said he could not make a drawing of the death he had witnessed, so instead he drew a jagged line across a paper to represent the events of that day. In one place on the drawing, the jagged line crossed over itself. The therapist asked, "Was this the hardest part of the day for you?"

"Yes," replied Tommy.

"Was this when you saw your brother hit by the car?"

"No," he said, *"this was the hardest part of the day,* when my parents left me at a neighbor's house and I didn't know what was happening."

Later, this family communicated openly about the death, and shared their conflicted feelings of grief, anger, and guilt. The parents found a way to include Tommy in all that was happening after the death: he drew pictures for his brother on the handmade wooden coffin, he helped plan the funeral service, and went to the ocean with his parents to help scatter his brother's ashes.

Reassurance and Understanding

Children sense and respond to the stress in the atmosphere when adults suppress their feelings. Open expressions of sadness and grief in the family have a releasing and healing effect, giving the child permission to grieve as well. Still, her feelings of insecurity and vulnerability may be exceptionally high. This is why children need extra reassurance, affection, and comfort during their bereavement. Grieving parents may not be able to care for all these needs, so they should ask relatives or friends to plan regular visits or outings with the children to supply this needed support.

When a parent dies, a child needs explicit reassurances that her life and her care will continue. At four years of age, my son seemed not to have this concern when his father died; but when Donovan was seven, we began discussing how both of us could prepare to survive an earthquake. Suddenly he realized—with great anxiety—that I could die unexpectedly. "What will happen to *me?*" Donovan asked. I assured him that neighbors or emergency personnel would locate other members of our family, and that I had already asked Donovan's uncle to be his guardian in the event of my death. It is important for a child to know that his or her parents have made a plan and prepared for their possible death, and that someone the child knows will take care of her.

It's not uncommon for very young children to report seeing or communicating with the deceased person. Instead of denying her perception, we must respect the child's experience and allow her to talk about it, accepting that we don't know everything about death.

Just as adults need to heal and conclude their relationship with the deceased, and offer spiritual support through their meditation and prayers, children can be encouraged to do the same. For most children, regular prayers and simple rituals on behalf of the person who died feel natural and appropriate, and can diminish their feelings of insecurity.

Sometimes a child may seem exceptionally troubled after a death, and she may lack the words to express her feelings or fears. Two ways of exploring a child's inner world are through drawings or play. We can invite her to draw a picture of her home and family, and then ask her what each person in the drawing is doing or feeling. Playing a common family scene with dolls may begin to reveal the source of the child's distress. Simply spending time together, one-on-one, can build a feeling of trust so that the child eventually feels safe asking about or expressing what is bothering her.

Children need our understanding and acceptance when they experience grief. It's important to be aware that their feelings may be different from ours, and that they experience and express their grief in other ways besides sadness and tears. Their responses to death and bereavement will also vary depending on their age and level of exposure to death.

VERY YOUNG CHILDREN'S RESPONSES TO DEATH

Children under the age of four often consider that death is only a temporary state; they may expect the dead person to come back to life. Just as the person has disappeared, he or she may reappear. Thus *before* a cremation or burial takes place, very young children need special clarification about the fact that a person who died no longer has any physical feeling, and therefore cannot feel pain; and reassurance that he or she will not come back to life.

A very young child's principal fear about death is a personal fear of separation or abandonment. Children are frequently left out of events surrounding dying and death and discouraged from attending funerals or memorial services with the rest of the family. I favor an approach that includes children of every age, wherever possible, in each ritual or passage the family experiences, so that spiritually and emotionally they feel included in the full circle of family life.

Remember that small children have a different sense of time than adults. If we tell them someone is going to die, they will think that means within the next few weeks at most. If the dying process is likely to be a long one, we may decide to tell them a person is dying when the time of death is imminent.

A young child's grief does not resemble an adult's feeling of sadness for having lost a relationship. Her grief is expressed largely as a heightened insecurity and vulnerability. Thus a young child may temporarily regress to behavior of a younger age, wanting to take a bottle again or sleep with her parents, or she may act out her emotions in uncontrolled mood swings. Instead of shaming or judging a child's erratic behavior in the weeks and months following a death, we should realize that she is mourning in her own way, and offer her extra attention and reassurance.

It was a beautiful September morning, and Donovan insisted he wanted to go to the beach with his uncle, not to the hospital to see his father. He was four years old, and didn't realize the import of this day. I explained to Donovan that he was going to the hospital to visit his father, only for ten minutes, before going to the beach. And, as his father was dying, I told Donovan that he should really be present when he was with his father, since this might be the last time he saw him. That day in the hospital, Donovan's father gave him a pack of his favorite chewing gum, and this is the only memory of his father he still retains.

After spending a wonderful afternoon at the beach, when his uncle told him it was time to go home, Donovan adamantly refused to get into the car. He was almost hysterical for a half hour, refusing to go home, until finally my brother had to forcefully put him in the car. When my brother told me what happened, we were both mystified by this unusual behavior. Later I realized that Donovan was imagining that when he came home, his father would be dead; and he had acted out his grief, and heightened insecurity and fear, with a temper tantrum.

THE RESPONSE OF FOUR- TO SEVEN-YEAR-OLDS

Children between the ages of four and seven understand that death is a final, permanent state, but they imagine that, given the right conditions, they can personally escape death. They imagine death as an external danger—like a bogeyman or robber—a fearsome intruder who can be outwitted or overcome as in a cartoon show. During this stage of development, children are intensely interested in the physical body and all of the things which happen to it. A child may be full of questions, which she asks repeatedly: What does death look like? How do you die? What happens after someone dies? What *caused* him to die?

Since children this age want to learn how to avoid their own death, many of our honest answers will not reassure them. We can gain insights into a child's unexpressed thoughts and feelings by paying close attention to her stories or dreams, messages expressed in symbolic language.

As he grew up, I would ask my son regularly if he wanted to talk about his father or his father's death. By the time he was six, Donovan regularly asked me how his father died, and after explaining each time that no one knows what causes leukemia, I noticed a certain pattern emerging in his response. After I failed to explain the "cause" of his father's illness and death, Donovan proceeded to describe in vivid detail what he would do if a bank robber broke into our house; in each scenario he heroically trapped or disarmed the intruder. At first I tried to reassure him that a bank robber breaking into our house was highly unlikely, since we had a big dog who barked loudly at strangers, and we had nothing valuable to steal.

One day I realized that Donovan was describing his fear of death symbolically. I encouraged him to draw pictures of these scenes he had imagined, and one of his father in heaven. Once we could see the images and talk about them, his fears abated.

When children between four and seven grieve, they may experience only temporary moments of sadness, and then go back outside to play. Like very young children, four- to seven-year-old children often express their fears and grief in unexpected or distressing behavioral changes: stealing, missing school, bedwetting, increased aggression, or withdrawal from the family. If children are allowed to talk about the death and their feelings, and are given extra attention and reassurance, these temporary behaviors will gradually subside. Teachers and parents need to be educated about children's grief, so they understand the source of these behaviors and find humane alternatives to condemnation or punishment.

OLDER CHILDREN

Children eight years of age and older understand that death is both final and inevitable, and that one day *they* will eventually die.

Their experience of the death of a family member or friend is the poignant sadness of losing a cherished relationship. Right after my husband died, Donovan did not especially feel a painful sadness at his loss. At four years old, he had no expectation that things should be different. But when he was nine years old, I gave Donovan some of his father's belongings, and he began asking me the meaning of certain medals his father had been awarded while serving in the Navy during the Vietnam War. I apologized to Donovan, because I had forgotten the reason for each medal. That is when I first saw him weep for his father, as he said, "I wish my dad were here; he could tell me what these medals were for."

Older children and teens are often angry at the many ways a prolonged illness or a death in the family can disrupt their normal lives or limit their activities. Their frustration is normal, and needs to be acknowledged.

Like an adult, older children and adolescents will mourn the loss of their relationship with the person who died, although their grief will generally be less prolonged if it is not complicated by unfinished business. At this age, it is especially important that children be allowed to share their feelings and sadness with parents and siblings. When they are encouraged to respond to suffering with compassion and prayer, they will feel less isolated and helpless in their mourning.

ADOLESCENTS

Adolescence is the very hardest time in which to experience the grief of a loved one's death. A teenager is suspended between the vulnerability of childhood that she wants to put behind her, and the assumption of maturity and adult responsibility she hopes to earn. Thus she fears that feeling or expressing her deep sadness and pain may return her to the state of childlike vulnerability and dependency.

After the death or loss of a friend or family member, an adolescent will experience extremely high levels of isolation, stress, and painfully disorienting grief. Especially when a parent dies or leaves, a teenager experiences both the loss of a significant person in her life, and also the loss of an intact family, so she is doubly bereft.

If an adolescent lacks a spiritual perspective on life and death, she may consider death to be a destructive, chaotic force that strikes at random. Teenagers are exposed daily to disasters, tragedies, and assassinations in the news, and their personal experiences of death may even include friends dying suddenly in accidents or shootings.

Since death can strike without warning, many adolescents become stuck in anger in their bereavement, and conclude that life is meaningless. They may adopt a nihilistic attitude: "Why should I care, since we're all going to die anyway?" Some may develop a strange fascination with death, engaging in risky behaviors to gain a sense of control over it.

Teenagers are at a high risk for suicide, and even those who don't attempt it have certainly considered it during periods of intense emotional pain, isolation, or stress. Emotions are often magnified during adolescence, and so any grief or emotional distress is felt intensely. A teenager may not yet have learned how to cope with or ease her emotional suffering, and thus suicide may seem to be the only way out.

After suffering a significant loss, if a teen mentions that she is considering suicide, we should take her seriously, and bring her to a mental health professional or crisis center. A suicide threat is often a cry for help, and we must learn to recognize the subtle "cries" that may precede and warn us of a person's inability to bear their suffering alone.

Feelings of anger and guilt are often intense. Especially when a close friend dies in an accident, the teenager may feel guilty for being alive, or angry toward whoever she believes is responsible for the death. If a teen begins to act out her anger in other life-threatening ways, or seems to be turning it inward and becoming chronically depressed, those who love her—her support person, a counselor, or a family member she respects—may have to intervene to help her release her anger so that she can begin to mourn and accept her loss.

A bereaved teenager can expect little emotional support from her peers. If she is lucky, she may have one friend who gives her permission to grieve, but usually her classmates will encourage her to suppress her grief, as it evokes their own uncomfortable feelings of vulnerability. And while yearning for her parent's attention and comfort, the teenager will simultaneously avoid or reject it, by becoming withdrawn, rebellious, or unavailable physically or emotionally.

If she's to get through her grief without self-destructing, and if she cannot turn to her parents, who are also experiencing the painful dislocation of bereavement, it is up to others to help the teen find a support group, counselor, or another adult in her life she trusts. When a close family friend or relative is willing to spend time sharing recreational activities together with her, this may slowly build a trust that will enable the bereaved teen to share her feelings openly. Like anyone experiencing grief, a teenager needs to feel safe to grieve, and have her feelings validated. Rapport is often established not through talking but by sharing enjoyable activities together.

Connecting with nature, physical activity, or artistic expression can channel the heightened energy of grief in a life-affirming way. Teens can be encouraged to plan their own ritual, or dedicate something they are creating to the person who has died.

Grieving adolescents often blame their parents for not relieving their pain. With the smaller heartbreaks of childhood, a parent seemed to reduce the pain magically and make things right within a few days. Now the teen's expectation that her parents can relieve her pain is unrealistic, but she may not fully comprehend this. She is experiencing a deep and painful loss for the first time as any adult would. It will take time, love, and courage to heal.

When a Child Is Dying

There is nothing as painful as losing a child. Parents suffer tremendously on so many levels: wishing they could take their child's place; fearing they have failed at protecting their child; blaming themselves for not giving their child a better life or stronger health; and feeling as though they are losing not only a child, but an integral part of their future.

When parents cannot protect their child from illness and physical pain, they may try to protect her from emotional pain by withholding the truth about her condition and suppressing their grief in her presence. Yet, as we have seen, hiding and pretense cause many more difficulties than they prevent. When a child asks what is wrong and everyone skirts the truth, their secrecy triggers her fear that she has done something wrong and is being punished. A child facing death may fear that her parents will reject her if they know she's dying, so she will pretend along with them that all is well, and hide her true feelings.

An ill or dying child knows, much more than we realize, what is happening to her. She goes through the same emotional process in facing and accepting death as adults do, yet much more quickly. Her suffering will intensify, however, if she is never told she is dying. This is why we must rise to the situation with all the courage and strength we can muster.

As we break the news to a child, we must attune ourselves to her needs and fears, encouraging her to ask questions while responding with clear and well-thought-out answers. Since her principal fears of dying will be of abandonment and pain, we should be prepared to respond to these fears from the beginning. For instance, being hospitalized provokes a very young child's deepest fear—that of being separated from her home and parents. If an ill or dying child is left alone for long periods, she may feel rejected, and worry that her painful illness and death—along with her sense of isolation—are a punishment for having been bad.

Parents could plan ahead and arrange to take turns spending the night in the hospital room, so that their child is not left alone. They can reassure her repeatedly that she has done nothing bad to cause her physical problems. And, whenever possible, in the last weeks of life the parents can solicit the support of a hospice team to enable them to bring their child home to die.

When they are dying, children have the same needs as adults (see Chapter 3). Yet children will also have additional anxieties about the unfamiliar hospital environment and painful medical procedures. A child's heightened fear and frustration is often expressed as angry words, acting out, crying, or complaining. It's important to understand and acknowledge her feelings, yet we should continue to set healthy limits on her behavior.

It is tempting to pamper or spoil an ill or dying child. Occasional gifts may bring temporary joy, but if we respond to the child's every dictate, she will lose her own sense of boundaries, and her siblings will grow increasingly resentful throughout her illness. In truth, what a dying child needs to help her through her difficulties and pain is our genuine communication, affection, and love. If we focus only on giving her material things, we will relinquish our crucial role in helping our child develop and nurture a good heart.

Among the main sources of suffering for children who face death are their parents' strong attachment to them and their parents' blocked emotions and grief. It is vital for parents to seek outside support to help them release their charged emotions, so that they can begin grieving and coming to terms with their eventual loss. When parents try to "go it alone," their emotional pain and attachment can create a powerful inner pressure and blockage, resulting in more suffering for the dying child, as well as for other children in the family and themselves. With support, parents are able to get a wider perspective on what is happening, feel more compassion for themselves, and gain more understanding about their crucial role in loving and supporting their child through the time of dying.

To die with peace of mind, a child needs her parents' comfort, presence, and loving reassurance that it is all right to let go. Giving such reassurance is not easy; it is probably the most painful expression of love imaginable. Yet as we begin releasing our attachment and fear, we may discover what is lasting and true: the real love we have for our child. Although our child will die, as Elisabeth Kübler-Ross reminds us: "Real love doesn't die." This is the task parents are challenged with—to prepare to let go when the time comes, with all their heart, allowing their child to leave freely.

Stephen Levine describes a story that a nurse shared in one of his seminars. An eight-year-old boy had been in a coma for six months, and even after his life support was discontinued, he did not die. Mark's body remained an inert bundle of flesh and wasted away to twenty-five pounds. His appearance was so distressing that his parents could barely visit, and no one could understand why Mark was unable to die.

But one day, the nurse told us, "I spent some very special time with Mark, massaging him and speaking to him and playing music and receiving a sense, almost a communication, that what was keeping him from being able to let go was his concern for his parents' well-being. After work I called his parents and told them of what my experience had been that day, and how I sensed that Mark was holding on because he didn't want to hurt his parents by dying. . . ."

Later in the evening the nurse said she received a phone call from Mark's tearful mother saying, "We went up to the room and played some of his favorite music on the tape recorder you left by the bed and told him that he would be okay if he died and so would we. And the nurse put his thin, thin body in my arms and I was just rocking him back and forth, loving him and telling him we would be okay when all of a sudden there was a stillness in the room and Mark just let go and died in my arms."[1]

OTHER CONCERNS OF DYING CHILDREN

Older children have great difficulty with the physical limitations imposed by their illness. They are jealous of their healthy peers, and chronically frustrated, which can cause them to become more rebellious, complaining, or withdrawn. These feelings are natural, especially if they had been previously active and healthy. They are simultaneously grieving the loss of their relationships, and will suffer if friends stop coming by and sharing their lives. And as they become more dependent on others, and lose control of bodily functions in the process of dying, older children may struggle with feelings of shame.

Dying adolescents suffer from the awareness that they are dying before enjoying the longed-for freedom and promise of adulthood and the fear that their life, their suffering and dying are meaningless. The dying teen will grieve her lost future, the loss of her former way of life, friends who have fallen by the wayside, and the anticipated loss of everyone else in her life. Her grief is normal and should be validated. Even if she is never told she is dying, an adolescent will have these painful feelings but they will seem even worse if she senses that it is unsafe to begin expressing them.

An older child or teenager can be encouraged to apply herself to one or all of the Four Tasks of Living and Dying, enabling her to feel she has accomplished something even in her short life and given her dying a greater meaning.

Children of all ages need encouragement to find symbols or images of hope from their own religious tradition that will help them transcend their suffering and death. If we propose positive, spiritual responses to suffering such as devotion, taking refuge, or compassion, we may discover that our children are receptive vessels for this vital form of support. Some children may want to learn from their parents how to rely on prayer or psalms, or be interested in learning meditations such as Tonglen or Essential Phowa. Others may want simply to visualize a loving, radiant, and powerful image of God, Buddha, or a Divine Presence they can invoke and call out to for help.

Preparing for the death, grieving together, and healing relationships can release painful burdens and contribute to a loving atmosphere of peace and letting go at the time of death. And when parents share their living spiritual tradition with their children, when they rely on their faith and spiritual practice in times of crises, their children will also learn to appreciate the larger spiritual perspective that embraces the whole of life and death. They will know without a doubt that no matter what happens, they are not alone. There is no greater gift we can give our children.

Chapter 14

CAREGIVING AS SPIRITUAL PRACTICE

Marisa, a vibrant and pretty doctor in her mid-thirties, asked me how to deal with an angry, demanding patient. I suggested that she try one of the Buddhist meditations she had learned, especially before going into the patient's room.

Marisa took time to do the compassion practices of Seeing the Other as Another You and Exchanging Places (described in Chapter 7). "When I exchanged places with my patient, suddenly I was this old woman who had constant pain, who felt ugly, helpless, and unwanted," recalled Marisa. "And when I saw this attractive young doctor coming into my room full of smiles, I hated her more than anything."

The next time Marisa went into her patient's room, she wasn't smiling cheerfully. Feeling genuine understanding and love for the old woman, Marisa was able to meet her gaze, even while the woman continued to scream in anger at her.

"I knew just how she felt. In my heart, I told her that I understood her anger, and that it was all right. She continued to be demanding, but after she saw I wasn't reacting anymore, her tone grew quieter. When I left her room and walked down the corridor, my mind was peaceful and centered as though the meditation was still continuing."

I asked Marisa what happened when she went to see the next patient. "That man was very sweet and kind, and immediately I reacted with pleasure." She laughed. "That's when I realized I had lost my equanimity, and how important it is to keep my meditation going in every situation, whether it is difficult or pleasant."

Working with the elderly, ill, or dying is a demanding vocation. It's very difficult to witness other people's suffering when you cannot relieve all of their emotional or physical pain. And when you grow close to your patients and they die, you feel the added burden of each new grief. Besides the suffering you must face and respond to in your patients, you experience the changes, struggles, and pressures of your personal life as well. You may have to deal with staff conflicts, or decide how to respond when ordered to do something you feel is not in a patient's best interests. Even if you have a committed spiritual practice, you may feel that your work environment draws you back into a fearful or defensive attitude. You may be putting in long hours, and the work may be physically and emotionally exhausting.

Don't lose heart. As a caregiver, I invite you to consider that *your place of work is your shrine,* your place of meditation or prayer. You may have compartmentalized parts of your life—physical, emotional, spiritual, and professional—and relegated them to different times of the day. The vision presented in this book is more integrated and profound. The path of life is already a journey toward death, and once you decide to make that journey a spiritual one, then every aspect of life, including your caregiving work, gives a positive momentum to your spiritual path.

Reflecting in your daily meditation on the suffering of all beings, and praying deeply that you might be able to relieve their suffering, is one way of training the mind in compassion. And, as a professional or volunteer caregiver, you are also actively expressing compassion by *doing* something for those in your care. Thus everything you do at work—even the personal difficulties you endure—has more merit than meditation or prayer alone. *Your work is a very potent form of spiritual practice.*

How can you keep your meditation practice alive in a busy hospital or nursing home when there is nothing in the environment to support it? Training yourself daily to rely on the Three Noble Principles—establishing a motivation of profound compassion; sustaining the attitude of nongrasping; and sealing the practice through dedication—will shift your perspective on everything you encounter at work. The next step is to sustain your effort until your compassionate motivation and your spiritual practice become part of your flesh and bones. Once you have changed the attitude in your mind and heart, then no matter how distressing your work environment, you can be happy.

ESTABLISHING A MOTIVATION OF
PROFOUND COMPASSION

Generating a deep compassion makes our spiritual practice and prayers more potent in helping those in distress. Before beginning your daily meditation, spend some time reflecting on the suffering in the world or on your friends' or patients' suffering, and as their suffering touches and opens your heart, let your compassion grow even deeper and your intention to help even stronger. Dedicate your meditation and prayers to those who are suffering terribly. You could even imagine that they are gathered around and practicing with you, and that you are all receiving the blessings together.

Each day, then, reestablish your sacred intention for your spiritual path and your entire life: recognizing the many degrees of suffering that all beings everywhere experience, pray that they all may have happiness and become free of suffering, and that all attain liberation. Inspired with this intention, you might eventually decide that the best way you could benefit others and free them from suffering is to dedicate your life to attaining enlightenment.

You might pray: "May everything I do today be beneficial. Through remembering my spiritual practice throughout the day, may I gain more confidence in the wisdom and compassion of my true nature. And through this realization, may every contact I have with others bring us both benefit, relieving suffering, bringing healing and happiness, and furthering us along the path to freedom. May kindness and wisdom increase in the world, and through my efforts today, may I contribute to the betterment of life for all. *Bless me into usefulness.*"

Arousing this motivation at work creates a sacred atmosphere for all our activities. When difficulties arise, we will be able to welcome them as reminders to transform our perspective once again. Instead of always trying to change others or judge them, we will learn how to see the pain and fear behind their actions and generate compassion for them.

Of course, sometimes we make mistakes. In caring for others we may get feedback that we have said or done something unhelpful. Or we may feel regret or frustration when forced to do something we don't agree with. Instead of getting lost in our reactions, we must remember our motivation—to be of immediate and ultimate service to all beings—since it is the motivation behind our actions that counts. As soon as we recognize our error, we can ask for forgiveness, let go of the mistake, and train ourselves in keeping our heart and mind pure. Each day we can resolve to do better and become more aware, more compassionate, and more skillful.

SUSTAINING THE ATTITUDE OF NONGRASPING

Next, resolve to sustain the view of your true nature throughout your day. From the vast openness and clarity of your innermost essence, an unconditional love and compassion radiates toward all beings; allow this to resonate in your being as long as possible after meditating. Even if you do not directly connect with the nature of mind in meditation, by simply *trusting* it is there you can release your grasping and become more at ease with yourself. When you shift your perspective even a little, you bring a quality of letting go and letting be—a "nonstick" mind—to your workplace.

You may have noticed how easy it is to fixate on one problem at work, leading you to feel tense, angry, or upset. Once you grasp on to and solidify the problem, then it becomes your whole reality, and you can no longer be present for anyone else. When you are tense, you make even more mistakes, and have more misunderstandings and communication problems. Instead, contemplate Chagdud Rinpoche's advice:

Always recognize the dreamlike qualities of life and reduce attachment and aversion. Practice good-heartedness toward all beings. Be loving and compassionate, no matter what others do to you. What they will do will not matter so much when you see it as a dream. The trick is to have positive intention during the dream. This is the essential point. This is true spirituality.[1]

When you recognize that everything is impermanent, you take things a bit more lightly, with more humor. Resolve that whenever you find yourself falling back into emotional, grasping patterns, you will recall your fundamental skylike nature and allow changes to pass through you.

This is also how you can begin breaking down the artificial division between your spiritual practice and daily work. Allow the inspiration and spacious generosity of your meditation to transform your perception of those you meet; allow it to inform your choices and responses so that your life becomes a continuous and active expression of your deepest motivation.

SEALING THE PRACTICE THROUGH DEDICATION

As you conclude your practice each day, reflect on the gift you have received: a spiritual path which can free you from suffering. With a deep wish that your patients, friends, and family and all other beings become free as well, dedicate your practice and everything you do, all of your work and even your difficulties, to the benefit of all beings. Dedicating at the end of each workday ensures that the goodness of what you've done is never lost.

Through spiritual training, you are reducing your selfishness and territoriality. After you've done something good, however, your ego may react: "Wasn't that a great and noble thing! I hope someone will notice and thank me for it!" To free yourself of this subtle grasping, think instead: "May every kindness I do be unseen by others. May I share with all others the merit and positive power of my practice and my work, so that everyone enjoys good circumstances in their life and is free of suffering. May all my positive efforts contribute to the enlightenment of all beings."

Integrating Meditation with Daily Life

The deep peace of our true nature isn't something to glimpse momentarily while meditating and then forget. We must keep coming back to the pure presence and natural simplicity of our being until our mind has stabilized in this state. Thus, along with learning to meditate, it's necessary to train in these five points for integrating meditation and life:

- Practice meditation every day.
- Extend the meditation into your next activity.
- Use every experience as a reminder of the practice.
- Practice frequently throughout the day.
- Make your spiritual development a priority.

PRACTICE MEDITATION EVERY DAY

To say "My life is my spiritual practice" is not enough. Having a good heart and wishing to help others is a wonderful beginning, yet without meditation we will still live and relate in a dualistic way, lost in the busyness of life, with our old habits entrenched.

A daily meditation practice connects us with our wisdom nature again and again, so that our familiarity and confidence deepen. Meditation can inspire our heart and mind with profound love and compassion; and it is this that we bring into the room of someone suffering and dying. Isn't this the kind of caregiver each of us wants when we ourselves are dying?

Because of severe complications arising from his leukemia, my husband was frequently hospitalized in the first months of his illness. Sometimes that hospitalization felt like an open-ended prison sentence, stretching out until it became three weeks out of each month. Lyttle hated being in the hospital, and one day in particular he was severely depressed.

The man in the room next to Lyttle was exuberant and high-spirited. We could hear his loud voice as he spoke on the phone and the crashing of soda cans against the wall as he tried to make baskets into the trash can. Even though he was alone most of the time, it always sounded as if a party was going on in his room.

During the afternoon I used the bathroom that adjoined both hospital rooms, and I could hear the nurse in the other man's room bantering with him energetically, joking and teasing him. Lyttle and I were close with this nurse, yet I thought: She is not going to be in the right mood for my husband today.

As the nurse entered Lyttle's room a few minutes later, I saw that she was completely present and clear, aware of his sadness and adjusting her way of being to his needs.

The Buddhist teachings emphasize learning to become completely open, infinitely flexible, letting go of each past moment in order to be fully present and aware in the current moment. Meditation helps us come home to ourselves, dissolving our concepts and agendas so we can be appropriate and present with those who are suffering in a deep and meaningful way.

EXTEND THE MEDITATION INTO
YOUR NEXT ACTIVITY

The practice of meditation is not as important as the state of mind we are in when we conclude it. It's important to plan a peaceful transition from our practice into our next activity. If possible, choose one that facilitates continued mindfulness and awareness: listening to music, cleaning, eating a meal in silence, or going for a walk.

Sometimes your meditation practice seems to be nothing more than a period of complete distraction, and you may feel discouraged. Your mind was everywhere, thoughts and emotions ran riot, and you couldn't concentrate on the object of your meditation beyond the first few seconds. Don't judge your practice as either good or bad, and don't give up. You are training in something new, and old habits may come back stronger for a while. With time, discipline, and consistent practice, meditation will help your mind to release those distracting thoughts and emotions, and resume its essential bliss and clarity.

As Sogyal Rinpoche writes: "In the stillness and silence of meditation, we glimpse and return to that deep inner nature that we have so long ago lost sight of amid the busyness and distraction of our minds."[2] *Sometimes the real state of meditation may be revealed when you get up from your cushion or chair.* But if you jump up, "change gears," and rush off, you will miss it!

USE EVERY EXPERIENCE AS A
REMINDER OF THE PRACTICE

Bring the clear awareness of your true nature to the way you perceive and relate to others. From that perspective, every moment is the flow of meditation, every activity is prayer, everyone you meet is a potential buddha, worthy of respect. Train yourself to relate to each person with pure perception and a good heart, always from the intention of benefiting others. Mother Teresa describes seeing each of her dying patients as "Christ in his most distressing disguise"; for her, physically caring for their bodies is caring for the suffering and dying body of Jesus Christ.

Throughout the day, you can find many creative ways to integrate your activities and your spiritual practice:

- On waking, reflect with gratitude on the kindness you have received.
- Instead of gossiping, speak well of other people.
- Instead of cursing someone, send them your blessing.
- When walking, consider you are walking toward the truth.
- When preparing to eat, reflect with gratitude on all those whose sacrifice brought you the food; then mentally offer your meal and your enjoyment of it to all enlightened beings.
- When cleaning, imagine you are cleaning your negative habits.
- When putting on clean clothes, or receiving something new, offer your enjoyment.
- When you see someone happy, rejoice with them.
- When you see someone suffering, instead of turning away in fear, turn toward them in love, and give what you can in that moment.

When you are suffering physical or emotional pain, instead of letting this become an obstacle, make your difficulties a strong incentive to turn your heart and mind back to the practice. Thus everything you do, and every circumstance you encounter, can be joined with your spiritual path. As Dilgo Khyentse Rinpoche writes:

> The obstacles that can arise from both good and bad circumstances should never deter us or dominate us. We should be like the earth, which supports all living beings, without regard to distinctions of good or bad, favorable or unfavorable. The earth simply abides.[3]

PRACTICE FREQUENTLY THROUGHOUT THE DAY

Look for opportunities to bring your heart and mind back to your spiritual practice—resting in meditation, reflecting on gratitude or devotion, arousing compassion, or reciting short prayers or a mantra—even if only for a few moments at a time. Many frequent sessions of practice, scattered throughout the day, will have a greater impact on your mind and way of being than one longer session.

Look for little gaps in the day when your mind and heart are free to practice—while you're waiting on the phone, traveling to and from work, walking down a long hallway, breaks when you can go outside and walk in silence. Without formally meditating, you may find sometimes that you are in a state of natural ease and inspired openness; take a few minutes then to sustain that naturally arising clarity and presence.

Slowly you will find that your meditation practice inspires your life and your life inspires your meditation. If you practice continually throughout the day in formal and informal ways, then, as Sogyal Rinpoche says, the false separation between spiritual practice and daily life will dissolve, and "you will find yourself increasingly in your natural pure presence, without distraction."[4]

MAKE YOUR SPIRITUAL DEVELOPMENT A PRIORITY

Discipline means having the courage and quiet determination to remember always what is most important in life. And then to simplify our life, so we can do it. If we truly want to evolve spiritually, it is necessary to decide that spiritual practice and study will be the main focus of our life.

If you want to learn any skill, you have to make a plan, don't you? You must arrange to go to classes, schedule time in your appointment calendar, and organize your life so you can study and practice again and again. Look at all the appointments that are presently in your calendar and ask yourself: Will any of these activities help me when I die? *What is the most important thing, and how much time am I giving to it?*

To really change, to really nurture and develop confidence in our true nature, we must begin listening to and hearing the teachings of our spiritual path; reflecting on them until they become part of our being; and practicing meditation regularly and sometimes intensively, applying what we've studied to our entire way of life. We should set aside special periods of retreat throughout the year to concentrate on spiritual practice and study.

It's possible to design regular weeklong "retreats in life," where, besides going to work each day, we devote all our remaining free time to practice and study. If we want to evolve toward our highest potential and prepare in the most comprehensive way for death, we must, as His Holiness the Dalai Lama says, "make a plan for enlightenment."

A bird needs two wings in order to fly. By making spiritual study and practice priorities in our life, we will develop the two wings that will help us most in our caregiving work: skillful means and wisdom.

Integrating the Essential Phowa Practice

There are two reasons the Essential Phowa can bring invaluable spiritual support to those who suffer: first, the dire circumstances the person is in, and second, the unlimited ability of enlightened beings to bring their compassion and blessings to the person for whom we are praying. Those of us who practice in the Nyingma tradition invoke the presence and blessings of Padmasambhava, seeing him as the embodiment of the perfect wisdom and limitless compassion and power of all enlightened beings, buddhas, and lineage masters. Padmasambhava is considered to be a very special and powerful buddha for this time, whose presence is immediately available to bring spiritual support to those facing great suffering, disasters, or death.

Even though enlightened beings are present as soon as we invoke them, the strength of their presence and blessings can be heightened by the strength of our genuine devotion. Whichever enlightened presence you choose to invoke, it's important to establish a relationship of openness, gratitude, longing, and respect, and to pray sincerely, from the depths of your being, for the purifying and empowering blessings streaming from this Presence to fully enter you and awaken your wisdom nature.

After concluding your practice of Essential Phowa, to help you sustain the clarity and presence of pure awareness throughout the day, visualize that this Divine Presence is always in the sky in front of you and is above the head or in the heart of everyone you meet. Then your every action, word, or thought becomes a living prayer, a continual expression of devotion and wisdom.

If we generate such a deep and sincere devotion in our daily spiritual practice, then when we do the Essential Phowa for a person who is suffering or dying, we will be able to invoke this Divine

Presence and bring his or her compassionate blessings even more powerfully to the person in distress.

Those who work in emergency rooms have asked me: "How can I offer spiritual care for people who are dying, in the midst of a medical crisis? I am doing my best to save one person's life, but right after they die I have to rush over and work on the next patient. Even when it's not so busy, if we've failed to save a person's life, everyone just walks away from the body."

When you train in medicine, especially emergency resuscitation, you learn and repeatedly practice many lifesaving techniques, so that in a crisis situation you'll be able to act without thinking, reflexively. You need to train in your spiritual practice the same way, so you can bring its benefits spontaneously to every situation of work and life. Even the emergency room is your meditation shrine.

Practice the Essential Phowa every day before going to work, with a strong compassionate intention that your practice may truly benefit and help all those who suffer. At the conclusion of the practice, dissolve your being into the Buddha, Christ, or whichever enlightened being you have invoked, and once again enter your daily activities. Bring this Divine Presence with you into the hospital or your workplace, continually invoking and praying to the Presence as you care for your patients or clients.

Then, if your patient is on the edge of life and death, pray fervently and ask the Divine Presence to help him or her. Visualize that the Divine Presence or Buddha shines powerful light rays of compassion and blessing onto your patient, purifying any fear or anguish in his heart and mind. Pray that, if possible, he may be healed and survive this crisis. If he dies in spite of your efforts to save him, then visualize his consciousness in the form of a small sphere of light flashing out from his body like a shooting star and dissolving completely into the heart and mind of the Divine Presence. After coming home from work, take the time to do the Essential Phowa practice in a more complete way for all the patients you attended during the day.

David, an emergency-room doctor in a major city hospital, told me how stressful his job used to be, and how his experience has changed since he began integrating his spiritual practice at work.

"Families panic at the time of death, call 911, and bring their loved one to the emergency room to die. When they arrive, they're not prepared in any way for what is about to happen. What I see is enormous fear, confusion, anxiety, and helplessness. The way I used to deal with the situation was through detachment. Outside of doing my best for the patient, I figured there was no way I could impact their situation at all.

"Telling a family that their loved one has died or is dying was one of the things I hated most about my job. Often the family reacted to me with hostility and anger. The work was fearful and unpleasant for me.

"Since I started doing spiritual practice in the emergency room, I've watched the person's expression in the final few minutes of life change to one of acceptance, sometimes even a gentle smile, replacing the fear and anxiety. It looks like an opening, a release. Then, when I have to go and tell a family that their loved one has died, I notice an enormous difference in their reaction. Family members often will thank me and even come up and hug me. This new experience I'm having since doing my spiritual practice in the hospital has transformed my life and my medical practice."

A Different Perspective on Burnout

There are three common sources of burnout: loss of perspective; an accumulation of grief and unfinished business; and exhaustion and stress.

From the point of view of your ordinary mind and ego, burnout is a real danger. But from the perspective of your true nature, it is not possible to get burned out giving to others. Your compassionate essence is like the sun—the more you radiate generosity, the more powerful your connection with the source of wisdom becomes. Instead of draining you, the expression of this transcendent compassion recharges you so that you have even more to give. The question is: Which perspective are you usually coming from?

For professionals or loved ones caring for the dying, the Four Tasks of Living and Dying are not optional. We won't be able to support another person in healing his grief and unfinished business if we have not acknowledged and released our own. Preparing meaningfully for our death will give us invaluable insights and the confidence to work lovingly and appropriately with others who are suffering. The artificial distinction between "helper" and "helped" will break down when we see that both of us are in the same boat—facing death in every moment.

TONGLEN FOR CAREGIVERS

The Tonglen practice is especially relevant for caregivers; it can help you relate to suffering in an entirely new way. When you work with people suffering, you generally feel both fear and hope—you are afraid to have your patients' illness or pain, and you hope that you can successfully relieve all of their suffering. This perspective leads to frustration and burnout, as you cannot possibly ease every person's suffering, and the fear you feel while witnessing their difficulties only closes down your heart. And when you have aversion toward your patient's suffering, he will sense your fear and your rejection, and it will become even more difficult for him to accept himself and his own condition.

Before you do the Tonglen for Others, you may need to spend time first doing the Loving Kindness and Self-Tonglen meditations each day to open your heart and heal your fears and accumulated grief. Once you have transformed your own emotional pain, doing the Tonglen for Others enables you to accept and love the other person exactly as he is.

Imagine for a moment how a saint or buddha might feel toward our suffering. How does a loving mother feel when seeing her child in great pain? She doesn't reject her child's suffering and turn away; she yearns to take it from him and would wish more than anything to bring him peace of mind. Surely the boundless compassion of an enlightened being toward us would be similar.

Since the true nature of an enlightened being cannot be harmed by suffering, or burned out from giving love, connecting with our wisdom nature will bring us a confident joy in fearlessly "giving and receiving." When we approach the practice with this perspective, it will be more powerful and beneficial to those for whom we practice, as well as ourselves.

Each of the compassion practices described in Chapters 6 and 7 can be integrated with caregiving work exceptionally well. But with the main Tonglen practice, I suggest that you first train in it thoroughly at home, doing the "giving and receiving" with each breath as part of your daily meditation. Once you can practice confidently, then begin to integrate the Tonglen with your care-giving work.

BE KIND TO YOURSELF

Each time you pray for all beings to have happiness and be free of suffering, remember to include yourself! When you offer to serve others, you must also be willing to care for and nurture yourself so that you are able to give consistently. Becoming exhausted and stressed as a result of thinking you are indispensable is not exercising compassion. Being out of touch with your body and failing to take care of yourself are another aspect of your ego. It's important to periodically "check in" with yourself and determine whether you are making yourself busy helping others in order to avoid facing your own difficulties and inner pain.

If you realize this is happening, be creative in working with yourself. You might read passages from spiritual teachings, or listen to tapes which open your mind and heart. If your emotional pain has left you closed down and avoiding meditation, then take a lit-tle time each day to nurture yourself with the Loving Kindness or Self-Tonglen practices.

Take good breaks for yourself. Relaxing well allows you to recharge and inspire yourself so that you can continue to bring inspiration to your work for others. Recognize also that setting limits—saying no to some of your patients' requests or refusing to take extra shifts at work—can be an important expression of a fun-damental love toward yourself.

Stress in the workplace can be minimized when caregivers acknowledge their mutual difficulties and recognize their need for a supportive atmosphere in which to work. Several successful hospice and hospital teams have described the elements of a sup-portive environment: an agreement among staff members that they will speak about problems as soon as possible after they come up; frequent team meetings and regular supervision meetings with a counselor or social worker; rotation of hospital personnel to dif-ferent wards where death is less frequent; the implicit permission to request time out during a shift, or a longer period of time off to work through disabling levels of grief or stress.

Remember always that you cannot survive the deepest pain and crises of your life alone. Once you recognize you are in trouble, be willing to ask for and receive support. Find professional counselors or turn to friends who are good listeners. Ask a circle of friends to share a mutual "pick up the phone" agreement. When any of you is in distress, you feel free to call anyone else on the list. You understand that the person you've called will honestly tell you if he doesn't have the time to listen at the moment. When this happens, you arrange to call him at another time, or phone another friend on your list.

You need to establish a sane routine for yourself—not filling up every break in your day or week with plans and activities. Leave time just for you, to restore yourself. If you have had an especially difficult day, find ways to give yourself time and space to settle your feelings *before* reentering home and family life: perhaps a half hour of quiet meditation, a hot bath, listening to music, going for a walk in nature, or writing in a journal.

Each week, cultivate other creative interests that help nurture and restore your whole being—body, emotions, heart, and mind— so that you keep a balance in your life between helping others and relaxation and play.

If you are providing long-term care for an elderly or disabled loved one at home, he will likely feel better when he sees you taking time for yourself, and feel that he is less of a burden when he sees you continuing with other activities.

Finally, real compassion includes the exercise of intelligence and discrimination, so that in responding to others' suffering, you do what you can and then let go of any tension or worry. Keep in mind the message of the Serenity Prayer:

> God, grant me the serenity to accept the things I cannot change,
> The courage to change the things I can,
> And the wisdom to know the difference.

As the great Buddhist saint and master of compassion Shantideva wrote: "If you can do something about your problem, then there is no need to worry about it; and if you can't do anything, then what's the use in worrying?" So instead of troubling yourself over situations where your help is ineffective or unwanted, bring the wisdom of discriminating awareness, along with all your skill and acumen, to find the potential areas where you *can* make a difference in the quality of your patients' lives and in their deaths.

Impermanence and change are in every moment; you cannot flow with the next unfolding moment in time if you haven't let go of the preceding one. *There are some situations where you cannot really do anything to make things better, so relax.*

Nurture a Vast Perspective

What does it mean to find hope when we are facing suffering or death? Real hope comes as we begin discovering and nurturing a vast perspective on life—an outlook that views the whole cycle of life and death from the deeper dimension of our true nature.

When we cultivate such a perspective, we do what we can for those who suffer, but we don't look upon their situations as irrevocable tragedies. And we don't shoulder all their burdens ourselves. When another person's burden weighs too heavily, then we have lost this larger perspective and are no longer able to help. As the Zen master Suzuki Roshi wrote:

> To live in the realm of Buddha nature means to die as a small being, moment after moment. When we lose our balance we die, but at the same time, we also develop ourselves, we grow. Whatever we see is changing, losing its balance. The reason everything looks beautiful is because it is out of balance, but its background is always in perfect harmony. This is how everything exists in the realm of Buddha nature, losing its balance against a background of perfect balance. So if you see things without realizing the background of Buddha nature, everything appears to be in the form of suffering. But if you understand the background of existence, you realize that suffering itself is how we live, and how we extend our life.[5]

The spiritual view that embraces all of life and death transforms our view of our patients as well. A nurse working in a hospice for many years put it this way: "I've learned to see and appreciate the real person inside of each patient, the true human being who is always there, underneath his physical appearance or emotional state."

Learning to acknowledge with compassion our own suffering will give birth to a limitless compassion in our heart for the suffering others experience and a reverence for all life. Through sustained spiritual practice and study, we cultivate a joy in developing our potential, and begin to appreciate the sacred potential within each person we provide care for. Don't let their appearance or their suffering ever make you forget who they truly are. *In the essence of their being, no matter how they appear, each person is perfect, whole, and complete.*

EPILOGUE

AFTER MY HUSBAND, LYTTLE, DIED, I REFLECTED WITH gratitude on what went well in our last year together and also on my mistakes. Writing the following poem after his death enabled me to express my regrets and make peace with myself. If you have had a loved one die, I invite you to do the same: forgive yourself for any failures, and trust that if you really loved the other person as best you could, your loved one who has died truly knows it.

YOU CAN GROW LESS BEAUTIFUL

Your hair is falling out, and
you are not so beautiful.
Your eyes have dark shadows,
your body is bloated: arms covered with
    bruises and needlemarks;
    legs swollen and useless.
Your body and spirit
are weakened with toxic chemicals
urine smells like antibiotics,
    even the sweat
that bathes your whole body
in the early hours of morning
reeks of dicloxacillin and methotrexate.

You are nauseous all the time—
I am afraid to move on the bed
for fear of waking you
    to moan
and lean over the edge
vomiting into the bag.

Epilogue

I curl up fetally
    withdraw into my dreams
with a frightened back to you—
    I'm scared
    and I'm hiding
but I love you so much;
this truth does not change.

Years ago,
when I met you, as we were falling in love,
your beauty attracted me:
  long, golden-brown hair
  clear and peaceful green eyes
    high cheekbones and long smooth muscles
but you know
I fell in love with your soul
    the real essence of you
and this cannot grow less beautiful.

Sometimes these days
even your soul is cloudy
    but I still recognize you.

We may be frightened
    and hiding our sorrow
it may take a little longer
to acknowledge the truth,
      yet I would not want to be anywhere else:

I am here   with you
you can grow less beautiful to the world
  you are safe—
I will always love you.

Perhaps reading this book was a challenge for you; writing it was certainly one for me. I was unequivocally brought face to face with the still unfinished aspects of my life: withheld forgiveness, unresolved fears, old grief, and painful experiences that needed acknowledgment. Some new losses and significant endings unfolded as I committed these words to paper. Thus, while describing the teachings and spiritual practices offered in this book, I've had to apply them to my own suffering: compassionately acknowledging my emotional and physical pain, reaching out to friends and a counselor for support, facing and healing unfinished business, and contemplating the spiritual teachings anew. I've had to meditate and pray, sometimes while I was in the midst of weeping.

At the start of my spiritual journey, I had hoped for a dramatic deliverance from all my suffering and fears. From the base of the mountain gazing toward the snowcapped peak, I imagined a swift and painless journey to the top. Yet the spiritual path whose promise holds out so much hope also leaves me responsible for myself. I must make the arduous journey and do the necessary work to heal my life, my attitudes, and selfish habits. And everything that happens—every loss or frustration—reveals new challenges.

Above all, what I've learned is the importance of being very kind to ourselves as we follow our path. Life is not easy, and it can be so tempting *not* to forgive ourselves for our flaws and mistakes. But this is the human condition. We must acknowledge our mistakes and then forgive ourselves, moving into the next moment with a clean heart and no trace of judgment. Everyone suffers, and so many people have no framework of understanding to show them a way through or offer a beacon of hope. If our own suffering enables us to develop a compassionate heart that grows increasingly vast and all-encompassing, then we have something genuine to offer others.

My wish is that this book opens doors of hope, forgiveness, and healing for you. My wish is that through learning of the suffering, mistakes, and insights that I and others have experienced—and working with these teachings and spiritual practices—you find the strength to begin living with courage, with compassion, with a sense of direction and purpose, taking the risk to lend support to others with your own deep confidence and love. May the unnecessary suffering of living and dying be thereby increasingly relieved for us all.

If you have "practiced dying" throughout life; if you can gracefully surrender your attachments and "offer up" all that you are leaving behind; if you can look into your heart and discover a wellspring of love; and if you can rest undistracted in the vast expanse of your true nature, then death can be like walking out of a centuries-old prison that dissolves behind you, like an image in a dream.

As I write these words, it is the twentieth anniversary of Lyttle's death. This book is one way in which I have dedicated his suffering to the benefit of everyone who is presently ill or dying, and to their loved ones and caregivers: My prayer is that each of us recognizes the sacred potential within and shines with the presence of wisdom and limitless compassion, bringing more happiness and peace into the world, until finally we all attain liberation.

QUIETNESS

Inside this new love, die.
Your way begins on the other side.
Become the sky.
Take an axe to the prison wall.
Escape.
Walk out like someone suddenly born into color.
Do it now.
You're covered with thick clouds.
Slide out the side. Die,
and be quiet. Quietness is the surest sign
that you've died.
Your old life was a frantic running
from silence.

The speechless full moon
comes out now.

—Rumi[1]

NOTES

CHAPTER 1

1. This story, told by Sogyal Rinpoche, first appeared in the April 1977 issue of *Psychology Today* in an article titled "New Evidence for the Survival of Consciousness" by Daniel Goleman. A more complete version appears in Sogyal Rinpoche's *The Tibetan Book of Living and Dying* (San Francisco: HarperCollins, 1992), 228.

CHAPTER 4

1. Sogyal Rinpoche, *The Tibetan Book of Living and Dying* (San Francisco: HarperCollins, 1992), 12.

2. Kenneth Ring, *Life at Death: A Scientific Investigation of the Near-Death Experience* (New York: Quill, 1982), 45.

3. Margot Grey, *Return from Death: An Exploration of the Near-Death Experience* (Boston: Arkana, 1985), 47.

4. Michael Sabom, M.D., *Recollections of Death: A Medical Investigation of the Near-Death Experience* (New York: Harper & Row, 1982), 66.

5. Grey, *Return from Death,* 47.

6. Grey, *Return from Death,* 53.

7. Raymond A. Moody, Jr., M.D., *Reflections on Life After Life* (New York: Bantam, 1977), 35.

8. P. M. H. Atwater, *Coming Back to Life* (New York: Dodd, Mead, 1988), 36.

9. Sogyal Rinpoche, *The Tibetan Book of Living and Dying,* 14.

CHAPTER 5

1. Pesach Krauss, *Why Me? Coping with Grief, Loss, and Change* (New York: Bantam, 1988), 66.

Notes

2. The Four Noble Truths are traditionally formulated as: the truth of suffering, the truth of the cause of suffering, the truth of the cessation of suffering, and the truth of the path leading to the cessation of suffering.

3. Elisabeth Kübler-Ross, "Death Does Not Exist," a talk given at the Association for Holistic Health in 1976, reprinted in *The Holistic Health Handbook* (Berkeley, CA: Berkeley Holistic Health Center, And/Or Press, 1978), 349.

CHAPTER 6

1. Ken Wilber, *Grace and Grit: Spirituality and Healing in the Life and Death of Treya Killam Wilber* (Boston: Shambhala, 1991), 360.

2. *Bodhicitta* is a Sanskrit word meaning "the heart of the enlightened mind." Absolute bodhicitta refers to our wisdom nature, while relative bodhicitta is a pure, unconditional love and compassion for all beings which radiates from our wisdom essence.

3. Sogyal Rinpoche, *The Tibetan Book of Living and Dying* (San Francisco: HarperCollins, 1992), 57.

4. Sogyal Rinpoche, *The Tibetan Book of Living and Dying*, 201.

5. Wilber, *Grace and Grit,* 250.

6. Sogyal Rinpoche, *The Tibetan Book of Living and Dying,* 60.

CHAPTER 7

1. Sogyal Rinpoche, *The Tibetan Book of Living and Dying* (San Francisco: HarperCollins, 1992), 317.

CHAPTER 9

1. Mother Teresa, *Meditations from a Simple Path* (New York: Ballantine, 1996), 50.

2. John 14:14.

3. Ruth Hatch in "The Way to Life," an editorial in the newspaper *Community Spirit,* Monterey, CA, 1983.

4. International Committee on English in the Liturgy, *Pastoral Care of the Sick—Rite of Anointing and Viaticum* (New York: Catholic Book Publishing, 1983), 210.

5. This is the short version of *Viduy,* the confession prayer for the time of death in the Jewish tradition, as printed in Rabbi

Chaim Binyamin Goldberg's *Mourning in Halachah* (Brooklyn, NY: Mesorah Publications, 1991), 442.

6. Living wills are not always legally binding by themselves, and doctors, hospital administrators, or family members have been able to overturn the dying person's directives; a "Durable Power of Attorney for Health Care" is a legally binding document.

7. *The Tibetan Book of the Dead,* Francesca Fremantle and Chögyam Trungpa, trans. (Boston: Shambhala, 1975), 37.

8. Sogyal Rinpoche, *The Tibetan Book of Living and Dying* (San Francisco: HarperCollins, 1992), 238.

9. *The Tibetan Book of the Dead,* 36.

10. In the Nyingma tradition, we would invoke Padmasambhava and recite his mantra, *Om Ah Hum Vajra Guru Padma Siddhi Hum.* Many people have told me they have felt more confidence in God's presence and more receptive to His forgiveness and blessing when they are reciting a short, inspiring prayer from their own tradition while doing the Essential Phowa.

11. Another practice for the moment of death is to whisper the names of certain buddhas, such as Amitabha, Avalokiteshvara, or Padmasambhava, into the ear of the dying person, or to recite their mantras, which invokes the buddhas' presence and blessings in the dying person's room and in her heart.

12. Nyoshul Khenpo, *Natural Great Perfection* (Ithaca, NY: Snow Lion, 1995), 56.

13. The meaning of the *Mani* mantra, the mantra of Avalokiteshvara, is described thoroughly in Sogyal Rinpoche's *The Tibetan Book of Living and Dying,* 389–91.

14. This practice is described in *The Way of a Pilgrim and The Pilgrim Continues His Way,* R. M. French, trans. (Harper San Francisco, 1965); and in *The Path of Prayer* by St. Theophan the Recluse (Newbury, MA: Praxis Institute Press, 1992).

CHAPTER 10

1. Leo Tolstoy, *The Death of Ivan Ilych* (New York: Penguin, 1960), 152–55.

2. Stephen Covey, *First Things First* (New York: Simon & Schuster, 1994), 17.

3. Kenneth Ring, *Life at Death: A Scientific Investigation of the Near-Death Experience* (New York: Quill, 1982), 143.

4. Ring, *Life at Death,* 157.

5. Margot Grey, *Return from Death: An Exploration of the Near-Death Experience* (Boston: Arkana, 1985), 100.

6. Sogyal Rinpoche, *The Tibetan Book of Living and Dying* (San Francisco: HarperCollins, 1992), 213.

7. Mwalimu Imara, "Dying as the Last Stage of Growth," in Elisabeth Kübler-Ross, *Death: The Final Stage of Growth*. (Englewood Cliffs, NJ: Prentice-Hall, 1975), 154.

8. Shunryu Suzuki, *Zen Mind, Beginner's Mind* (New York: Weatherhill, 1970), 87–88.

9. Viktor Frankl, *Man's Search for Meaning* (New York: Simon & Schuster, 1959), 104–5.

10. Sandol Stoddard, *The Hospice Movement: A Better Way to Care for the Dying* (New York: Random House, 1991), 123.

11. Pesach Krauss, *Why Me? Coping with Grief, Loss, and Change* (New York: Bantam, 1988), xiv.

12. *The Essential Rumi*, Coleman Barks, trans. (San Francisco: HarperCollins, 1995), 31–32.

13. Brother David Steindl-Rast, quoted in the "Hanuman Foundation Newsletter," 1981, vol. 2, 12.

CHAPTER 11

1. Judy Tatelbaum, *The Courage to Grieve: Creative Living, Recovery and Growth Through Grief* (New York: Harper & Row, 1980), 107.

2. Tatelbaum, *The Courage to Grieve*, 9.

3. The national contact for Compassionate Friends is: P.O. Box 3696, Oakbrook, IL 60522. Telephone: (708) 990-0010; fax: (708) 990-0246. To locate other resources for grief therapy, contact your local hospice. You can obtain the telephone number in your phone book, or by contacting the National Hospice Organization, 1901 North Moore Street #901, Arlington, VA 22209-1714. Hospice referral line: (800) 658-8898; telephone: (703) 243-5900; fax: (703) 525-5762.

4. Tatelbaum, *The Courage to Grieve*, 160.

5. C. S. Lewis, *A Grief Observed* (New York: Bantam, 1963).

CHAPTER 12

1. Sogyal Rinpoche, *The Tibetan Book of Living and Dying* (San Francisco: HarperCollins, 1992), 263.

Notes

2. Michael Sabom, M.D., *Recollections of Death: A Medical Investigation of the Near-Death Experience* (New York: Harper & Row, 1982), 37.

3. This was observed and written about by two hospice nurses, Maggie Callanan and Patricia Kelley, in their book *Final Gifts: Understanding the Special Awareness, Needs and Communications of the Dying* (New York: Bantam, 1992).

4. George Ritchie, M.D., *Return from Tomorrow* (Grand Rapids: Baker Book House, 1978).

5. Padmasambhava, as quoted by Tsele Natsok Rangdröl in *The Mirror of Mindfulness: The Cycle of the Four Bardos* (Boston: Shambhala, 1987), 73.

6. Mary Oliver, "In Blackwater Woods," from *American Primitive* (Boston: Little, Brown, 1983), 82.

7. Pesach Krauss, *Why Me? Coping with Grief, Loss, and Change* (New York: Bantam, 1988), 170.

CHAPTER 13

1. Stephen Levine, "Coma Stories," published in *Co-Evolution Quarterly* (Sausalito, CA, Winter 1983), 46.

CHAPTER 14

1. Chagdud Tulku Rinpoche, *Life in Relation to Death* (Cottage Grove, OR: Padma Publishing, 1987), 28.

2. Sogyal Rinpoche, *The Tibetan Book of Living and Dying* (San Francisco: HarperCollins, 1992), 59.

3. Dilgo Khyentse, *The Wish-Fulfilling Jewel* (Boston: Shambhala, 1988), 75.

4. Sogyal Rinpoche, *The Tibetan Book of Living and Dying,* 78.

5. Shunryu Suzuki, *Zen Mind, Beginner's Mind* (New York: Weatherhill, 1970), 31.

EPILOGUE

1. *The Essential Rumi,* Coleman Barks, trans. (San Francisco: Harper, 1995), 22.

ACKNOWLEDGMENTS

My deepest gratitude goes to every one of my spiritual masters, whose teachings, blessings, and unfailing encouragement are the source and inspiration of my work: my primary teachers, Sogyal Rinpoche and Nyoshul Khen Rinpoche, as well as Tulku Urgyen, Dzongsar Jamyang Khyentse Rinpoche, and Dodrupchen Rinpoche, and the great Tibetan masters of this century who have generously imparted their blessings, teachings, and protection in my life: His Holiness the Dalai Lama, His Holiness the 16th Gyalwang Karmapa, His Holiness Dudjom Rinpoche, His Holiness Dilgo Khyentse Rinpoche, Khandro Tsering Chödrön, His Holiness Sakya Trizin, and His Holiness Penor Rinpoche. May their tireless compassionate activity for the benefit of beings meet with ever-growing fulfillment and may their heritage of wisdom continue for ages to come.

For helping me complete this book, my deep thanks go to Frank Zechner, who offered his support and assistance in researching and reading the text, and suggested many improvements. I am indebted to D. Patrick Miller and Phyllis Hatfield, who provided invaluable editing skill, creativity, patience, and immeasurable kindness in helping to shape the book. My thanks also go to Patrick Gaffney, who helped clarify crucial points in the presentation, and who is a constant source of inspiration to me, both in his skill as a writer and in his entire way of being.

There are so many others to whom I am indebted, but I would especially like to thank all those who offered their assistance,

245

Acknowledgments

research, or suggestions, including: Ringu Tulku, Gabriel Berdé, Richard Bredsteen, Leslie Snider, Kieran Bahn, Anne Sadie, Ruth Yeomans, Marion Kuiper, and Robin Phillips.

I am also grateful to all those who offered their encouragement and personal and practical support over the many years it took to compile this work, including: Diane Exeriede, Michael Pope, Sandra Scales, Joe and Becky Williams, Sally Mitchell, my friends at Seminarhaus Engl—Wolfgang, Heike, and Ute—the Muckle family, Carol Wadsworth, Annie Eichenholz, Erric Solomon, the Brombachs and staff at Hospiz Elizabeth, and my parents.

Within Rigpa and the Spiritual Care for Living and Dying program, so many have helped contribute to my work over the years, I offer my heartfelt thanks to them all. I would like to especially express my deep gratitude to those who offered many years of support in the formation of the Spiritual Care program and my work: Sandra Pawula, Lisa Brewer, Alan Javurek, Tim McKnight, Karin Behrendt, Christa Reichert, and Angela Bork-Krahmer, who coordinates my European teaching program with great kindness and skill.

I am particularly grateful to my agents, Nancy Rose and Robert Levine, my friend Geoffrey Menin, and my editor at Doubleday, Betsy Lerner, for their encouragement, guidance, and vital support in bringing this book into being.

Finally, my deep appreciation goes to my son, Donovan, whose unconditional love enriches my life, and my late husband, Lyttle, whose life, suffering, and death inspired me to enter a spiritual path and find a greater meaning to my own life.

To all those whose stories and insights appear in these pages, I offer this book as an expression of my gratitude to them; for in learning of their experiences, many others are now encouraged and inspired to heal their lives and find hope in death.

APPENDIX A

Recommended Further Reading

DYING AND DEATH

Callahan, Daniel. *The Troubled Dream of Life: Living with Mortality.* New York: Simon & Schuster, 1993.

DeSpelder, Lynne Ann, and Albert Lee Strickland, eds. *The Path Ahead: Readings in Death and Dying.* Mountain View, CA: Mayfield, 1995.

Jury, Mark and Dan. *Gramps: A Man Ages and Dies.* New York: Penguin, 1976.

Kavanaugh, Robert. *Facing Death.* New York: Penguin, 1972.

Krauss, Pesach. *Why Me? Coping with Grief, Loss, and Change.* New York: Bantam, 1988.

Kübler-Ross, Elisabeth. *On Death and Dying.* New York: Macmillan, 1969.

―――. *Questions and Answers on Death and Dying.* New York: Macmillan, 1974.

―――. *Death: The Final Stage of Growth.* Englewood Cliffs, NJ: Prentice-Hall, 1975.

Lund, Doris. *Eric.* Philadelphia: J. B. Lippincott, 1974.

Ruskin, Cindy. *The Quilt: Stories from the Names Project.* New York: Pocket Books, 1988.

Tolstoy, Leo. *The Death of Ivan Ilych.* New York: Penguin, 1960.

Appendix A

HOSPICE AND HOME CARE

Brown, Rebecca. *The Gifts of the Body.* New York: HarperCollins, 1994.

Callanan, Maggie, and Patricia Kelley. *Final Gifts: Understanding the Special Awareness, Needs and Communications of the Dying.* New York: Bantam, 1992.

Duda, Deborah. *Coming Home: A Guide to Dying at Home with Dignity.* New York: Aurora Press, 1987.

Dunn, Hank. *Hard Choices for Loving People: CPR, Artificial Feeding, Comfort Measures Only and the Elderly Patient.* Herndon, VA: A & A Publishers, 1994.

Eidson, Ted, ed. *The AIDS Caregiver's Handbook.* New York: St. Martin's Press, 1993.

Grollman, Earl, ed. *Concerning Death: A Practical Guide for the Living.* Boston: Beacon, 1974.

Mace, Nancy L., and Peter V. Rabins. *The 36-Hour Day: A Family Guide to Caring for Persons with Alzheimer's.* Baltimore: Johns Hopkins University Press, 1991.

Saunders, Cicely, M.D., and Mary Baines, M.D. *Living with Dying: The Management of Terminal Disease.* Oxford and New York: Oxford University Press, 1989.

Stoddard, Sandol. *The Hospice Movement: A Better Way to Care for the Dying.* New York: Random House, 1991.

BEREAVEMENT

Caine, Lynn. *Widow.* New York: William Morrow, 1974.

Froman, Paul Kent. *After You Say Goodbye: When Someone You Love Dies of AIDS.* San Francisco: Chronicle Books, 1992.

Gilbert, Kathleen R., and Laura S. Smart. *Coping with Infant or Fetal Loss: The Couple's Healing Process.* New York: Bruner-Mazel, 1992.

Guest, Judith. *Ordinary People.* New York: Viking, 1976.

Lewis, C. S. *A Grief Observed.* New York: Bantam, 1963.

Lukas, Christopher, and Henry Seiden. *Silent Grief: Living in the Wake of Suicide.* New York: Bantam, 1987.

Murray Parkes, Colin, and Robert Weiss. *Recovering from Bereavement.* New York: Basic Books, 1983.

Sarnoff Schiff, Harriet. *The Bereaved Parent.* New York: Viking Penguin, 1977.

———. *Living Through Mourning.* New York: Viking Penguin, 1986.

Stillion, Judith M., Eugene E. McDowell, and Jacque H. May. *Suicide Across the Life Span: Premature Exits.* New York: Hemisphere, 1989.

Tatelbaum, Judy. *The Courage to Grieve: Creative Living, Recovery and Growth Through Grief.* New York: Harper & Row, 1980.

Volkan, Vamik D., and Elizabeth Zintl. *Life After Loss: The Lessons of Grief.* New York: Collier, 1994.

CHILDREN AND DEATH

Bluebond-Langer, Myra. *The Private Worlds of Dying Children.* Princeton: Princeton University Press, 1980.

Corr, Charles A., and Donna M. Corr. *Helping Children Cope with Death and Bereavement.* New York: Springer, 1995.

Grollman, Earl. *Talking About Death: A Dialogue Between Parent and Child.* Boston: Beacon, 1976.

Kübler-Ross, Elisabeth. *On Children and Death.* New York: Macmillan, 1983.

NEAR-DEATH EXPERIENCES

Atwater, P. M. H. *Beyond the Light.* New York: Avon, 1994.

Grey, Margot. *Return from Death: An Exploration of the Near-Death Experience.* Boston: Arkana, 1985.

Moody, Raymond, Jr., M.D. *Life After Life.* New York: Bantam, 1975.

———. *Reflections on Life After Life.* New York: Bantam, 1977.

Morse, Melvin, M.D. *Closer to the Light: Learning from the Near-Death Experiences of Children.* New York: Ballantine, 1990.

Ring, Kenneth. *Life at Death: A Scientific Investigation of the Near-Death Experience.* New York: Quill, 1982.

Appendix A

────────. *Heading Toward Omega: In Search for the Meaning of the Near-Death Experience.* New York: William Morrow, 1984.

Ritchie, George, M.D. *Return from Tomorrow.* Grand Rapids: Baker Book House, 1978.

Sabom, Michael, M.D. *Recollections of Death: A Medical Investigation of the Near-Death Experience.* New York: Harper & Row, 1982.

Buddhist Teachings on Death and Dying

Chagdud Tulku Rinpoche. *Life in Relation to Death.* Cottage Grove, OR: Padma Publishing, 1987.

Fremantle, Francesca, and Chögyam Trungpa, trans. *The Tibetan Book of the Dead.* Boston: Shambhala, 1975.

Kapleau, Philip, ed. *The Wheel of Death: A Collection of Writings from Zen Buddhist and Other Sources on Death, Rebirth, Dying.* New York: Harper & Row, 1971.

Mullin, Glenn H. *Death and Dying: The Tibetan Tradition.* Boston: Arkana, 1986.

Rangdröl, Tsele Natsok. *The Mirror of Mindfulness: The Cycle of the Four Bardos.* Boston: Shambhala, 1987.

Rinpoche, Sogyal. *The Tibetan Book of Living and Dying.* San Francisco: HarperCollins, 1992.

Other Spiritual Perspectives

Beck, Charlotte Joko. *Nothing Special.* San Francisco: HarperCollins, 1993.

Chödrön, Pema. *Start Where You Are.* Boston: Shambhala, 1994.

Dalai Lama, the Fourteenth. *Kindness, Clarity and Insight.* Ithaca, NY: Snow Lion, 1984.

Dass, Ram, and Paul Gorman. *How Can I Help?* New York: Alfred A. Knopf, 1985.

Dossey, Larry, M.D. *Recovering the Soul: A Scientific and Spiritual Search.* New York: Bantam, 1989.

Fox, Matthew. *A Spirituality Named Compassion.* Harper San Francisco, 1979.

Frankl, Viktor. *Man's Search for Meaning.* New York: Simon & Schuster, 1959.

French, R. M., trans. *The Way of a Pilgrim and The Pilgrim Continues His Way.* Harper San Francisco, 1965.

Goldberg, Rabbi Chaim Binyamin. *Mourning in Halachah.* Brooklyn, NY: Mesorah Publications, 1991.

Harrison, Gavin. *In the Lap of the Buddha.* Boston: Shambhala, 1994.

Hellwig, Monika. *What Are They Saying About Death and Christian Hope?* New York: Paulist Press, 1978.

Jampolsky, Gerald, M.D. *Good-bye to Guilt: Releasing Fear Through Forgiveness.* New York: Bantam, 1985.

Kabat-Zinn, Jon. *Wherever You Go, There You Are: Mindfulness Meditation in Everyday Life.* New York: Hyperion, 1993.

Khenpo, Nyoshul. *Natural Great Perfection.* Ithaca, NY: Snow Lion, 1995.

Khyentse, Dilgo. *The Wish-Fulfilling Jewel: The Practice of Guru Yoga According to the Longchen Nyingtig Tradition.* Boston: Shambhala, 1988.

Krishnamurti, J. *Think on These Things.* New York: Harper & Row, 1964.

Kushner, Harold. *When Bad Things Happen to Good People.* New York: Schocken, 1981.

Levine, Stephen. *Who Dies? An Investigation of Conscious Living and Conscious Dying.* New York: Doubleday, 1982.

May, Gerald, M.D. *The Awakened Heart: Living Beyond Addiction.* San Francisco: HarperCollins, 1991.

Merton, Thomas. *Contemplative Prayer.* New York: Doubleday, 1969.

Nhat Hanh, Thich. *Being Peace.* Berkeley: Parallax Press, 1987.

Pastoral Care of the Sick. New York: Catholic Book Publishing Co., 1983.

Riemer, Jack, ed. *Jewish Reflections on Death.* New York: Schocken, 1974.

Steindl-Rast, Brother David. *A Listening Heart: The Art of Contemplative Living.* New York: Crossroads, 1983.

Appendix A

————. *Gratefulness, the Heart of Prayer: An Approach to Life in Fullness.* Ramsey, NJ: Paulist Press, 1984.

Suzuki, Shunryu. *Zen Mind, Beginner's Mind.* New York: Weatherhill, 1970.

Teresa, Mother. *A Simple Path.* New York: Ballantine, 1995.

Theophan, St., the Recluse. *The Path of Prayer.* Newbury, MA: Praxis Institute Press, 1992.

Trungpa, Chögyam. *Training the Mind and Cultivating Loving-Kindness.* Boston: Shambhala, 1993.

Wilber, Ken. *Grace and Grit: Spirituality and Healing in the Life and Death of Treya Killam Wilber.* Boston: Shambhala, 1991.

APPENDIX B

The Spiritual Care for Living and Dying Program

If you would like to find out more about what you have read in this book, you may be interested in the work of Spiritual Care for Living and Dying, an education and training program designed to help those concerned with the issues around death and dying.

Born out of the work of Rigpa, and inspired by Sogyal Rinpoche's *The Tibetan Book of Living and Dying,* Spiritual Care for Living and Dying seeks to apply the compassion and wisdom of the Buddhist teachings to the needs of people today: living, dying, or bereaved.

Seminars are offered in North America, Europe, and Australia by Christine Longaker and others, and there is a growing network of study and practice groups that provide support for caregivers working in the fields of medicine, healthcare, and human services. The development of a service program is underway with the creation of a hospice and healing center in Ireland.

To find out more or to become a member of Spiritual Care for Living and Dying, please write or call:

> Spiritual Care for Living and Dying
> P.O. Box 607
> Santa Cruz, California 95061-0607
> (408) 454-9352

Appendix B

AUDIOCASSETTES

For a current catalog of audiocassettes by Sogyal Rinpoche and Christine Longaker, please contact:

> Rigpa Publications
> P.O. Box 607
> Santa Cruz, California 95061-0607
> (800) 256-5262 in United States and Canada
> (408) 454-9242

INDEX

Index

Index

Index

About the Author

CHRISTINE LONGAKER has been a student of Sogyal Rinpoche (author of *The Tibetan Book of Living and Dying*) since 1980, and served for nine years as the principal coordinator of Rigpa Fellowship, the association sponsoring Buddhist teachings under Rinpoche's guidance in the United States. Her direct experiences of caregiving, and of healing her grief after her husband's death twenty years ago, led her to become a pioneer in the hospice movement; she helped to establish the Hospice of Santa Cruz County in California, and became its president.

Since ceasing her hospice work, Christine has given hundreds of training seminars on the care of the dying throughout the United States, Canada, and Europe. She has taught college courses on death and dying, provided training for nurses, ministers, and hospice caregivers, and counseled the dying and their families for many years. Currently, she is working closely with Rinpoche to develop the comprehensive education and training program Spiritual Care for Living and Dying, which applies the compassion and wisdom of the Buddhist teachings to the needs of people today: living, dying, and bereaved. In addition to Christine's seminars, the program supports a growing network of study and practice groups for health-care professionals who are integrating the teachings into their life and work.